# The Women's
# Seder
# Sourcebook

# The Women's Seder Sourcebook

## Rituals & Readings
### for Use at the Passover Seder

Edited by Sharon Cohen Anisfeld,
Tara Mohr & Catherine Spector

**JEWISH LIGHTS Publishing**
Woodstock, Vermont

*The Women's Seder Sourcebook:*
*Rituals and Readings for Use at the Passover Seder*

© 2003 by Sharon Cohen Anisfeld, Tara Mohr, and Catherine Spector

**Library of Congress Cataloging-in-Publication Data**
The women's seder sourcebook : rituals and readings for use at the Passover seder / edited by Sharon Cohen Anisfeld, Tara Mohr, and Catherine Spector.
   p.   cm.
Includes bibliographical references.
ISBN 1-58023-136-5 (HC)
1. Haggadah—Adaptations. 2. Passover—Prayer-books and devotions. 3. Seder. 4. Jewish women—Prayer-books and devotions—English. 5. Passover—Literary collections. 6. Feminism—Religious Aspects—Judaism. I. Anisfeld, Sharon Cohen, 1960– II. Mohr, Tara, 1978– III. Spector, Catherine, 1978–
BM674.795 .W66 2003
296.4'5371'082—dc21

                                                                2002151375


10  9  8  7  6  5  4  3  2  1

Manufactured in the United States of America

Published by Jewish Lights Publishing
A Division of LongHill Partners, Inc.
Sunset Farm Offices, Route 4, P.O. Box 237
Woodstock, VT  05091
Tel: (802) 457-4000     Fax: (802) 457-4004
www.jewishlights.com

*Dedicated to the extraordinary women*
*of the Jewish community at Yale University*
*whose wisdom and courage*
*provided the inspiration for this book*

# Contents

# Preface

Playwright Lillian Hellman once wrote, "Nothing, of course, begins at the time you think it did."[1] Reflecting on the origins and development of *The Women's Passover Companion* and *The Women's Seder Sourcebook,* we appreciate the wisdom of her words. For while we began formal work on the then-titled *Yale Women's Haggadah Project* in the spring of 2000, our efforts stood upon a foundation laid by many other women throughout the 1990s.

The seeds of this project lie in Jewish Women at Yale, a student group whose members have been creating superior women's programming on the Yale University campus for many years. With the leadership of Rabbi Sharon Cohen Anisfeld, then associate rabbi of Joseph Slifka Center for Jewish Life at Yale, the group held the first Yale Women's Seder in 1993. This event quickly became a beloved annual tradition that provided a unique forum for students, professors, and community members to come together. For the first seder, students wrote the *Yale Women's Haggadah,* which included commentaries, alternative texts, and creative writing on the traditional haggadah and themes of the holiday. Over the course of eight years, undergraduates revised and enhanced this unique piece of liturgy.

The *Yale Women's Haggadah* was but one manifestation of what became a vibrant Jewish feminist community at the university. In 1996, a student proposed hosting the first national Jewish women's conference for young women. During the next several months, a diverse group of students and faculty shaped what evolved into a ground-breaking, three-day event that attracted hundreds of college students from around the country. Inspired by its success, a new generation of students began work two years later on a second conference, this time centered on the theme of Jewish women and freedom.

A provocative and powerful conversation—across religious denominations, generations, and national boundaries—emerged among presenters and participants. Jewish Women at Yale wanted, and indeed felt they had an obligation, to capture this dialogue and share it with a wider audience. At the same time, some students began talking about the possibility of expanding and potentially publishing the *Yale Women's Haggadah*.

In the fall of 1999, these two projects converged. A group of undergraduate women led by Rabbi Cohen Anisfeld began work on a feminist haggadah that would include student writings as well as commentaries from the authors, activists, artists, and scholars who had been part of the conferences. The small committee soon realized, however, that creating this haggadah would be more than a part-time, extracurricular activity. In order to complete the project, Tara Mohr and Catherine Spector decided to spend a postgraduate year in New Haven working on the haggadah with Sharon Cohen Anisfeld. The three of us began serious work on the project together in the fall of 2000. With the help of many supporting individuals and institutions, Tara and Catherine were able to work full time on what became a two-year endeavor.

From its earliest stages, the project aimed to use the framework of the haggadah to create a comprehensive, pluralistic resource that would further Jewish women's explorations of significant questions about freedom, oppression, spirituality, feminism, and tradition and change. As time went on, however, we confronted the challenges of creating pluralistic liturgy. In addition, we struggled with how to achieve our goal of creating a feminist haggadah that could easily be used at family seders. As we spoke with dozens of women's seder organizers around the country, we learned that many communities had chosen to create their own women's haggadahs not simply because of the dearth of available resources but also because they felt that the process of putting together the haggadahs had great inherent value. As seder organizers who had experienced the impact of this process ourselves, we shared this feeling. Furthermore, as the project developed, we decided that our circle of contributing authors should extend beyond those who been part of the conferences, the Yale Women's Seder, or Jewish Women at Yale. These concerns gradually led us to conceive a new vision for the book that would better meet our goals: Rather than producing another women's haggadah, we would create a women's sourcebook for Passover.

As we further refined this vision, we considered what kind of materials we ourselves desired, both as seder organizers and as individuals celebrating the holiday. We felt it was important that the anthology address all aspects of women's relationships to the Passover holiday, from cleaning for the holiday to sitting at the family seder table to organizing a women's seder. Thus, we decided to feature readings and rituals to be included in the seder as well as longer essays to be read in advance or during the week of Passover. It soon became clear that there was enough important material to merit expanding the book into two volumes. One volume would include essays and the other would consist of material for the actual seder; the two could be used separately or in conjunction with each other. In this way, we would be able to fulfill the many needs of the different women and men who we hoped would find these anthologies meaningful.

These are some of the central considerations and influences that have guided the development of *The Women's Passover Companion* and *The Women's Seder Sourcebook*. The result is a collection featuring diverse voices writing in a myriad of forms: poetry, prose, essays, memoirs, commentaries, and creative and traditional exegesis. These writings discuss biblical texts, seder rituals, and passages from the haggadah, as well as Jewish women's history, personal experiences, and relevant political concerns. The writers are scholars, activists, rabbis, authors, artists, political leaders, and students.

Over the past two years, we have had the extraordinary privilege of working inside a fascinating dialogue currently occurring among these Jewish women. And we have had the extraordinary blessing of sharing an intensely collaborative process and a true labor of love. Our hope is that these volumes will help the Jewish community hear, respect, and include women's voices. And we hope that they inspire you for many Passovers to come.

# Acknowledgments

We are deeply grateful to the many supporters who have made it possible for us to see this project through to completion. We wish to thank the women whose advice steered us in the right direction at so many crucial points in the project: Paula Hyman, Claire Sufrin, Hilary Kaplan, Laura Wexler, Sydney Perry, Carol Diament, Karyn Kedar, Linda Altshuler, Peri Smilow, Merle Feld, Shulamit Reinharz, Naomi Danis, and the staff of the Jewish Women's Resource Center. Your counsel and encouragement were invaluable to us.

Those who took the time to read our manuscript offered insightful and important feedback: Judith Plaskow, Eve Landau, Rachel Cymrot, Sarah Anne Minkin, and, in particular, Ruth Kaplan. Your questions, concerns, and editorial suggestions improved the manuscript and helped us include the full breadth of voices represented in the anthology.

The Joseph Slifka Center for Jewish Life at Yale was instrumental in both the genesis and the development of this project. Slifka Center's support of student-initiated women's programming at Yale and its continued involvement with these books over the past two years has been remarkable. It was a great blessing to work at the Slifka Center during the initial year of the project, and we wish to thank the staff who enriched our year through conversation and friendship: Amy Aaland, David Cavill, Leah and Ilan Haber, Robbie Hobson, Susan Jeanette,

Karen Medin, Dennis Panasci, James and Elana Ponet, Catherine Satula, Jordana Schuster, and Jeanette Vega.

In addition to those with whom we worked directly at the Slifka Center, we thank each of the women who wrote the *Yale Women's Haggadah,* as well as the women who created Yale's two conferences on Jewish women in 1997 and 1999. Your work—courageous, innovative, and inspiring—is the foundation of this project. We owe a particular debt of gratitude to Sara Meirowitz, whose vision was the inspiration for the first conference and whose guidance and support has been vital to us during the project.

We were overwhelmed and heartened by the thorough, impassioned responses we received to our survey of women's seder organizers. The ideas, advice, and memories, as well as the original women's haggadahs that these women shared with us, shaped our research throughout this project. We are especially appreciative of Hadassah and the National Council for Jewish Women, which helped the surveys reach seder organizers.

In an independent project such as this one, specific needs for help and resources often arise. Ilana Kurshan, Doreen Semel, and Yossi Abromowitz and Susan Berrin at Jewish Family and Life! each gave generously to this project, offering help with kindness and enthusiasm.

The staff at Jewish Lights has been attentive, considerate, and thoughtful throughout this project. We are grateful for the experience of a richly collaborative and enjoyable editorial process. Thank you to Emily Wichland, managing editor of Jewish Lights, for her guidance, and to Alys R. Yablon for her perceptive and helpful editing, which greatly improved these volumes. Our thanks also to Stuart M. Matlins, publisher of Jewish Lights, for understanding the need for this anthology and valuing the material enough to feel it merited two volumes.

We want to express our deepest gratitude to those individuals and foundations whose support made this project possible; without it, a book of this scope and size could never have been created. Even more significantly, their support demonstrated a faith in this project that has sustained and inspired us in our work. We wish to thank The Dobkin

Family Foundation, Judy Katz and the Miriam Horowitz Fund, Diane Troderman and the Harold Grinspoon Charitable Trust, Brenda and Al Curtis, Sarah and Will Richmond, The Eugene Lang Foundation, The Hadassah Foundation, The Shefa Fund, and The Bronfman Youth Fellowships in Israel. We want to express a particular thank-you to the Charles and Lynn Schusterman Family Foundation, which offered funding to the project in its earliest stages. To David and Goldie Blanksteen: We have been moved by your ongoing involvement in this project, and we are enormously thankful for your passionate interest in its subject and in each of us. It has been a joy to share this work with you. Finally, we extend a profound personal thank-you to Barbara Dobkin, who not only made these books possible but, through her faith, guidance, and generosity, also made the experience all the more meaningful for us.

And to our friends and family: Your encouragement, support, and optimism were there when we most needed it. At times, you provided more than counsel, and we were touched by your offers to contribute so much of your time and talent to this endeavor. Thanks to Laura Crescimano for her extensive help with graphic and web design and to Andrew Krause for his wise editorial advice.

In addition, we would each like to offer some personal words of gratitude. From Tara: Thank you to Eric Ries for the hundreds of ways you have supported the project and enriched my life as I have been working on it; William and Harriet Mohr for your help and encouragement over the past two—and indeed twenty-four—years; and my teachers Judith Komoroske, Melissa Wilson, and Katherine Rowe, to whom more than a small share of this accomplishment is due.

From Catherine: Thank you to Nancy, Ken, David, and Rebecca Spector, my family, for their unwavering support and advice through the many struggles and successes of this project; and the friends who have played the roles of cheerleader, commiserator, and counselor, Laura Chen, Caitrin Moran, Liz Schroeder, and Rasika Jayasekera.

From Sharon: Thank you to my first and most important teachers, my parents, Jules and Doris Cohen, who have always encouraged me to search for the right questions; to my husband, Shimon Anisfeld, whose companionship, wisdom, and sense of humor have sustained me throughout this project; to my children, Daniel and Tali Anisfeld, whose sweet exuberance and love inspire me every day; to my friends Susan Fendrick, Sharon Kleinbaum, and Dianne Cohler-Esses, who have deeply influenced my understanding of Torah and who have given generously of themselves to make these volumes a reality.

We would also like to thank one another. Two years ago, we encountered one anothers' very different ways of thinking, reading, and writing. Over the course of working together, we have not only developed the deepest appreciation for one another but also learned from one another in countless ways.

And the deep collaboration of this project extends far beyond the three of us, to the more than one hundred and fifty generous, enthusiastic, and talented women who have given the entire Jewish community words that will inspire and teach for years to come. We are in awe of your accomplishment, and we give you our deepest thanks.

# Introduction

*I sing, I sing,*
*until the lands*
*sing to each other.*

—MURIEL RUKEYSER, "MIRIAM: THE RED SEA"

Miriam's song has become an increasingly important theme at women's seders over the past thirty years. Earlier women's haggadahs from the 1970s and 1980s, such as *The Telling* and the *San Diego Women's Haggadah,* scarcely mention Miriam's song, while newer haggadahs, such as *The Journey Continues,* make it a focal point. One recently published haggadah even draws on this image for its title: *The Dancing with Miriam Haggadah.* For many women, singing Miriam's song at the seder, in one of its contemporary renditions, is a highlight of the event. Numerous poems and readings in recent women's haggadahs take Miriam's song as their subject. What accounts for the widespread interest in the idea of Miriam's song?

It is often pointed out that while Moses begins his song in the first person singular—"I will sing to the Lord, for the Lord has triumphed gloriously"—Miriam begins in the second person plural: "Sing (all of you) to the Lord, for the Lord has triumphed gloriously," calling our attention to the fact that Miriam invites the other women to join her song. Significantly, then, Miriam did not sing alone at the shores of the sea. Her song was not the song of a lone prophet, but the simultaneous, spontaneous outpouring of all the women who went forth from Egypt.

In the interpretation of the Lubavitcher Rebbe, who lectured on this topic in 1992, this song was a "female version" of the two songs sung at the sea:

> Actually, there are two versions of the Song at the Sea—a male version and a female version. After Moses and the Children of Israel sang their song, "Miriam the prophetess, the sister of Aaron, took the tambourine in her hand; and all the women followed her with tambourines and dances. And Miriam called to them: "Sing to God, for He is most exalted; horse and rider He cast in the sea...."[1]

The women, he suggests, possessed a unique understanding of both slavery and liberation—one that needed to be expressed to make complete our people's song at the sea.

And yet, Miriam's song itself appears truncated and incomplete as it is recorded in the Torah. It is, after all, only two short verses: "Sing to God, for God is most exalted, horse and rider God cast in the sea...." Indeed, this song is not really a song at all, but rather a call—an invitation—to sing!

Perhaps this is the power of Miriam's song for our own day. It hints at the idea of a collective women's song yet to be fully expressed. As women, as feminists, we have made enormous strides; we have achieved unprecedented levels of access and participation for women in Jewish life. But the task now in front of us is to hear the diverse and robust voices of Jewish women, to think about what they sound like and what they contribute, to imagine a Judaism that truly reflects the wisdom and vitality of the entire Jewish people. This is the promise of Miriam's song. It is up to us, as it will be up to our daughters, to carry on what Miriam began when she first lifted her tambourine and invited the women to add their voices to the song of our people.

*The Women's Seder Sourcebook* is one contemporary expression of Miriam's song. It gathers the voices of more than a hundred women in the form of readings, personal and creative reflections, commentaries, blessings, and ritual suggestions for the Passover seder. It is a resource for women's and feminist seders as well as family and communal seders, for all women and men planning their own seders and creating their own haggadahs.

Among the sources included here are texts from unpublished women's haggadahs created by campus Hillels, chapters of Jewish women's organizations, federations, congregations, and individual women. Until now, these important texts have remained, for the most part, in the filing cabinets and attics of their creators. Here they are made available to a wider community. *The Women's Seder Sourcebook* also collects some of the most interesting and powerful reflections found in the small number of published women's haggadahs.

The vast majority of writings, however, are original pieces solicited from individual women whose perspectives are essential to our evolving understanding of Passover. What new insights do our female rabbis and Judaic scholars such as Lynn Gottlieb, Sandy Eisenberg Sasso, Ellen Frankel, and Susannah Heschel offer on the texts of the haggadah and the Book of Exodus? What wisdom does a Supreme Court Justice—Ruth Bader Ginsburg—have to share about the pursuit of justice and *tikkun olam?* What challenges and perspectives do brave Jewish activists such as Naomi Klein, Eve Ensler, and Ruth Messinger contribute to the seder table? What new language do our poets—Marge Piercy, Alicia Suskin Ostriker, and Maxine Kumin—give us for the telling? How do our policy makers such as congresswomen Barbara Boxer and Jan Schakowsky understand revolution, liberation, and leadership?

Equally important are other authors' attempts to discover how women's personal experiences shed light on the central ideas of the holiday. In this volume, a recovering anorexic guides us to a new understanding of "Let All Who Are Hungry Come and Eat." A breast cancer survivor teaches us how to appreciate our blessings even in the most difficult situations through a reflection on the meaning of *Dayeinu.* An adoptive mother sheds new light on the courage and character of Pharaoh's daughter.

When Miriam stood at the shores of the sea, she invited *all* of the women to join in expressing their praise and joy. In this spirit, *The Women's Seder Sourcebook* collects the voices of women from a wide variety of fields and backgrounds, who contribute their perspectives on the texts and themes of Passover. This volume reflects and furthers a dialogue among contemporary Jewish women and offers women's seder participants a sense of the larger community that joins them—metaphorically—at the seder table. We hope it will enhance the possibilities for future women's seders as it dramatically expands the range of perspectives brought to bear on the Passover story and the seder experience. Moreover, we hope it will offer families and communities a way to bring women's voices to their seder tables.

What new insights do these diverse women offer? What new questions do they bring to the seder table? As we return to the seder each year, let us listen closely for what they might teach us about the sound of Miriam's song. For what was true at the shores of the sea is true today. When Jewish women raise their voices, they make a vital contribution to our people's song. May we, like Muriel Rukeyser's Miriam, continue to sing until the lands sing to one another.

# How to Use This Book

I n recent decades, American Jews have increasingly chosen to create their own unique materials for the Passover seder. Whether compiling a haggadah from scratch or supplementing an existing one, individuals preparing for a family or women's seder often incorporate readings from a variety of haggadahs as well as sources from other contexts.

From this project's outset, we have aimed to support this emerging trend. It is an extremely rewarding process for those who undertake it, offering an educational experience that stretches individuals to think critically about their seders. It reflects a growing sense that one can— and should—take an active role in shaping one's own Jewish religious experiences. It allows for the kind of creativity that keeps the seder fresh and relevant each year. In addition, this openness to adapting, supplementing, and creating anew has facilitated the introduction of feminist innovations and women's voices into the Passover seder.

Building on this phenomenon, we have collected in this sourcebook more than two hundred rituals, readings, commentaries, and blessings for the seder. The materials here do not constitute a complete haggadah, and, of course, far more materials are included in this volume than could possibly be incorporated into a single seder. As the reader, you will be introduced to an incredible range of perspectives and will choose the questions, ideas, and voices you would like to bring to the seder table each year.

## Organization of *The Women's Seder Sourcebook*

*The Women's Seder Sourcebook* is organized according to the order of the seder. Each chapter of the book is devoted to a particular section of the seder and has two parts: a short introduction and a selection of readings and rituals.

The introduction to the section provides accessible and vivid background information on the particular part of the seder. It also gives an overview of how this aspect of the Passover ritual has been reinterpreted in a feminist context. Whether you wish to orient yourself before attending a seder or refresh your knowledge before leading one, the introductions will provide you with a concise and useful resource. In addition, because the introductions discuss the variety of ways in which women's seders have approached this aspect of the ritual, women's seder organizers may wish to refer to them when making their planning decisions.

The sources constitute the heart of each chapter and include readings, commentaries, blessings, and rituals. Each chapter features a diverse array of perspectives and interpretations. In some cases, these materials serve as substitutes for traditional passages of the haggadah; in other cases, they are intended to be used as supplements to the traditional text. Offering new interpretations and insightful commentaries, the sources can also be read at leisure as part of your preparation for the holiday.

We have placed each reading or ritual into a section of the seder where it can be used so that you are able to easily incorporate these sources into your seder. Indeed, most of the pieces included in this volume focus on a particular part of the seder. However, because the same themes, symbols, and questions are addressed in a variety of ways throughout the haggadah, some of the readings could be incorporated at different points during the ritual. Sections that include several such pieces are Reflections on Preparing for Passover in "Opening the Seder,"

Reflections on Feminine God Language in "Candlelighting," Readings on the Women of Exodus in "Go Forth and Learn," and Readings on the Holocaust in "Elijah's Cup." We encourage you to incorporate these pieces wherever you feel they will most enhance your seder.

## How to Use *The Women's Seder Sourcebook*

Depending on your particular needs, you may want to use the book in any of the following ways:

**If you are creating a haggadah for a women's or family seder,** we recommend that you take some time, well in advance of the seder, to sit down with a haggadah, *The Women's Seder Sourcebook,* and any additional secondary sources you might like to include in your seder. Spend some time familiarizing yourself with the materials in front of you. If you are unfamiliar with the traditional haggadah, plan to devote time to reading and learning during this process. You may review *The Women's Seder Sourcebook*'s introductions on each part of the haggadah to get some concise background of the seder. For more extensive information, we recommend Ron Wolfson's thorough and accessible *Passover: The Family Guide to Spiritual Celebration* (Jewish Lights Publishing).

Next, begin to make decisions about the haggadah you would like to create. We suggest that you follow the traditional framework of the seder—which, after all, means "order." For each section of the seder, you will need to decide whether you would like to simply include the haggadah's traditional text or whether you would prefer to replace or supplement this text with a more creative reading.

**If you are hosting a seder and want to add some new readings to your haggadah,** begin by briefly reviewing the haggadah you plan to use. In addition, take a bit of time to think about the new ideas and information you would like your seder to include. What unaddressed topics, missing voices, or important insights would you like to incorporate or give more emphasis to? For example, would you like to tell the stories of the women of Exodus in greater depth? Include readings written by contemporary Jewish women? Offer the option of feminine God language in a blessing? Address a particular political or social issue? Have more discussion or participatory components?

If you are short on time or are overwhelmed by the prospect of looking through the entire haggadah to make these choices, simply turn to *The Women's Seder Sourcebook* and select a few favorite readings to supplement the haggadah.

**If you are preparing to be a participant at a family or women's seder,** there are several different ways to use this book. You may read through some of the materials in order to mark your favorite readings and share them at the seder. Or bring *The Women's Seder Sourcebook* with you and follow along in the book as the group proceeds through the seder, adding a new idea or reading a piece as you come across it.

If you do not wish to introduce new materials to the seder, read from *The Women's Seder Sourcebook* in advance of the seder in order to bring new questions, insights, or interpretations from your reading to the discussion at the seder table.

Beyond these practical applications, reading the materials in advance of the seder will enrich your experience of the holiday. If you have attended seders throughout your life, this book will offer you an array of new perspectives and ideas. If this is your first seder, it serves as a vibrant, engaging introduction to the rituals of the seder and their rich meanings.

Two things to keep in mind when using readings from *The Women's Seder Sourcebook* at the seder:

- Be respectful of copyrights and the requirement for permission (see p. iv) before copying material, and be careful to cite the author of the piece as well as *The Women's Seder Sourcebook* in any work you use from the volume. To find the original sources of previously published readings and rituals, refer to the permissions list at the end of the book (pp. 325–28).
- Responsive readings can work wonderfully at the seder, drawing each guest into an active role in reading the hag-

gadah. We encourage you to read some of these pieces responsively at your seder, marking the parts for the leader and the group yourself.

## Finding Rituals and Readings in *The Women's Seder Sourcebook*

There are several different ways to locate specific readings:

- If you would like to incorporate a ritual or reading for a particular part of the seder, refer to the table of contents to find the chapter of *The Women's Seder Sourcebook* focusing on that part of the seder and select a favorite reading from that section.

- If you would like to feature the voice of a particular woman, refer to the index by author.

- If you would like to include a reading on a particular topic, biblical figure, or feminist issue, refer to the topical index.

It is our hope that *The Women's Seder Sourcebook* will be a useful resource for its readers for many Passovers and that it will guide you in taking an increasingly active role in shaping a meaningful seder.

# Opening the Seder

Each year we return to the seder table with memory and hope, with nostalgia and expectation. We come to the table anticipating familiar melodies and favorite recipes; we come with memories of previous Passover celebrations in our own lives; we come longing to connect with generations of Jews who have sat at the seder table before us. Thus, the seder must be familiar and resonant with memory. But we also hope that our seder will feel transformative. We hope to discover some new insights, some new connection to the Passover story. For if we do not, we have not fulfilled the central imperative of the holiday: "In every generation, each person is obligated to see herself as if she had personally gone forth out of Egypt."

In deciding how to begin your seder, it is important to consider who will be gathered around the table. What words will welcome? What words will exclude? What will make the seder feel comfortable and familiar? What will make it come alive? To bring participants together and set the tone for the evening, many women's seders include an opening ritual, reading, or song before beginning the traditional seder rituals.

Women's seders have initiated the custom of having each woman introduce herself as the daughter of her mother, grandmother,

1

great-grandmother, and so forth, going as far back through her family as she can. This tradition both honors the women who have come before us and dramatically asserts how this seder is different from all other seders: At this seder, we come together as mothers and daughters; at this seder, when we share our genealogy, we hear the sounds of women's names.

In some communities, it is customary to begin the seder by reflecting on the extensive work of cleaning for Passover that must be performed before the seder. This provides a meaningful opportunity for women to remember the devoted labor of their mothers and grandmothers as well as to contemplate their own preparation—both physical and spiritual—for the Passover holiday.

∽

## Introductions

We will begin by introducing ourselves by our matrilineage: "I am
_____ daughter of _____ daughter of _____," or "I am
_____ *bat* _____ *bat* _____," tracing back through as
many generations as possible.

Alternatively, participants may choose to name other women who have acted as mothers and grandmothers in their lives.

## Our Mothers' Daughters

We begin by introducing ourselves as our mothers' daughters. Who among us has considered what that means? We inherit our mothers' legacies. We inherit their stories. And we move forward, telling our own stories, creating our own legacies.

How can we thank our mothers for what they have given us?
Should we be grateful for what they have provided?
Must we accept what they have offered?

—SARA BUCHDAHL LEVINE

## Opening Meditation for a Women's Seder

We come together from our separate lives, each of us bringing our concerns, our preoccupations, our hopes, and our dreams. We are not yet
fully present: The traffic, the last-minute cooking, the final details still
cling to us. Our bodies hold the rush of the past few hours.

It is now time to let go of these pressures and really arrive at this
seder. We do this by meditating together. Make yourself comfortable;
you can close your eyes if you wish. Now take a few deep breaths, and
as you exhale, let go of the tensions in your body. You'll begin to quiet
within.

When you're ready, repeat silently to yourself: *"Hineini,"* or "Here
I am." *Hineini* is used in the Torah to signify being present in body,
mind, and spirit. It means settling into where we are and simply being
"here."

If you prefer, you can visualize the word. Let the word become
filled with your breath. Merge with it, so that you experience being
fully present. Everything drops away, and you're left in the unbound-
ed state of here-ness. When a thought arises, just notice it and return to
*hineini* again and again. Let yourself be held in the state of *hineini*.

Meditate in this way for several minutes, long enough to become
more present. Slowly open your eyes, and look around the room at
the women in your circle. Now, we begin our journey together.

—NAN FINK GEFEN

## To Remember and to Build

Tonight, each woman has come from a different place and has brought
with her different experiences. For some, a woman's seder is a familiar
event; for others, it is something new. Some have been looking forward
to the seder all year; others are not sure why they have set aside these
hours. Each woman, surely, has come for a different reason. Yet, the
fact that we are here together assumes that we all have something in
common, some shared experiences, some shared commitments, some
shared longings.

By definition, a women's seder is old. It is a seder, an ancient celebration marking an even older event of liberation. It is a time for thanking and for giving praise. It is a time for remembering. Yet, by
definition, women's seders are also new. No one can be sure what they
will look like. In what language should we speak? What images should
we embrace? What stories should we tell? In each place and in each
year, the answers will be different.

We are here to form a community, and we do so by embracing
both our similarities and our differences. We do so by acknowledging
the tension of creating something new that is also something old. We
do so by affirming that what we create together has the power, in turn,
to change us as a group and as individuals.

Women's seders arose in response to a need for women's experiences to be shared, preserved, and remembered. When we speak, our
words will become a bridge connecting us all. They will shape our community, our seder, and our future. Through our retellings, women's
voices will be heard more clearly in the Judaism of the present and of
the future. Our goal is to remember and to build.

—CLAIRE SUFRIN

## Joining Together

Tonight we sit at this Passover seder as a family. We, the daughters
and sons of Judaism, seek to find again the purest spirit of our heritage.

The seder is an invitation to all of us in this room to work together to make a sanctuary of blessings for our daughters and sons equally:
in our hearts, in our homes, in our neighborhoods, and in our country.

Each year, the celebration of Passover demands that we become
aware of injustice and oppression wherever they might exist. Here we
participate in the reenactment of the ancient drama of slavery and liberation and honor the deep need for redemption in us all. And so we
say together:

As we celebrate here,
We join with women and men everywhere

Who are working to break down the barriers,
To bring equality between our daughters and sons
For the sake of the earth and its children.

—SHARON L. SOBEL

## Daughters of Sarah

Where are the daughters of Sarah?

Sarah, the matriarch, is the mother of all Jewish women, for the line of the covenant is traced through her flesh. A woman of wisdom and beauty, she was a priestess in her own right. Perhaps more than anything else, Sarah is remembered for her laughter. In this way, she teaches us to take note of all the joys of life.

All Jewish women, everywhere—we are Sarah's daughters.


Are Miriam's daughters here?

Miriam led the Children of Israel out of Egypt and danced at the shores of the sea. Sister of Moses and Aaron, she was a prophetess, a leader, and a great musician. Miriam inspires us to celebrate our victories, despite the bitter oppression we have endured.

Every Jewish woman who raises her voice or instrument in song and music, or who moves her body in dance and celebration—we are Miriam's daughters.


The daughters of Ruth: Where are they?

Ruth, a Moabite who married into an Israelite family, followed her mother-in-law, Naomi, back to the Land of Israel after the death of her husband. Hers was a free choice to follow a woman she loved. Ruth told Naomi, "Wherever you go, I will go; wherever you lodge, I will lodge; your people shall be my people, and your God my God" (Ruth 1:16).

Every woman who makes the difficult choice to cast her lot with the Jewish people, and every woman who chooses to follow other women, out of loyalty or out of love—we are Ruth's daughters.

Esther's daughters: Are they with us?

Esther was a Persian Jew who found herself suddenly in a position of power when she was chosen to become the wife of King Ahashuerus. She could have enjoyed her status as a beauty queen and lived a life of leisure in the palace. But when the Jews were endangered by Haman, she risked her life to save her people. Esther's bravery enabled the Persian Jewish community to survive and thrive for thousands of years.

Every woman who has rebelled against the stereotype of women as sex symbols or Jewish princesses, every woman who has taken a stand for her political beliefs—we are Esther's daughters.

Do we number Beruriah's daughters among us?

Beruriah was a talmudic scholar whose insights were quoted by our sages for centuries. Her love of learning and Jewish law remains a shining exception to the male dominance of Jewish scholarship.

Every Jewish woman who has thirsted for study and knowledge, created her own midrash, interpreted the Torah's laws, or felt enraptured by a Hebrew prayer—we are Beruriah's daughters.

Are Doña Gracia Nasi's daughters here?

Doña Gracia Nasi was born into a *marrano* family shortly after the expulsion of the Jews from Portugal. Widowed as a young woman, she fled the Spanish Inquisition. As she moved from Portugal to Antwerp to Venice to Constantinople, she also helped other Jews escape through an "underground railroad."

Every woman who has succeeded on her own or who has had to deny some part of herself to survive, every woman whose bravery helped others survive—we are Doña Gracia's daughters.

Are Hannah Rachel Werbermacher's daughters here?

Hannah Rachel Werbermacher, often known as the Maid of Ludomir, is one of the few female mystics and Chasidic scholars whose name has come down to us. She taught both men and women and was called *Rebbe*.

Every woman who has explored the mystical texts of our tradition, every woman who has searched for religious innovation and meaning— we are Hannah Rachel's daughters.

Where are Emma Goldman's daughters?

Born in Russia in 1869, Emma Goldman was an anarchist leader as well as an early advocate for birth control, unionization, free speech, anti-conscription, and the eight-hour workday. She was imprisoned and deported from the United States for her activism. Even among her political allies, she was considered radical, bravely voicing her support for the rights of women and homosexuals.

Every woman who stands behind her principles and voices her beliefs despite the risks, every woman who works for social change—we are Emma's daughters.

The daughters of Hannah Senesh: Are they here?

Hannah Senesh went to Palestine as one of the earliest Zionist pioneers. During the Holocaust, she returned to Nazi Europe to rescue fellow Jews. Captured and tortured, she died at the age of twenty-three. Hannah Senesh, a true hero, left us her powerful poems.

Every Jewish woman fighter, Zionist, or poet—we are Hannah's daughters.

And the daughters of the unnamed ones: Where are they?

They are all the unnamed women, known only as daughter of, wife of, mother of. Women whose names are unknown and whose voices are unheard. We could not be here today without you, and we will speak up because you could not.

All of us, well known or anonymous, quiet or vocal—we are all, all of us, your daughters.

—ELAINE MOISE AND REBECCA SCHWARTZ

## Passover Miracle

that we find our spring selves again,
that we shed the thick protective layers
of winter that shield but
separate us from the world out there.

At the seder table we sit refreshed—
tired yes from all the work of preparation
but in spirit, refreshed.

We sit at the seder table
and encounter our younger selves
wide-eyed, asking questions.

We become each year once again
the four sons, we become child-like,
spring-like, ready each year once again
to go out from Egypt

with nothing
but a pack on our back
ready to walk once again
out into the wilderness
in search of our freedom
and our God.

—MERLE FELD

# Reflections on Preparing for Passover

## Finding Our Place

The hollow of my outstretched palms cradles an old wooden chopping bowl, its own hollow an etching, crosshatched like the faces of the women whose kitchens sanctified my childhood Pesach. Without the fish, there is no Sabbath. So goes the old Yiddish saying. Without women, there is no Pesach, I would say.

My *bubbe*, my aunts, my mother: I remember how they lay the sleeping babies crosswise on the beds and slipped their aprons off when *zayde*, dressed like a king, adjusted his snowy *kittel*, leaned to the left on his pillows in a great easy chair, and surveyed the seder table these women had prepared for us.

Weeks before, they polished windows with crumpled newsprint, opening the eyes of our houses to spring's first thin sunlight. They beat the winter salt out of carpets, saw to the wall washing, got out the mismatched Passover dishes where they were stored in the basement. They took us shopping for *yontif* outfits with such room to grow we looked like urchins out of the *shtetl*, then still found time to put up the hems and take up the sleeves so we wouldn't shame them when we sat down to the seder.

Days before, in the wooden chopping bowl, its bottom rounded as the bellies our mothers first carried us in, *bubbe* chopped fish into submission, then shaped it in her palms gently, but firmly, the way she had shaped the growing of her sons. I remember the roundness: circles of ruddy carrot to decorate the *gefilte* fish, matzah balls puffing with pride in boiling water, golden coins of fat floating in the nectar of her chicken soup. And the ubiquitous eggs, chattering away as their sides bumped against each other, hardboiling in the chipped enamel pot.

On seder nights, when we girls looked for our place in the haggadah, the women of our family were everywhere, shushing the children while the husbands and sons said *kiddush*, mopping the inevitable wine spills, and later, sucking in their bellies as they passed each other in *bubbe*'s tiny kitchen, stiffly balancing plates of chicken soup in their palms so as not to lose a single drop. Meanwhile, the men discussed the magical number four: four cups of wine, four sons, four questions, four commandments for observing the seder. Some say that the number four honors the Four Matriarchs, whose piety and modesty caused us to be redeemed, but we didn't learn that until so much later.

So the years of my childhood passed, each Pesach the same as the very first, the seasons coming round in a satisfying circle. Now I am the grandmother who makes the seder. I caress the hollow of *bubbe*'s chopping bowl and think of Yocheved nestling her baby in the hollow of a basket, her faith in God, an emblem of our people's destiny. The women I speak of are gone, but others take their place, linking one generation to the next. This year my daughter will recline at the table's head and lead us through the seder we women have once again prepared. So, as much as things are the same, some things are different. This year, leafing through the haggadah as women have done for centuries, we will have no trouble finding our place.

—FAYE MOSKOWITZ

## A Woman's Seder

It starts a week before.
Each drawer, each shelf,
   is stripped and scrubbed;
A rite performed each spring
   since Pharaoh forced
The chosen ones to flee
   before their bread could rise.
I wash a dish, streaked black
   from last year's news
And filled with years of
   family seders,
And think of Miriam,
The woman who began
Our journey to the promised land.
Did she lament the flat and
   tasteless bread
She served her men?
Or did she know that we
   would share her deed
Each spring as we recall
   her exodus from bondage,
That has still to be complete?
As smells of spring
   and chicken soup mix pleasingly,
I peel an apple, chop the nuts
   and sip the wine,

Remembering the bricks
   that stood between
Each ghetto girl and study
of the Torah.
The shankbone roasts
   and fills the air
Within my modern home
With smells of sacrifice
   that women made
So that there would be seders
   every year.
I fill a dish with bitter herbs,
But feel no bitterness,
Because I know that
   each small task links me
With every Hebrew woman
   who prepared
A seder meal since God proclaimed
   that Jews
Should celebrate their freedom
   every year.

Surely God never meant
For women to be passed over.

—*SAN DIEGO WOMEN'S HAGGADAH*

## Preparing for the Pilgrimage

"It's so much work!" remains the refrain around women's preparations for Passover. The rigorous work of cleaning, shopping, and cooking are tasks we rarely consider in their own right. Most often, we think about them in terms of the goal and reward of the seder, not as rituals.

But preparing for Passover could be very different if approached from a new perspective: Pesach is one of the three pilgrimage holidays, and the preparations for a pilgrimage enrich the process.

People going on a serious climb or trek train by walking around their neighborhoods with heavy backpacks to prepare for the adventure.

We clean, search, and labor in our homes. Might this also constitute an important ritual preparation for our journey toward freedom?

For as we clean we can sort through the accumulations of the past year and decide, "Do I really need this?" As we gaze at an object or reread a note, we can examine our relationship to it and to the memories and associations it holds. Some things will remain precious; others no longer engage us. We may learn that we have completed the chapter of our lives it belonged to, or that we have integrated the memory into our very beings and can let it go. We may want to throw certain things away, to create a space for a reinvention of some part of ourselves. With these reflections, a transformation is taking place—whether or not we choose it.

As we let go of what we no longer need, we challenge the stagnation in our personal lives. Cleaning becomes a meditation during which we address the emotional crumbs and clogs. We can ask ourselves, "Is this a crumb of the past that is not my present? What is my attachment to this thing? Can I let it go? Am I freer having this or letting it go? Do I have these things because there is a hole in my spirit that needs to be filled?" And as we search for *chametz*, we can imagine each crumb as some aspect of our lives or ourselves that no longer serves us. Are we willing to release that crumb even if there is nothing but empty space left behind, a space to grow into?

We can also reflect on perceiving this cleaning as a burden. Did we feel discomfort with this disruption to the flow of our ordinary lives, resentment that we have to unearth things that were just fine when they were hidden? We can ask ourselves, "Am I grateful for these Passover dishes, or are they a burden to me? What burdens do I carry or create in my life? Are they real, or something I hide behind? By thinking of Passover preparations as a burden, am I hiding from the opportunity for self-reflection that is waiting for me?"

The preparations for a pilgrimage are work, but they are sacred work. The cleaning ritual prepares us for pilgrimage because we are challenged to decide what is essential in this life. What do we each need or want to have as we go forward, knowing that our space and time are limited? By freeing ourselves of things, we create space to allow the unknown and the unexpected to enter. And if we allow the ultimate Unknown to be present with us, these moments may reveal hidden spaces in each of us that unfold in a life of their own.

—JUDY SIROTA ROSENTHAL

## Spring Cleaning Ritual on the Eve of the Full Moon Nisan

Removing the Hametz
In the month of nisan
with the death of winter
and the coming of spring
our ancient mothers
cleaned out their houses.

They gathered brooms, mops, brushes,
rags, stone, and lime
they washed down walls
swept floors
beat rugs
scoured pots
changed over all the dishes in the house.

They opened windows to the sun
hung linens for the airing out of blankets and covers
using fire
air
and water
in the cleaning.

In the month of nisan
before the parting seas
called them out of the old life
our ancient mothers
went down to the river
they went down to the river
to prepare their garments for the spring.

Hands pounded rock
voices drummed out song
there is new life inside us
*Shekhinah*
prepares for Her birth.

So we labor all women
cleaning and washing
now with our brothers
now with our sons
cleaning the inner house
through the moon of nisan.

On the eve of the full moon
we search our houses
by the light of a candle
for the last trace of winter
for the last crumbs grown stale inside us
for the last darkness still in our hearts.

Washing our hands
we say a blessing
over water...
We light a candle
and search in the listening silence
search the high places
and the low places
inside you
search the attic and the basement
the crevices and crannies
the corners of unused rooms.

Look in your pockets
and the pockets of those around you
for traces of Mitzrayim.

Some use a feather
some use a knife
to enter the hard places.

Some destroy Hametz with fire
others throw it to the wind
others toss it to the sea.

Look deep for the Hametz
which still gives you pleasure
and cast it to the burning.

When the looking is done
we say:

All that rises up bitter
All that rises up prideful
All that rises up in old ways no longer fruitful
All Hametz still in my possession
but unknown to me
which I have not seen
nor disposed of
may it find common grave
with the dust of the earth
amen amen
*selah....*

—LYNN GOTTLIEB

# Candlelighting

The Book of Genesis establishes the most basic rhythm of Jewish time in its account of Creation: "There was evening, and there was morning; the first day" (Genesis 1:5). Following this formulation, in Jewish tradition, each new day begins at night. Sunset, rather than sunrise, punctuates our transition from one day to the next.

Thus, the Sabbath begins at sundown, as does every Jewish festival. As we enter holy time, we greet the darkness by kindling lights. Traditionally, we light at least two candles and recite a blessing. Our act of kindling these lights links us to the Divine, whose work of Creation began with the words "Let there be light" (Genesis 1:3). The candles reflect both the light of Creation and the light of God's presence in our world.

Candlelighting has historically been performed in the home by women and therefore has particular resonance at a women's seder. Many communities highlight the special role of women in fulfilling this *mitzvah*.

At some women's seders, the blessing over candlelighting—the first formal blessing of the evening—raises questions about the language we use when we speak to and about God. Traditionally, Jewish prayers address God using primarily masculine metaphors, such as Father or King. Women's seders provide a unique ritual opportunity for participants to explore alternative language and imagery for God. Many women's haggadahs draw on references within Jewish mystical tradition to the *Shekhinah* as the feminine aspect of the Divine. Experimentation with God language at a women's seder allows participants to reflect on significant questions such as these: What emotions are evoked when we recite a blessing using feminine language for God? How is our understanding of God transformed when we explore feminine imagery for the Divine? How does this transformation affect our vision of ourselves, as human beings created in God's image? Including alternative liturgy for the candlelighting blessing, or a reading contemplating these questions, signals to participants that these important issues will be among those addressed at your seder table.

## The Radiance of the Infinite

We begin our celebration of the holiday by lighting the Passover candles. These lights mark the separation of profane from holy time. Lighting candles to mark holidays has traditionally been one of women's responsibilities. Tonight we light these candles in celebration of that duty and praise *Shekhinah,* the feminine face of the Eternal.

May the light of the candles we kindle together tonight cast their glow on the earth and bring the radiance of the Infinite to all who still live in darkness.

May this season, marking the deliverance of our people from Pharaoh, rouse us against anyone who keeps others in servitude.

In gratitude for the freedom we enjoy as women and as Jews here, may we strive to bring about the liberation of Jewish women within Judaism, and of all people everywhere.

—*WILLIAMS COLLEGE FEMINIST HAGGADAH*

# In Sarah's Tent

It began in Sarah's tent: a gleam of light, continuous in its intensity. The flame went out upon the death of our matriarch Sarah, and although Abraham continued to light the candles, they did not miraculously burn from one Friday to the next, as Sarah's had. This flame reignited only when Rebecca entered Sarah's home as Isaac's bride. Out of this midrash on the biblical story of our foremothers emerged the idea that Jewish women bring spirituality into their homes through the act of candlelighting.

How? How does a mere flame, albeit miraculous in its strength, draw spirituality into a concrete, physical surrounding? In the time of the *mishkan*, when God's presence presided with all its glory in God's home, there burned in the main sanctuary a constant flame, the *ner tamid*, lit each morning by the priests. If Godliness was palpable in the Tabernacle, and the Divine Light awesome, what need was there for a human-kindled flame? Despite the Spirit permeating the *mishkan*, it was necessary to have a tangible object connecting the spiritual and physical realms. The *ner tamid* was spirituality made manifest through a visible light. It thus paralleled the candles lit by Sarah and Rebecca, as the structure of the Temple mimics the homes of the matriarchs in its design.

A candle's flame is powerful. It can dispel darkness and brighten its surroundings with a peaceful glow. For the Jewish people, candlelighting has been and remains a symbol of the bond between the Divine Light and the inner spark that every Jew possesses. The flame of the candle merges with the light of the soul, bestowing an overwhelming sense of peace in the home. This peace brings blessings, happiness, and the promise of everlasting unity with God.

It is no small thing that one of the *mitzvot* that women traditionally perform is lighting this flame on every Friday evening and festival, sanctifying it with a blessing and welcoming the holiness of the day into our homes. Although the commandment of candlelighting was given to both men and women alike, long-standing custom entrusts this *mitzvah* to women, who are likewise entrusted with maintaining the spiritual atmosphere of the home. Women have channeled this spiritual energy, transmitting it through time, woman to woman, constantly rekindling this profound relationship between a Jewish home and the Creator.

Just as a flame flickers upward, the act of candlelighting uplifts and connects us to a higher, infinite source. As we light these candles tonight, we continue a tradition that began three thousand seven hundred years ago in the tent of our mother Sarah.

—TOBY HECHT

## A Passover *Tkhine*

The following prayer is a *tkhine*, one of the devotions in Yiddish recited by central and Eastern European Jewish women beginning in the sixteenth century.[1] The prayer translated below is from a *machzor*, a special festival prayer book for Passover.[2]

One feature of this text, typical of many later *tkhines*, is the interplay between Hebrew and Yiddish. Each short paragraph begins with a sentence in Hebrew, often echoing phrases from the Tanach or the prayer book, and continues with an expansion and interpretation of the Hebrew in Yiddish. The translation of the Hebrew is in bold type; the Yiddish translation is in regular type.

This *tkhine* is to be recited on the first and second nights of Passover after kindling the lights.

> **You are the Lord God who creates heaven and earth.** You are God, the God who has created the high heavens and the earth with all the creatures found therein.
>
> **For you perform miracles for us at every moment.** For you, God, work wonders and miracles for us at every moment; therefore, work wonders for me as well, accepting my words, although I know I am not worthy of it.
>
> **You brought us forth from Egypt to be your beloved people.** You took us out of Egypt and brought great plagues and blows upon the Egyptians, and you chose us to be your beloved people.

**And upon me, your handmaid, who knocks at the gates of compassion, may your mercies stir.** And upon me, _____, your handmaid, daughter of _____, your handmaid, who now comes knocking at the gates of mercy, may your mercies stir, that you may have compassion upon me and upon my husband and upon my children.

**And may no illness or injury come upon us.** And just as you protected your children, the People of Israel, from the plagues you brought upon the Egyptians, so may you protect us from all illness and plague.

**And by the merit of our eating unleavened bread, may you protect us from the "bread of affliction."** And by the merit of our keeping your holy commandment to eat unleavened bread for the entire festival—for matzah is called "bread of poverty"—may you protect us for our entire lives from poverty and hunger.

**Look down from the heavens and see the toil of your people.** Lord of the Universe, look down from heaven and see how much work and effort your dear children, the People of Israel, put out to honor the Passover holiday, and how much money they spend for the sake of the holy festival.

**They strive with all their might to fulfill your commandments.** They toil with all their substance to observe the commandment you have commanded them, to remove completely all leaven *[chametz]* from their houses and to eat unleavened bread for all seven days.

**Remember the merit of your tribes who entered the Sea of Reeds.** Dear God, remember to our credit the merit of the hosts of your People Israel, who themselves entered into the depths of the sea and had faith in you that you would save them so that they would not drown.

**Please accept with favor my blessing over the candles.** I pray you, dear God, merciful God, that you may accept with good will the blessing I have made over the candles which I kindled in honor of the holy festival.

**And may you enlighten the eyes of my husband and my children in your holy Torah.** And may you enlighten the eyes of my husband and my children in your holy Torah,

by the merit of my lighting my home with the candles for
the festival.

**And cause light to shine in the darkness of Jerusalem and
the Temple.** And may you cause light to shine in the darkness of Jerusalem and of the Temple, which have been dark
now for a very long time.

**And may we bring the paschal sacrifice to the fire on the
altar.** And may we be worthy to sacrifice the paschal lamb
upon the fire of the altar, speedily in our days, amen and
amen, so may it be God's will.

—FROM *MAHZOR MISHLEI YEHUDAH,* TRANSLATED AND
WITH AN INTRODUCTION BY CHAVA WEISSLER

## *Tachat Kanfei ha Shekhinah*

*Shekhinah:* you are the indwelling presence of God. You are present in
our lights: the *ner tamid,* Shabbat candles, our Yom Tov lights, in
every act of kindness that occurs in this world. You illuminated the
Western Wall until you went with our People Israel into exile. You are
the wandering female presence of God, trying to find your place in
the world; just as we, the Jewish women, must search for ours.

*Shekhinah:* when we are weary in our search, may we rest *tachat
kanfei ha Shekhinah,* beneath your wings of kindness.

We are troubled by the blank spaces in our Torah where we know
you once stood. We are startled when we listen and cannot hear our
voices. Comfort us; strengthen and remind us that you are with us in
our search. Let us continue to search together.

—STEPHANIE AARON

## Kindling a New Light

We sit here together in the darkness, preparing to begin our women's
seder. We're here to tell the story of our people. In doing so, we are
stepping into a familiar ritual: telling the story of our going out from
Egypt. But tonight we are stepping into the unknown as well, for we
are taking the risk of telling new stories and of finding old stories that

were lost. We are inviting ourselves into a tradition that is our own and yet has not always made us feel welcome, and we are inviting Judaism to have a place in our lives. As we relive the story of our escape from bondage and oppression we are moving toward the freedom of making choices—a freedom that comes as we begin to know ourselves. This seder, then, is also a search—a search for what is missing and a search for answers. We begin with searching for a way to speak of the dynamic Power that takes us out of our many Egypts and brings us home.

We know the names our fathers used in prayer. But for many of us, these words are incomplete. We do not know what She is called, but we are searching for names that will open us up to a Wonder that is nameless.

The seder begins with the kindling of lights. With this first ritual and blessing, we take up the challenge of naming. Creating new names may feel uncomfortable; yet, in doing so we hope to unearth and re-create our spirituality, our history. In our stories tonight, we begin to shed light on the dark places, to enrich our vision, and to open ourselves to new understanding. Let us gain strength for the journey as we kindle a new light.

—*OBERLIN COLLEGE HAGGADAH*

## Reflections on Feminine God Language

### Third hymn to the *shekhina*

I    *Ur*

You are hard for me, Lady
I'm still
Breaking my teeth on your name.
For that matter I'm
Hard for myself—
Breasts, hair, secret

Uncovenanted parts—All
That I struggle with. There's
Something you have to teach me
And I don't want to learn.
I keep
Trying
Holding back
Trying.

II    *Sinai*

All the prayers I make you are
Flashy
Like new silver.
It's too much
Being alone with you. I want a
*Rebbe,* a *minyan,* a
Thousand generations to put
A patina on these words—
I want a crowd around this mountain

III    *Meribah*

I should be
A Samuel for you but
Here I am
Wild, sullen, creeping close, then
Leaping away as if
You'd never touched me.
I should be
A David for you but
I don't want to sing.
I'm angry at you
Pushing, making me change.
I wanted to pray as if there
There were no women and
You wouldn't let me. I'm
Angry at you. You're not
Other enough or I'm not
Far enough beneath you.

Be more awesome. Let's have some
Magnificence here. Come
Clothed in crown and majesty. I'm
Angry at you; I'm
Afraid.

IV    *Gilui Shekhina*

Don't show me your face, please don't
Please
Don't
Show me your
Face your
Rachel face your
Battered your bereft your
Lost your longing your
Imperfect, incomplete
Translucent your
Transcendent your
Triumphant face—
Dark
Woman with eyes
Familiar with destruction
Leaning your forehead against
A crumbling wall.

—RACHEL ADLER

## the shekhinah as exile

hidden one: when the temple fell
when Jerusalem arose and fell and whenever
we were persecuted and scattered
by the nations,
to follow us in pain and exile
you folded wings patched coats
dragged mattresses pans in peasant carts, lived your life
laboring praying and giving birth, you also
swam across the hard Atlantic
landed in the golden land

they called you greenhorn
you danced in cafes
you went in the factory
bargained pushcart goods ice shoes Hester Street
put on makeup threw away wigs
and you learned new languages
now you speak everything
lady, but part of you is earth
part of you is wounds
part of you is words
and part is smoke
because whoever was burned over there, you were burned
you died forever with the sheep
whoever survived, you speak in our tongues
open your wings, instruct us
say what we are
do not confuse us
with the sanhedrin of the loud speakers
who have no ear for your voice
but we who thirst for your new
instructions, source of life
come into our thoughts
our mouth. Speak to us
voice of the beloved

help us
say what we are
say what we are to do

—ALICIA SUSKIN OSTRIKER

## God at a Women's Seder

To change the word King, to alter the term He,
Is not to make a statement. It is to ask
A question, to throw a what-if into temple air.

Judaism joys in the unanswerable questions, poured
Into portions by the infinite book. Here is a question
Outside the book. Unanswered, because it asks

Not the book we hold, but the one that holds us
Not the words we speak, but the words that speak us.

Women do not know what it means to live
In the house that they have lived in, where walls
Are covered in His image, and air ever echoes His name.

Under an ancient sun, our fathers answered questions
Of the book. We ask the question
Lying at its edge, floating out the window in red.
Do not ask in words; we do not yet know the language
Of possibility. Our answer has no verse, no passage,
No garden of black type.

New methods: strain to peek over the wall
Of consciousness and history. Strain for precipice and limit.
Sweat by exertion of the imagination. Fly the what-if
Into the air. Find, under muscles, in the space between cells,
The beating of a vision streaming light outside this Egypt.

—TARA MOHR

## Candlelighting Using Feminine God Language

בְּרוּכָה אַתְּ יָהּ
אֱלֹהֵינוּ רוּחַ הָעוֹלָם
אֲשֶׁר קִדְּשָׁתְנוּ בְּמִצְוֹתֶיהָ וְצִוַּתְנוּ
לְהַדְלִיק נֵר שֶׁל (שַׁבָּת וְשֶׁל) יוֹם טוֹב.

*B'rucha at yah eloheinu ruach ha'olam asher kid'shatnu
b'mitzvoteha v'tzivatnu l'hadlik ner shel (shabbat
v'shel) yom tov.*

You are Blessed, Our God, Spirit of the World, who
makes us holy with *mitzvot* and commands us to kindle the light of (Shabbat and of) the festival day.

*—THE JOURNEY CONTINUES: THE MA'YAN PASSOVER HAGGADAH*

# *Kadesh*

*adesh* comes from the Hebrew word that means "to sanctify" or "to set apart." As on every Sabbath and festival, we recite *kiddush* over a glass of wine or grape juice at the seder. With this blessing, we proclaim the holiness of the day.

Our ability to recite *kiddush*—to sanctify time—is itself an expression of our status as free men and women. Arguably, the most fundamental freedom denied to a slave is the freedom to determine how time is structured and spent. Slavery is a timeless existence in which nothing interrupts one essential reality: The slave must acquiesce to her master's wishes and come when her master calls.

Significantly, the words of the Sabbath and festival *kiddush* recall our Exodus from Egypt, emphasizing the profound link between freedom and the consciousness of sacred time. On Passover, this connection is intensified: We recline for the first time during the seder as we drink this first cup of wine. To further highlight our dignity as free people, it is customary for participants to refrain from pouring their own wine at the seder; instead, we pour for one another.

The Passover *kiddush* concludes with the *shehecheyanu*, traditionally known as *birkat ha'zman*, or the blessing over time. We recite this blessing at the beginning of Jewish holidays and to mark other special occasions. With the stirring words of the *shehecheyanu* blessing, we acknowledge the One who is truly the Master of our time on this earth, the One "who has kept us alive, and sustained us, and enabled us to reach this season."

## *Kiddush*

> Drink four cups of wine
> for the earth ever-turning
> for those who kept faith
> for Adonai who still waits
> for those of us, returning

—GERTRUDE RUBIN

## A Sip of *Kadosh*

> Blessed are You, Adonai,
> For reminding us that
> With holiness comes separation
> And for separating us, now, to remind us of
> Our holiness, even ours                     again ours
> Because with separation comes new space
> With new space, movement
> With movement, becoming
> With becoming, memory
> With memory, again, holiness
> A sip of *kadosh*.

—KIERA LEVINE

## Sanctification Over Wine for Passover

> Let us bless the source of life
> that ripens fruit on the vine
> as we hallow the Passover festival
> to commemorate our liberation.

קִדּוּשׁ לְחַג הַמַּצּוֹת

נְבָרֵךְ אֶת עֵין הַחַיִּים
מַצְמִיחַת פְּרִי הַגָּפֶן
וּנְקַדֵּשׁ אֶת חַג הַמַּצּוֹת,
זְמַן חֵרוּתֵנוּ,
זֵכֶר לִיצִיאַת מִצְרָיִם.

—MARCIA FALK

## Sanctification Over Wine for Sabbath and Passover

There was evening and there was morning, the sixth day.
The heavens and earth were complete, with all their hosts.
  (Genesis 1:31–2:1)

Let us bless the source of life
that ripens fruit on the vine
as we hallow the seventh day—
the Sabbath day—
in remembrance of creation,
and as we hallow the Passover festival
to commemorate our liberation.

קִדּוּשׁ לְלֵיל שַׁבָּת וְחַג הַמַּצּוֹת

וַיְהִי־עֶרֶב וַיְהִי־בֹקֶר, יוֹם הַשִּׁשִּׁי.
וַיְכֻלּוּ הַשָּׁמַיִם וְהָאָרֶץ וְכָל־צְבָאָם.
בראשית א:לא - ב:א

נְבָרֵךְ אֶת עֵין הַחַיִּים
מַצְמִיחַת פְּרִי הַגָּפֶן
וּנְקַדֵּשׁ אֶת יוֹם הַשְּׁבִיעִי —
יוֹם הַשַּׁבָּת —
זִכָּרוֹן לְמַעֲשֵׂה בְרֵאשִׁית,

וּנְקַדֵּשׁ אֶת חַג הַמַּצוֹת,
זְמַן חֵרוּתֵנוּ,
זֵכֶר לִיצִיאַת מִצְרָיִם.

—MARCIA FALK

## Sanctification Over Wine with Feminine God Language

בְּרוּכָה אַתְּ יָהּ
אֱלֹהֵינוּ רוּחַ הָעוֹלָם
בּוֹרֵאת פְּרִי הַגֶּפֶן.

*B'rucha at yah eloheinu ruach ha'olam boreit p'ri
hagefen.*

You are Blessed, Our God, Spirit of the World, who
creates the fruit of the vine.

—*THE JOURNEY CONTINUES: THE MA'YAN PASSOVER HAGGADAH*

## Festival *Kiddush* with Feminine God Language

Begin here on Friday night:

(וַיְהִי־עֶרֶב וַיְהִי־בֹקֶר יוֹם הַשִּׁשִּׁי.
וַיְכֻלּוּ הַשָּׁמַיִם וְהָאָרֶץ
וְכָל־צְבָאָם.
וַתְּכַל אֱלֹהִים בַּיּוֹם הַשְּׁבִיעִי
מְלַאכְתָּהּ אֲשֶׁר עָשָׂתָה.
וַתִּשְׁבֹּת בַּיּוֹם הַשְּׁבִיעִי
מִכָּל־מְלַאכְתָּהּ אֲשֶׁר עָשָׂתָה.
וַתְּבָרֶךְ אֱלֹהִים אֶת־יוֹם הַשְּׁבִיעִי
וַתְּקַדֵּשׁ אֹתוֹ
כִּי בוֹ שָׁבְתָה מִכָּל־מְלַאכְתָּהּ
אֲשֶׁר־בָּרָאָה אֱלֹהִים לַעֲשׂוֹת.)

*(Vay'hi erev vay'hi voker yom hashishi. Vay'chulu
hashamayim v'ha'aretz v'chol tz'va'am. Va'techal elo-*

*him bayom hash'vi'i m'lachta asher asta. Va'tishbot*
*bayom hash'vi'i mikol m'lachta asher asta. Va'tevarech*
*elohim et yom hash'vi'i va'tekadeish oto, ki vo shavta*
*mikol m'lachta asher bar'a elohim la'asot.)*

Continue here, adding words in parentheses on Shabbat:

בְּרוּכָה אַתְּ יָהּ
אֱלֹהֵינוּ רוּחַ הָעוֹלָם
בּוֹרֵאת פְּרִי הַגָּפֶן.
בְּרוּכָה אַתְּ יָהּ
אֱלֹהֵינוּ רוּחַ הָעוֹלָם
אֲשֶׁר בָּחֲרָה־בָנוּ מִכָּל־עָם
וְרוֹמְמַתָנוּ מִכָּל־לָשׁוֹן
וְקִדְּשָׁתְנוּ בְּמִצְוֹתֶיהָ.
וַתִּתְּנִי־לָנוּ יָהּ, אֱלֹהֵינוּ
בְּאַהֲבָה (שַׁבָּתוֹת לִמְנוּחָה וּ)
מוֹעֲדִים לְשִׂמְחָה
חַגִּים וּזְמַנִּים לְשָׂשׂוֹן

אֶת יוֹם (הַשַּׁבָּת הַזֶּה וְאֶת יוֹם)
חַג הַמַּצּוֹת הַזֶּה
זְמַן חֵרוּתֵנוּ
(בְּאַהֲבָה) מִקְרָא קֹדֶשׁ
זֵכֶר לִיצִיאַת מִצְרָיִם.
כִּי בָנוּ בָחַרְתְּ וְאוֹתָנוּ קִדַּשְׁתְּ
מִכָּל־הָעַמִּים
(וְשַׁבָּת) וּמוֹעֲדֵי קָדְשֶׁךְ
(בְּאַהֲבָה וּבְרָצוֹן)
בְּשִׂמְחָה וּבְשָׂשׂוֹן הִנְחַלְתָּנוּ.
בְּרוּכָה אַתְּ יָהּ מְקַדֶּשֶׁת (הַשַּׁבָּת וְ)
יִשְׂרָאֵל וְהַזְּמַנִּים.

*B'rucha at yah eloheinu ruach ha'olam boreit p'ri*
*hagafen. B'rucha at yah eloheinu ruach ha'olam asher*

*bachara vanu mikol am, v'romematnu mikol lashon,*
*v'kid'shatnu b'mitzvoteiha. Vatit'ni'lanu, yah eloheinu,*
*b'ahava (shabbatot lim'nucha u') mo'adim l'simcha,*
*chagim uz'manim l'sason, et yom (hashabbat hazeh v'et*
*yom) chag hamatzot hazeh, z'man cheiruteinu, (b'aha-*
*va) mikra kodesh, zeicher litzi'at mitzrayim. Ki vanu*
*vachart, v'otanu kidasht, mikol ha'amim (v'shabbat)*
*umo'adei kodsheich (b'ahava uv'ratzon) b'simcha*
*uv'sason hinchalatnu. B'rucha at yah m'kadeshet*
*(hashabbat v') yisraeil v'haz'manim.*

On Saturday night, add the following to mark the division between
Shabbat and the festival:

בְּרוּכָה אַתְּ יָהּ אֱלֹהֵינוּ רוּחַ הָעוֹלָם
בּוֹרֵאת מְאוֹרֵי הָאֵשׁ:
בְּרוּכָה אַתְּ יָהּ אֱלֹהֵינוּ רוּחַ הָעוֹלָם
הַמַּבְדִילָה בֵּין קֹדֶשׁ לְחוֹל
בֵּין אוֹר לְחֹשֶׁךְ
בֵּין יִשְׂרָאֵל לָעַמִּים
בֵּין יוֹם הַשְּׁבִיעִי לְשֵׁשֶׁת יְמֵי הַמַּעֲשֶׂה:
בֵּין קְדֻשַּׁת שַׁבָּת לִקְדֻשַּׁת יוֹם טוֹב
הִבְדַּלְתְּ וְאֶת־יוֹם הַשְּׁבִיעִי
מִשֵּׁשֶׁת יְמֵי הַמַּעֲשֶׂה קִדַּשְׁתְּ.
הִבְדַּלְתְּ וְקִדַּשְׁתְּ אֶת עַמֵּךְ יִשְׂרָאֵל בִּקְדֻשָּׁתֵךְ.
בְּרוּכָה אַתְּ יָהּ הַמַּבְדִּילָה בֵּין קֹדֶשׁ לְחוֹל.

*Brucha at ya eloheinu ruach ha'olam boreit me'orei*
*ha'esh. Brucha at ya eloheinu ruach ha'olam hamavdi-*
*lah bein kodesh lechol bein or lechoshech, bein yisrael*
*la'amim bein yom hashevi'i lesheshet yemei hama'aseh.*
*Bein kedushat shabbat li'kedushat yom tov hivdalt ve'et*
*yom hashevi'i misheshet yemei hama'aseh kidasht. Hiv-*
*dalt vekidasht et ameich yisra'el bikdushatech. Brucha*
*at yah hamavdilah bein kodesh lechol.*

—*THE JOURNEY CONTINUES: THE MA'YAN PASSOVER HAGGADAH*

# Readings for Shehecheyanu

## This Special Occasion

The *shehecheyanu* prayer is used to mark special events in one's life as well as to mark the arrival of festivals throughout the year. We make this blessing tonight in honor of this special occasion—may there be many more to come.

—STEPHANIE AARON

## This First Night

We follow the blessing of the wine with the blessing that reminds us of the joy of life. This prayer is usually said only on "first nights." We recite it together on this night to acknowledge our first coming together as women at this season.

—NAIDA COHN

## Blessing for the New and for Renewal

Let us bless the flow of life
that revives us, sustains us,
and brings us to this time.

שֶׁהֶחֱיָנוּ

נְבָרֵךְ אֶת מַעְיַן חַיֵּינוּ
שֶׁהֶחֱיָנוּ וְקִיְּמָנוּ וְהִגִּיעָנוּ
לַזְּמַן הַזֶּה.

—MARCIA FALK

## *Shehecheyanu* with Feminine God Language

בְּרוּכָה אַתְּ יָהּ
אֱלֹהֵינוּ רוּחַ הָעוֹלָם
שֶׁהֶחֱיַתְנוּ וְקִיְּמַתְנוּ וְהִגִּיעַתְנוּ
לַזְּמַן הַזֶּה.

*B'rucha at yah eloheinu ruach ha'olam shehecheyatnu
v'kiy'matnu v'higiatnu laz'man hazeh.*

You are Blessed, Our God, Spirit of the World, who
keeps us in life, who sustains us, and who enables us
to reach this season.

*—THE JOURNEY CONTINUES: THE MA'YAN PASSOVER HAGGADAH*

# The Four Cups

Kadesh marks the first of four cups of wine that we will drink during the course of the seder. We recite *kadesh* over the first cup, *maggid* over the second, *barekh* over the third, and *hallel* over the fourth. Readings for each of the four cups are included here.

These cups are traditionally associated with God's four promises to the Israelites, recounted in the Book of Exodus: "I will free you from the burdens of the Egyptians. I will deliver you from their bondage. I will redeem you with an outstretched arm. I will take you to be My people and I will be your God" (Exodus 6:6–7). Many seders highlight this connection by including readings that elaborate on the meaning of the four divine promises.

At women's seders, it is customary to link the four cups to Jewish women who have been important sources of wisdom, courage, and inspiration throughout Jewish history and in our own time. Some communities select four women and explore their lives and accomplishments in depth, featuring different heroines each year. Others honor a group of women, acknowledging, for example, women from particular eras of history with each cup. Alternatively, some opt to honor women who have had a more personal impact on the lives of the women present, whether as role models, teachers, or friends.

## Out of the Shadows of the Past

The sages teach that the four cups of wine represent God's promises of redemption:

> Say, therefore, to the Israelite people: I am the Lord. *V'hotzaiti—I will free you* from the labors of the Egyptians, *V'hitzalti—and I will deliver you* from their bondage. *V'ga'alti—I will redeem you* with an outstretched arm and through extraordinary chastisements. *V'lakachti—And I will take you* to be My people, and I will be your God (Exodus 6:6–7).

Each expression marks a stage in the transition from slavery to freedom. So, too, let each cup mark for us a stage in the history of Jewish women. Let the four cups take our women out of the shadows of the past and bring them across time and space to our seder table.

### The First Cup: V'hotzaiti

With the first cup, we bring out the Jewish women of biblical Israel. Recall the matriarchs, Sarah, Rebecca, Leah, and Rachel, and all who were mothers; the prophetesses and the women who joined them—those who danced alongside Miriam and who went to war with Deborah; those who were wise, as was Hulda; those who prayed before the Lord, as did Hannah; those who were royal: Michal, Abigail, and Batsheva.

Let this cup also remind us of those unnamed: the mother who stood before Solomon, willing to surrender her child rather than see him cleaved in two; the women who worked in the fields beside Naomi and Ruth; and all those evoked by the proverbial woman of valor: "She girds herself with strength, and performs her tasks with vigor…let her works praise her in the gates" (Proverbs 31:17, 31).

### The Second Cup: V'hitzalti

With the second cup, we deliver from our past the women who lived in the long centuries that followed, from late antiquity to the cusp of the modern era. Recall those who prayed at the birth of a daughter, "May she sew, spin, weave, and be brought up to a life of good deeds"; the wives who ground corn, baked bread, cooked food, nursed their children, and conversed while spinning yarn in the moonlight; those who kept the Sabbaths, the festivals, the commandments concerning a woman's cycle; those who sewed Torah scrolls, made candles for the synagogue, and embroidered Hebrew inscriptions.

Bring forth some names from these long centuries: Rufina, "a Jewess, head of the synagogue," in second-century Smyrna; Beruriah, whose learning was so prized that, when the sages discussed her insights, they observed, "Rightly did Beruriah say"; Al-Wuhsha and Gluckel of Hameln, savvy businesswomen in twelfth-century Cairo and seventeenth-century Europe; Doña Gracia Nasi, the Sephardi patroness and philanthropist, who fled the Inquisition and helped others do the same; Sarah Rebecca Rachel Leah Horowitz, who wrote *tkhines*, women's devotional prayers, in eighteenth-century Poland.

Let us also remember with this cup the far too many who died cruel deaths, hacked by Crusaders' swords, burnt at the stake on false charges of ritual murder, and broken on the racks of the Inquisition.

### *The Third Cup:* V'ga'alti

With the third cup, we redeem and recall the voices of the women of the modern Jewish experience. Recall the German housewives who made their Jewish homes islands of serenity; the mothers of the *shtetl* who hawked wares in the marketplace; the daughters of the *shtetl* who sang, "Why was I born to be a seamstress, why?"; the ladies of the sisterhood who outfitted the Sunday schools; the *chalutzot* (pioneers) who labored in the kibbutzim.

As we get closer to our own moment in time, the most famous— Henrietta Szold, Golda Meir—burst forth. But with this cup, let us redeem those whose names are less well known: the writers Mary Antin and Pauline Wengeroff; the educators Rebecca Gratz and Sarah Schenirer; the activists Emma Goldman and Clara Lemlich Shavelson; the social workers Rebekah Kohut and Bertha Pappenheim; the religious leaders Mathilde Schechter and Regina Jonas; the Zionists Manya Shochat and Rahel.

And we must pause to remember in sorrow that in modern times too, Jews died as Jews. Edith Holländer Frank and her daughters, Anne and Margot, were but three among the millions slaughtered and gassed in the Holocaust.

### The Fourth Cup: V'lakachti

With the fourth cup, we take to this seder table contemporary Jewish women, those among us now. Celebrate those at this table and those not so near. For all belong to this, the most recent stage in the history of our women.

—PAMELA S. NADELL

## To Life!: The Four Cups of Feminist Judaism

### The First Cup

We dedicate this first cup to the individuals and institutions who glimpsed the barest vision of a Judaism that embraced women as full participants in Jewish life—as equals to men in religious participation and obligation, in leadership roles in the synagogue and in communal life, in the eyes of the rabbinical court.

We acknowledge the earliest efforts of the Reform movement in the nineteenth century, which abolished the *mechitzah* and established the precedent of family pews—males and females seated together—in the synagogue.

We take note of the Reconstructionist movement, which made its mark on the American Jewish scene with the celebration of the first bat mitzvah ceremony in 1922, and which began to call women to the Torah in the 1950s.[1]

We are grateful to the women's organization *Ezrat Nashim*, which challenged the Conservative movement in the 1970s and early 1980s to act on the "conviction that women are intellectually and spiritually equal to men and equally deserving of positions of authority within the synagogue and community." These efforts to foster egalitarianism within Judaism helped reimagine the sociological landscape of the Jewish community and transform Judaism as a religion.

## The Second Cup

Our second cup is raised high to Jewish feminists who sought the renewal of religious Jewish life through a strategy of liberation. These feminists did not want to participate as equals in a system they believed to be overwhelmingly male-oriented. They desired instead to transform this tradition into one that was more inclusive and more expansive—for their own sake, for the sake of their daughters, for the sake of their sons.

The advocates of this second stage of Jewish feminism began the task of forging new prayers and blessings, sometimes translating traditional male language into the feminine, at other times creating entirely new prayer formulas and images. In their pioneering efforts, they reclaimed less dominant theologies and fashioned new ones, moving beyond "*Avinu malkenu,* our Father, our King" to embrace such mystical images of the divine as *Shekhinah,* and such naturalistic images as *Hamakom,* the Omnipresent One, and *Eyn hahayim,* the Wellspring of Life.

They created an abundance of new ceremonies, including baby namings, rituals to mark the onset of puberty and menopause, and rituals to ease the suffering of rape survivors and of women unable to bear children.

We honor those who poured out their energies even as they could barely imagine a Judaism transcending its male focus, who labored on even as they were vilified as threats to the continuity of the chain of Jewish tradition. We drink gratefully for this generation's clarity, while acknowledging that redemption is not yet complete. Their vision enabled them to see that it was not necessary to choose between feminism and Judaism, but rather that women can be fully Jewish and fully female, and that including women in ways that mark the fullness of their lives enhances and enriches Jewish life for all Jews.

## The Third Cup

We have eaten richly of our festive meal; we are filled with gratitude for the efforts of those who have worked to create this evening of discussion and feasting and to create a world where women's rituals are increasingly celebrated.

We fill our third cup with sober recognition of the work that is yet to be done to fulfill the vision of feminist Judaism and to achieve a transformed Jewish life. While we celebrate the enormous strides taken to make Judaism more inclusive for women, we recognize that many Jews are still excluded, as women were for so long, from full participation in Jewish life. We acknowledge the work we must take on to create room at our table for the gloriously diverse members of the Jewish community.

We must reach out to all Jewish families as they are today—multiracial, interfaith, single-parent, or with two mothers or two fathers. We must redefine "family" so that we fully grasp that it is a sin to exclude or marginalize individuals who will never stand under a *chuppah* or who will never have biological children.

We must embrace Jews who identify as gay, lesbian, bisexual, transgendered. We must open our arms to non-Jewish partners. We must reform our organizational and communal institutions so that they are open to Jews from all socioeconomic backgrounds. We must ensure that individuals with physical disabilities and chronic illness are able to participate fully in our gatherings. We must take care not to prioritize the experiences of Eastern European ancestors over those of Jews of Spanish, North African, Asian, and Ethiopian descent.

The Rabbis wrote: "You are not obliged to complete the work, but neither are you free to set it aside." Let the wine nourish our spirits as we take hold of the rich legacy of our feminist forebears and further their work.

### The Fourth Cup

We sip from our fourth and final cup, imagining the sweet liquid as a taste of a redeemed world, when all of our daughters and all of our sons—be they biological children, adopted children, or spiritual heirs—are free to be fully and completely themselves, celebrated for who they are and what they accomplish, able to give of themselves generously to the Jewish community and to the wider world. To life! *L'Chayim!*

—DEBORAH WAXMAN

## Our Foremothers' Exodus

The four cups we drink at the seder derive from Exodus 6:6–7. In these verses, God uses four expressions to describe how Israel will be redeemed from Egypt: *hotzaiti* (I will bring you out), *hitzalti* (I will deliver), *ga'alti* (I will redeem), and *lakachti* (I will take you out).

Nahmanides, a thirteenth-century Spanish kabbalist, discusses these terms as referring to four stages in the process of Israel's redemption. *Hotzaiti* signifies that God will remove the physical burden of slavery from the Israelites. *Hitzalti* affirms that God will no longer allow Israel to be subjugated as slaves. *Ga'alti* expresses that the redemption will come at the price of the Egyptians' lives, in exchange for God's plagues and miracles. The word *lakachti* presages that the Israelites will become God's people when they experience revelation and receive the Torah. Tonight, we imagine how this four-step process would have been experienced by one of our foremothers.

### The First Cup: "I shall bring you out from under the burdens of Egypt"

It has become a part of me, this basket I carry on my head. I can barely feel it. I was born carrying this weight, as were my parents before me, and their parents before them. I am hunched over now, crushed into one older than her years.

Can my children really be spared? Yet, today my burden will be removed. I bow to my God even as I am released.

But I have grown accustomed to this life. What does it mean to throw off this basket? What does it mean to have freedom?

There was a time when I would dream of such things.
Throwing off that weight, and running far.
Now I no longer dream.
Yet I begin to feel it.

### The Second Cup: "I shall deliver you from their bondage"

God has released us. My great-grandchildren will not know this land. They will know nothing of my oppressors and will laugh in the morning sun. They will touch my scars and ask where they came from.

They will take my gnarled hands in their own, soft and dirty from play.

Should I feed them bitter herbs? Should I explain these scars? Describe my masters' faces to the last detail?

Or shall I pretend that age has taken away my memory and thereby take away theirs as well? Withhold these bitter herbs and hide my scars, wave away the past so it can't hurt them?

They must feel my scars, and touch my rough, misshapen hands.
To remember the pain is to know the past.
To know the past is to own the future
And to own anything at all is freedom.

### The Third Cup: "I shall redeem you with an outstretched arm and with great judgments"

God has bought my freedom.
Traded it for blood swirling into water,
Swarms of locusts, and crawling vermin,
Dazed mothers standing empty-handed,
Fire and smoke billowing above the tallest pyramids
One brave soul jumped in feet first, and the water rose
In spectacular structures all around us.

### The Fourth Cup: "I shall take you to be my people and I shall be your God"

I shall be Yours, God.
Through thunder and lightning and blasts of the horn
You shall be mine, God
Through fire and smoke and crying
I shall take You, God
You shall take me, God
With a low whisper in my ear
You have revealed Yourself to me.

—ISCAH WALDMAN

# Ur'chatz

**D**uring the seder, we wash our hands twice: once before dipping and eating the *karpas* and again before eating matzah, the bread of the Passover meal. The first handwashing, *ur'chatz*, is performed in silence; no liturgy accompanies this ritual act. Only later in the seder, with *rochtzah*, do we recite the handwashing blessing as we wash in preparation for the festival meal.

The silence of *ur'chatz* allows time for personal reflection. How have we used our hands since we last sat at the seder table? What have they created? What burdens have they carried? What does it mean to cleanse ourselves in preparation for the seder? What do we seek to wash away with the waters of *ur'chatz*? You may choose to reflect on these questions together or to preserve the silence of *ur'chatz*, suggesting that participants pause for quiet meditation during the handwashing.

In some communities, women wash one another's hands. This can be a wonderful way to create a sense of connection among participants at an early moment in the seder. As we wash one another's hands, we affirm that we will strive to use our hands to offer comfort and healing to others.

At other seders, particularly larger gatherings, the leader performs the handwashing on behalf of all the women present. Alternatively, one individual from each table can wash her hands, representing the others at her table. If you want each person at the seder to be able to wash her hands, you may choose to set up washing stations around the room or to place pitchers and basins on each table. It is worth noting that the process of handwashing can take a significant amount of time, depending on the size of your seder.

At many women's seders, *ur'chatz* has become a time to reflect on the centrality of water in the Exodus narrative. Throughout the story of our liberation from Egypt, water is a potent symbol of life and death, signifying both the risks and the possibilities in the journey from slavery to freedom. Significantly, from the banks of the Nile River to the shores of the Sea of Reeds, it is often women who, by hiding, rescuing, singing, and dancing, courageously transform the waters of despair into waters of hope and redemption.

## All These Things Are Possible

On all other nights, we wash our hands only before we bless and eat bread. Why do we wash our hands an extra time tonight, before dipping and eating the *karpas*?

Is it because we are about to take our first taste of this ritual meal? Is it because we are about to dip the *karpas* into a communal dish, one filled with the salt water of our tears and our hope? Or is it to spark our children, and ourselves with them, to ask these very questions: Why are we doing this, when on all other nights we do not?

As we wash our hands in silence, without even a blessing to break our concentration, we rediscover the answer—one we have known all along. We are together tonight because all these things are possible: our ritual, our family and community, our hope and tears, and our telling of the story. We were slaves to Pharaoh in Egypt, and now we are free.

—JORDANA SCHUSTER

## God's Children

In the story of the Exodus, water is associated both with sustaining life and bringing death. Moses' mother places him in the river to save his life. Pharaoh's daughter pulls him from the water to nurture him into adulthood. The Israelites are redeemed at the shore of the Sea of Reeds as it parts to let them pass into freedom. Following in pursuit, the Egyptians are swallowed by that same sea and drown as the waters crash around them.

At the water's edge, God reminds us that all people are God's creations. As the Israelites rejoice in their redemption from bondage God rebukes them for singing as God's other children were drowning. As we wash our hands in silence we honor the power of water and remember our kinship with all of God's children.

*—JEWISH FEDERATION OF METROPOLITAN DETROIT*
*WOMEN'S HAGGADAH*

## Women Who Met by the Water

Two remarkable women met by the water: Pharaoh's daughter and Miriam, the sister of Moses. The result of this interfaith encounter is the recovery of baby Moses and his royal "adoption." We do not know the name of Pharaoh's daughter but we do know that she defied her father's evil decree and risked his wrath by taking Moses into her home. She and Miriam together began the cycle of love, hope, and ultimately redemption.

—NAAMAH KELMAN

## In These Hands

A silent washing—another door to freedom
Hands open to receive the cool water
Our bodies awaken.

Listen as you begin to relax, let go of slaveries, habits, hurts—
    let go,
even of expectations for tonight.

Take a quiet moment.
What does the water of life feel like on your fingers, palm, on
    the back of your hand?

A silent washing

The blessing is in this silence.
In these hands.
In this moment.

Now we draw closer
To dip
To taste
To tell
To remember
To rejoice!

—SHEILA PELTZ WEINBERG

## Our Silent Handwashing

Our silent handwashing follows the words of *kiddush* with a power
akin to that of our hands themselves. Weaving, washing, braiding;
feeding and holding loved ones—our hands, according to midrash, are
created for the purpose of our work. In preparation for Pesach, our
hands have scraped and scrubbed, carried and cut, sweated and stirred.
In perpetual motion, they have performed a multitude of tasks.

Often we do not have a chance to pause or reflect on their work.
But at this moment, we pause, appreciate, honor. Are we cleansing?
Purifying? Dedicating? Sanctifying?

"*Avadim hayinu l'Pharaoh b'Mitzrayim va-yotzi'einu Adonai Eloheinu mishahm b'yad chazakah u'viz'roa n'tuyah.* We were slaves to
Pharaoh in Egypt, but Adonai our God brought us forth with a strong
hand and an outstretched arm." "Once we were slaves, now we are
free": free to paint, to make music, to write poetry; free to heal with
our hands, to caress one another, to feel the soothing water as it is
poured over our fingers.

The water refreshes, nurtures, and connects us to the original stream, the first flow. It reminds us that we have been birthed and that we give birth, in body and in spirit. It reminds us of the fluidity of all life, and the fluid within us. It tickles our hands so that they may dance the dance of freedom.

—ELANA PONET

# *Karpas*

**K**arpas is the first of the symbolic foods that we eat at the seder. It is specifically meant to arouse curiosity and questioning: Why *is* this night different from all other nights? Why, on this night, do we dip a vegetable in salt water before we eat the festival meal? In asking these questions, we undertake the process of inquiry that is so central to the Passover seder.

*Karpas* is usually a green vegetable, such as parsley, lettuce, or celery, although some communities use a potato instead. Interpretations of *karpas* abound, but it is most often understood as a symbol of springtime and renewal. In this sense, *karpas* offers a humble message of hope that complements Passover's grander vision of redemption. *Karpas* does not proclaim the existence of miraculous "signs and wonders"; it reminds us of the quiet reawakening of the earth each spring and the unseen possibilities for new life that are always just below the surface, waiting to blossom.

The *karpas* is dipped in salt water, evoking the salty tears that our ancestors wept while they were slaves in Egypt. The dipping of *karpas* asks us to do what our ancestors have done at seders throughout the ages: taste the tears of suffering intimately, on our own tongues, and yet recognize, bless, and savor the taste of hope.

Some women's seders use the *karpas* ritual as a time to reflect on our connection to the earth. It is an opportunity to express our commitment to treating the natural world and all its creatures with greater respect and care so that new life can indeed continue to spring forth from the earth.

## Come with Me

Come with me,
my love,
come away

For the long wet months are past,
the rains have fed the earth
and left it bright with blossoms

Birds wing in the low sky,
dove and songbird singing
in the open air above

Earth nourishing tree and vine,
green fig and tender grape,
green and tender fragrance

Come with me,
my love,
come away

—*THE SONG OF SONGS*, TRANSLATED BY MARCIA FALK

## Why Are All Other Nights Different from This Night?

*The following reading may be used to introduce the custom followed in many Mizrahi communities of dipping* karpas *in lemon juice at the seder.*

When I was a little girl, Ashkenazim regularly explained my family's "difference" with the following refrain: "Oh, you're from Iraq. You were under Arab influence. That's why you don't do things the normal way." I remember trying to wrap my brain around that statement, assuming the adults should know more than me. I thought that rabbis and teachers were aware that Sarah and Abraham came from Iraq, that the first yeshivas were in Iraq, and that the Talmud was written in Iraq. I thought they knew that Passover took place in Egypt and that Purim took place in Iran. I thought it was obvious to them that the Jewish holiday cycle was based on a Middle Eastern calendar and that Mizrahi and Sephardi communities predated Ashkenazi communities by thousands of years. So why, I wondered, do they see our traditions as being the result of Arab influence? If anything, why don't they see their traditions as being the result of European influence?

No amount of explaining seemed to persuade the Jewish community that non-Ashkenazi traditions were legitimate. And so, as much as my family tried to be a part of the Jewish community, we were regularly alienated from and insulted by it. When I was five years old, for example, guests stormed out of our home as soon as the Passover meal was served. Once word got out that we served rice on Passover, the local community declared our strictly Orthodox home "unkosher."

Today it is trendy for Ashkenazim to eat rice on Passover, but the rice remains a symbolic side dish at the collective Jewish table; for shifting practice without shifting consciousness is simply co-opting tradition. Until mainstream Jewish leadership reflects more than a token group of Jews of color, until non-Ashkenazi leaders are no longer expected to adjust to the Ashkenazi bias in Jewish organizations, and until Ashkenazi leaders are required to know and teach about non-Ashkenazi history, heritage, and religious traditions in order to be hired, the collective Jewish "table" will remain an exclusively Ashkenazi domain.

Jewish feminism has successfully challenged the male hegemony of Judaism but to date has left in place the Ashkenazi hegemony. This Passover, let us dedicate ourselves to shifting our consciousness and freeing all our Jewish sisters: Mizrahi, Sephardi, and Ethiopian Jewish women; Ashkenazi women of color; and white Ashkenazi women, all of us together.

For starters, as we bless the parsley and dip it in lemon juice, let us notice if we wonder, "Why lemon juice instead of salt water?" And if we do, let us begin to ask the question, "Why salt water instead of lemon juice?" As my mother always answers, "It's because they didn't have lemon trees in Poland!"

—LOOLWA KHAZZOOM

## Transforming *Karpas*

Western society historically connects women and earth—an association with which we may or may not comfortably identify. We are the "natural" ones, the "earth mothers." Sometimes there can be a positive spin to this link; other times, it is decisively negative. Remember Eve, who was kind to all animals and liked to try new foods?

But for a moment, let's accept the earth-woman connection.

In the traditional *karpas* ritual, the greens, symbol of nature, are drowned in the tragedy of the collective Jewish past. The salt water overshadows the innocuous parsley. For women, being overshadowed is a familiar situation. In the traditional seder, our stories are forgotten among those of the men.

In transforming the *karpas* ritual, we recognize this bit of nature as a symbol of ourselves. As we dip into the salt water that is our tears, we cry for the oppression of women throughout history, we cry for the oppression we suffered and continue to suffer. For these tears are not only in the past; as Jewish women, we are not yet free.

Remembering our connection to the natural world around us, we cry also for the oppression of the earth—a condition that need not be. But we willingly plunge ourselves into the sadness in order to emerge bathed in the waters that will stir our action and our renewal.

It is a *mikveh* in a salty Miriam's well. The fruit of the earth, which has thrived along with us in Miriam's fresh water, mixes with the water of the sea, nourisher of many plants and animals. The melding of land and sea awakens us to the life of the entire planet, which is ours to sustain even as it sustains us.

—HILARY KAPLAN

## The Tremor in the Seed

Long before the struggle upward begins,
There is tremor in the seed.
Self-protection cracks,
Roots reach down and grab hold.
The seed swells, and tender shoots
Push up toward light.
This is *karpas:* spring awakening growth.
A force so tough it can break stone.

And why do we dip *karpas* into salt water?

To remember the sweat and tears of our ancestors in
    bondage.

To taste the bitter tears of our earth, unable to fully renew
    itself this spring because of our waste, neglect, and greed.

To feel the sting of society's refusal to celebrate the blossom-
    ing of women's bodies and the full range of our capacity
    for love.

And why should salt water be touched by *karpas*?

To remind us that tears stop. Spring comes.
And with it the potential for change.

—RONNIE M. HORN

## All Life Needs Is Your Faithfulness

Often, when he came to visit, my grandfather would bring me a present....

Once he brought me a little paper cup.... "If you promise to put
some water in the cup every day, something may happen," he told me.

At the time, I was four years old and my nursery was on the sixth
floor of an apartment building in Manhattan. This whole thing made
no sense to me at all. I looked at him dubiously. He nodded with
encouragement. "Every day, *Neshume-le,*" he told me.

And so I promised. At first, curious to see what would happen, I did not mind doing this. But as the days went by and nothing changed, it got harder and harder to remember to put water in the cup. After a week, I asked my grandfather if it was time to stop yet. Shaking his head no, he said, "Every day, *Neshume-le*." The second week was even harder, and I became resentful of my promise to put water in the cup. When my grandfather came again, I tried to give it back to him but he refused to take it, saying simply, "Every day, *Neshume-le*." By the third week, I began to forget to put water in the cup. Often I would remember only after I had been put to bed and would have to get out of bed and water it in the dark. But I did not miss a single day. And one morning, there were two little green leaves that had not been there the night before.

I was completely astonished. Day by day they got bigger. I could not wait to tell my grandfather, certain that he would be as surprised as I was. But of course he was not. Carefully he explained to me that life is everywhere, hidden in the most ordinary and unlikely places. I was delighted. "And all it needs is water, Grandpa?" I asked him. Gently he touched me on the top of my head. "No, *Neshume-le*," he said. "All it needs is your faithfulness."

This was perhaps my first lesson in the power of service, but I did not understand it in this way then. My grandfather would not have used these words. He would have said that we need to remember to bless the life around us and the life within us. He would have said when we remember we can bless life, we can repair the world.

—RACHEL NAOMI REMEN

## Zecher L'Idit

We dip *karpas,* the leafy green vegetable that symbolizes growth and the renewal of life that comes with liberation, into a bowl of salt water, which represents the tears we shed under the oppression of slavery.

As we dip greens in salt water, we can also remember the tears of Lot's wife, unnamed in the Torah, who turned back toward Sodom as she and Lot left their home. Her turning was out of compassion for all human creatures and out of anguish for the life that was being destroyed. Tonight we give her back her name: Idit. Idit died in the month of Nisan, the time centuries later when we gather at the seder table to recall Israel's freedom from bondage.[1]

We taste this salt *zecher l'Idit,* in remembrance of Idit. May it be a reminder that redemption is bound to the tears that we weep—even at the suffering of our foes—and to our deeds of lovingkindness. May it be a remembrance of a pillar of salt that is testimony to the miracle of love. The witness, *zecher l'Idit*...salt of the earth.

—SANDY EISENBERG SASSO

## Blessing over the *Karpas*

Let us bless the wellspring of life
that nurtures the fruits of the earth.

כַּרְפַּס

נְבָרֵךְ אֶת עֵין הַחַיִּים
מַצְמִיחַת פְּרִי הָאֲדָמָה.

—MARCIA FALK

## Blessing over *Karpas* with Feminine God Language

בְּרוּכָה אַתְּ יָה אֱלֹהֵינוּ רוּחַ הָעוֹלָם
בּוֹרֵאת פְּרִי הָאֲדָמָה.

*B'rucha at yah eloheinu ruach ha'olam boreit p'ri ha'adama.*

You are Blessed, Our God, Spirit of the World, who creates the fruit of the earth.

—*THE JOURNEY CONTINUES: THE MA'YAN PASSOVER HAGGADAH*

# *Yachatz*

At any other festival meal, we break bread and eat it. At the seder, we break bread and hide it, reminding ourselves that the seder is not only a celebration but also a search. The seder is a search to understand the story of our ancestors, the meaning of our people's liberation, and the claims that our history makes on us. *Yachatz*, the breaking and hiding of the middle matzah, marks the beginning of that quest.

The leader takes the middle matzah from the seder plate and breaks it into two pieces. The larger piece becomes the *afikomen* and is either hidden by the leader or stolen by the children, who will ransom it at the end of the seder. The smaller piece is placed between the remaining two matzahs and will be eaten by the participants at the beginning of the meal.

At women's seders, *yachatz* is often used as an opportunity to reflect on the rich meanings of breaking, hiding, wholeness, and fragmentation. Because the matzah itself has dual connotations—as the bread of affliction and the bread of redemption—so the act of breaking the matzah has both positive and negative associations.

To break the bread of affliction is to symbolically enact the breaking of shackles that have bound slaves throughout history, from our own ancestors in ancient Egypt to those still enslaved in other parts of the world today. In this spirit, some women's seders interpret the act of breaking matzah as a positive symbol representing the breaking of boundaries that is needed to create new space in Judaism for women and others who have long been marginalized or silenced.

To break the bread of redemption, on the other hand, is to reflect the painful reality of fragmentation in our unredeemed world. The broken pieces of the matzah signify the broken pieces of our lives, and hold out a challenge before us: What will we do to heal the divisions that keep us from seeing and honoring the wholeness of all creation?

## How Much We Have Yet to Understand

We lift the middle matzah and break it in two.

Hear the sound of glass broken at the end of every Jewish wedding.
Hear the echo of stone tablets cast down and shattered at the foot of the mountain.
Hear the crack of the whip on the backs of slaves.
We carry our brokenness with us.

We lift the middle matzah and break it in two.
The larger piece is hidden.
To remind us that more is concealed than revealed.
To remind us how much we do not know.
How much we do not see.
How much we have yet to understand.

The larger piece is hidden and wrapped in a napkin.
This is the *afikomen*.
It will be up to the children to find it before the seder can come to an end.

In this game of hide and seek,
We remind ourselves that we do not begin to know all that our children will reveal to us.
We do not begin to understand the mysteries that they will uncover,

The broken pieces they will find,
The hidden fragments in need of repair.

"Behold I will send you Elijah the prophet
Before the coming of the great and awesome day of the Lord.
And he will turn the hearts of parents to children and the
hearts of children to parents—
Lest I come and smite the land with utter destruction."

On this night, may the hearts of parents and children turn
toward each other.
Together, may we make whole all that is broken.

—SHARON COHEN ANISFELD

## When We Think of War

*As we hear the breaking of the matzah, we remember the destruction and brokenness that war has brought to so many nations. Tonight, as we read the following reflection by playwright Eve Ensler, we remember not only the loss that we Jews have suffered in wars throughout centuries but also the shattered worlds that millions today must live in because of contemporary wars. We honor the healing work of women in these nations.*

When we think of war, we think of it as something that happens to men in fields or jungles. We think of hand grenades and Scud missiles. We think of the moment of violence—the blast, the explosion. But war is also a consequence—the effects of which are not known or felt for months, years, generations. And because consequences are usually not televised, by then the war is no longer sexy—the ratings are gone, consequences remain invisible. It is the bombing, the explosions in the dark, that keep us watching. As long as there are snipers outside of Sarajevo, Sarajevo exists. But after the bombing, after the snipers, that's when the real war begins.

It is found in the broken-down fabric of community, in the death of trust, in the destruction of the everyday patterns of living. It is found in trauma and depression, poverty and homelessness and starvation. It is found in the emasculation and rage of the victim, in the new violence; the traumatized soldier beating his wife, the teenage boys already plotting revenge, the ongoing panic of the children.

When we think of war, we do not think of women. Because the work of survival, of restoration, is not glamorous work. Like most women's work, it is undervalued, underpaid, and impossible. After war, men are often shattered, unable to function. Women not only work, but they also create peace networks, find ways to bring about healing. They teach in home schools when the school buildings are destroyed. They build gardens in the middle of abandoned railroad tracks. They pick up the pieces, although they usually haven't fired a gun.

—EVE ENSLER

## The Fourth Matzah

*Traditionally, we include three pieces of matzah on our seder plate. Tonight, add a fourth piece of matzah, and use the following reading:*

Three matzot are traditionally placed on the seder plate: two as symbols of the two loaves set out at the Temple in the ancient celebration of the holy day and one in honor of the Passover festival. In the past century, many of us added a fourth matzah to our seders, as a reminder of Jews of the former Soviet Union, who were once forbidden to practice their Judaism. We ate the fourth matzah for them, because they could not; we prayed for their liberation.

They are now able to practice Judaism, but we have kept the fourth matzah here, as a reminder that while any one person is enslaved anywhere and in any way, we are not entirely free. This fourth matzah is the matzah of hope.

—*WILLIAMS COLLEGE FEMINIST HAGGADAH*

## Breaking the Chains

Recently, my son brought home from school a special "user-friendly" haggadah. It was annotated and colorful, with quizzes, stories, and contests for children. I was intrigued by the particular way the editors of the haggadah chose to relate to the concept of freedom and liberty.

They demonstrated the denial of freedom through the contemporary tragedies of Israeli soldiers missing and held in captivity.

I thought that this was indeed an appropriate example, and it felt particularly apt to discuss these tragic cases during the most significant familial-religious celebration of the year. However, if we think about the deeper dimensions of the concept of liberty, the case of these soldiers almost seems the easy way out. It does not demand any self-reflection on the part of the Jewish community; in this situation, external enemies deprived the soldiers of their physical freedom.

At the seder, it is equally—if not more—important to mention deprivations of freedom occurring within our own community. The Jewish women who want to escape their marriages but cannot because their husbands have refused to grant them a *get,* the Jewish bill of divorce, are victims of an unjust denial of liberty. Even if a marriage is already dead, or violent, or abusive, or simply ceases to reflect the wife's will, Jewish law gives the husband the ultimate power over the *get,* and hence positions him as the ultimate guard of his wife's freedom. The plight of these women, modern-day *agunot,* chained in unwanted marriages, is a shame to Orthodox Judaism. The paralysis with which Orthodoxy has responded to this painful problem is disgraceful; the incompetence of the rabbinate to make use of halakhic precedents for overcoming recalcitrant husbands is inexcusable.

We cannot forget our own community's responsibility. This deprivation of freedom is internal to our system. We are all accountable. We all have a duty to act. In order to do so, we first need to raise awareness about the problem. And so tonight, it is our duty to remember our *agunot* sisters on this holiday of freedom, mourn their plight, and pray for them. As we break the matzah, let us pray that their chains will likewise be broken and that they will regain their freedom. Then, when the holiday is over, we must keep pressing the halakhic authorities, suggesting solutions, supporting the brave ones who dare to be more halakhically innovative and creative.

—RUTH HALPERIN-KADDARI

# Miriam's Cup

Rabbinic legend teaches that a magical well accompanied the Israelites on their journey from Egypt toward the Promised Land. This well is said to have appeared because of the merit of the prophetess Miriam. According to Jewish tradition, the waters of the well dried up after her death.

Elaborating on this beautiful legend, Jewish feminists have created a new Passover ritual known as Miriam's Cup, or *Kos Miryam,* which has been widely incorporated into women's, family, and community seders. *Kos Miryam* is a cup filled with spring water. The waters of *Kos Miryam* are said to draw from the miraculous, life-giving waters of Miriam's well.[1]

At many women's seders, the ritual of Miriam's Cup has become an occasion for the celebration of Miriam as a leader, prophetess, and inspiring foremother. *Kos Miryam* offers a time to draw on the wealth of traditional and contemporary legends about Miriam and her role in the liberation of our people from Egyptian slavery.

This ritual is often performed at the very beginning of women's seders, as a way of establishing Miriam's honored place at the table and setting a special tone for the evening. We have chosen to place Miriam's Cup here to suggest another alternative for women's and family seders that prefer not to begin the entire ritual with Miriam's Cup. This placement puts Miriam's Cup just before *maggid* and thus celebrates her as an important figure in the telling of our people's history.

Given the traditional haggadah's reluctance to elevate any human being, including Moses, in its recounting of our liberation from Egypt, some communities choose not to highlight Miriam's role in the Exodus story at all. In this spirit, Miriam's Cup may be introduced near the end of the seder—alongside Elijah's Cup—thus emphasizing Miram's role, not as a heroic figure from our past but as a messenger of hope for the future. Several of the readings in this chapter follow this approach. Both Miriam's Cup and Elijah's Cup hold out a vision of redemption. Miriam's Cup is filled with water, Elijah's with wine. Both cups beckon and ask: For what do you thirst?

## On Our Journeys

As we hold Miriam's Cup aloft tonight, some may feel that it stands for healing in its broadest sense. For others, it symbolizes the need to infuse women's perceptions into Judaism and into our own lives. For some of us, Miriam's Cup stands for the process—the trek through the wilderness—as opposed to the goal, the arrival at Canaan. For others, it represents women's special abilities to embrace struggle, change, and growth.

Miriam's Cup, glistening with water that energizes the soul, calls to us in confident invitation. Let all who are ready, come and fill it. Let all who are thirsty, come and drink.

May next year find us still on our journeys.

—SUSAN SCHNUR

## Miriam's Cup

Recently, Miriam's Cup has been added to many seder tables, in addition to Elijah's Cup of wine. A cup of fresh water, it represents Miriam's well, which followed the Children of Israel through the desert until she died. We associate this cup of water with the redemption occurring daily in our lives.

The cup of Elijah holds wine;
the cup of Miriam holds water.
Wine is more precious
until you have no water.

Water that flows in our veins,
water that is the stuff of life
for we are made of breath
and water, vision

and fact. Elijah is
the extraordinary; Miriam
brings the daily wonders:
the joy of a fresh morning

like a newly prepared table,
a white linen cloth on which
nothing has yet spilled.
The descent into the heavy

waters of sleep healing us.
The scent of baking bread,
roasting chicken, fresh herbs,
the faces of friends across

the table: what sustains us
every morning, every evening,
the common daily miracles
like the taste of cool water.

—MARGE PIERCY

## These Are the Living Waters

*Kos Miryam,* the Cup of Miriam—with this cup of pure spring water we remember God's gift of *mayim khayyim,* the living waters from Miriam's well. Elijah's Cup represents our future redemption in the messianic age, when peace will fill the world. The Cup of Miriam represents our past redemption, when our people were brought out of Egypt and delivered from slavery.

Miriam's well was said to hold divine power to heal, sustain, and renew. It became a special source of transformation for a people leaving slavery to form a new identity. Throughout our journey as a people, we have sought to rediscover these living waters for ourselves.

Tonight at our seder, we continue this journey. Just as the Holy One delivered Miriam and her people, just as they were sustained in the desert and transformed into a new people, so may we be delivered, sustained, and transformed on our own journey to a stronger sense of ourselves as individuals and as one community. May the living waters of Miriam's well nourish us and give us inspiration as we embark on our journey through the haggadah.

### Lift Cup

**Reader:** *Zot Kos Miryam, kos mayim khayyim.*
*Zeykher litzi'at mitzrayim.*
This is the Cup of Miriam, the cup of Living Waters.
Let us remember the Exodus from Egypt.

**All:** These are the living waters, God's gift to Miriam, which gave new life to Israel as we struggled with ourselves in the wilderness.
Blessed are You God, Who brings us from the narrows into the wilderness, sustains us with endless possibilities, and enables us to reach a new place.
*N'varekh et eyn ha-khayyim she-natnah lanu mayim khayyim.*
Let us bless the Source of Life, Who has given us living waters.
*Barukh ata Adonai, Eloheinu Melekh ha-Olam, she-ha-kol nih'yah bi-d'varo.*
Blessed are You, Adonai our God, Majestic Spirit of the Universe, by Whose word everything is created.

*Drink.*

—MATIA RANIA ANGELOU AND JANET BERKENFIELD

## Those Who Sustain Us

As we each pour spring water from our water glasses into the cup of Miriam on our table, we pause to share a brief comment about a woman who has nurtured, inspired, or helped us on our journeys.

We each pour water into Miriam's Cup and say: *"I pour this water in honor of (woman's name) who (brief comment)."*

These are the living waters, God's gift to Miriam, which gave new life to Israel as we struggled in the wilderness. May the cup of Miriam refresh and inspire us as we embark on our journey through the haggadah.[2]

—*LICHVOD PESACH: A WOMEN'S COMMUNITY SEDER HAGGADAH*

## Redemptions Yet to Come

*Many of us have come to invite Miriam the prophet to our Passover seder through rituals like Miriam's Cup. Including Miriam in our seder is not so much an act of remembrance of a beloved figure from our past— even Moses does not appear in the haggadah—as an act of dreaming forward, into the future. Miriam represents possibility, transition, miracles, and redemption.*

*In the following reading for your seder, paragraphs can be traded off by two readers, read sequentially by many individuals, or read as call and response between a leader and the other seder participants.*

Miriam, some say that you and your mother were Shifra and Puah, midwives to the other Hebrews, defying Pharaoh at every turn, saving babies as you ushered new life into this broken world. You heard their cries and saw the tears of their mothers and fathers; yours were the first hands to hold them.

Stay with us as we birth new possibilities in the face of challenge and danger. Hold us and make us strong as we move into uncharted waters.

When others packed clothing and other basic necessities, preparing for the arduous journey into the desert, you made the women believe that beyond mere escape, a time would come to celebrate. You urged them to pack drums and tambourines, knowing this would lift their hearts toward the better days you were sure would come, and ensuring they would be able to dance with joy after safely crossing the Reed Sea.

Remind us that liberation must be envisioned before it can be tasted. Dance with us. Help us believe that a time of safety and freedom for all people is within our reach. At every step of the journey, remind us not only to say *Dayeinu* but also to celebrate with all that we have.

One tradition holds that in a truly redeemed world, you will lead us all, men and women together, in a circle dance. While the world as we know it has roles that limit and define us, in a time to come our identities will serve only as a source of meaning and connection to others.

Guide us to a place where all the ways in which we wish to be known are seen by others and valued in community. Help us to remember that none of us can reach that place unless all of us are welcome there.

Because of your merit, a band of tired slaves had a traveling well from which to drink as we wandered in the desert. Your well now appears to us at the end of each Shabbat, when we sing of you and of the prophet Elijah, so that we may drink from its living waters and taste the redemptions yet to come.

Miriam, take us by the hand and guide us to the waters of redemption. Teach us to see the wells of possibility even in the most narrow places.

—SUSAN P. FENDRICK

## Redemption in Our Own Lives

We place Miriam's goblet on the seder table as a counterweight to the cup of Elijah. The latter is a symbol of messianic redemption at the end of time; the former, of redemption in our present lives. Elijah lived in the desert as a lone, howling visionary, focused on the millennium.

Miriam sojourned in the same wilderness, but she accompanied the Hebrew people. Tireless tribal parent, she offered hope and renewal at every stage of the journey.

We raise her goblet and recite this prayer:

> You abound in blessings, God, Creator of the universe, Who sustains us with living water. May we, like the Children of Israel leaving Egypt, be guarded and nurtured and kept alive in the wilderness, and may You give us wisdom to understand that the journey itself holds the promise of redemption.

—SUSAN SCHNUR

## Miriam's Well

*Kos Miryam* refers to a vessel containing the waters of Miriam's well, a legendary well said to have been created on the second day of Creation. From that time on, the well has been passed on to those whose merits caused them to deserve such a divine gift. Miriam received the well on behalf of the Children of Israel, who were wandering in the desert after their escape from Egypt. According to the legend, she was able to call forth water with her beautiful voice. When she died, the waters of her well dried up.

Miriam's well seems to reflect this history of the Jewish people, drying up in times of crisis and bubbling forth when called on in times of renewal. The Torah fed the people's spirit, but the waters of Miriam's well enabled them to survive physically in the desert. Without water to drink, they could not have lived long enough to receive the Torah at Sinai.

As the waters of Miriam's well offered sustenance to the Jewish people, the water from her cup makes this strength available now. A drink from Miriam's Cup proclaims that the existence of the prophetess is ongoing, just as a drink from Elijah's Cup professes his imminent arrival.

—PENINA ADELMAN

## Discovering the Cup of Miriam

In the late 1980s, Joyce Rosen led our Rosh Chodesh group in a meditation to Miriam's well. She invited us to take a goblet, fill it with the healing waters of Miriam's well, and drink. Stephanie Loo was so taken with the image of the well and the water that she began using a crystal goblet filled with spring water to remind her of the *mayim khayyim* (living waters) from Miriam's well. She called this goblet *Kos Miryam* (the Cup of Miriam) and used it every Friday evening to welcome Shabbat. It was Stephanie who gave the cup its name and who wrote the first ceremony using *Kos Miryam*.

It seems to me that Stephanie discovered this custom more than she created it. It's as though *Kos Miryam* had been lost in history, and that it is just now being rediscovered. As Penina Adelman has said:

> The ritual is "new" in the sense that such a cup had never been used on the seder table...or for a bat mitzvah celebration...or during any of the other myriad uses this particular group found for the Cup of Miriam. However, the ritual is "ancient" and even "traditional" in the sense that...it felt so natural to start blessing this cup full of pure spring water from Miriam's well, using it at the appropriate times.[3]

Indeed, we read in *The Book of Our Heritage:* "There is said to be a custom to draw water from a well at the end of Shabbat, for at that time, the water of the well of Miriam fills every other well and whoever comes in contact with it, or drinks it, is cured of all his ailments."[4]

Miriam died on the tenth day of the month of Nisan. Midrash tells us that when Miriam died, the miraculous well that had been given by God in her honor disappeared, leaving the Israelites without a source of water in the desert. In our generation, Miriam's well has become a symbol of our thirst for spiritual nourishment. It is fitting that *Kos Miryam* is being used at this time in Jewish history, because we are now rediscovering the women of the Torah and beginning to relate to them differently. We are ready spiritually to uncover these women's lessons and to understand their teachings in a new way. Now is the time for women's voices to be heard along with men's voices.

—MATIA RANIA ANGELOU

## Miriam Throughout History

In every generation, we must see ourselves as if we had gone out of Egypt. In every generation, we search for the threads that connect our present with our past. In every generation, we reclaim the heroines and heroes of Jewish history whose visions are truly timeless.

Miriam the prophetess is one such heroine. An instrumental part of the Exodus, she carefully watched over her brother Moses and joyously led the people in song after the crossing of the sea. While Miriam, like Moses, is not mentioned in the haggadah, her story has been retold throughout the centuries by Jews who look to her as a model of faith, forbearance, and leadership. Miriam's song is sung once again.

The Bible tells us that Miriam "took a timbrel in her hand" and sang, "Sing unto God, for God is great; a horse and its chariot have drowned in the sea." However, the Bible does not record the full text of Miriam's song.

A complete version of the song of Miriam was found among the Dead Sea Scrolls (first century B.C.E.):

> God, You are great, the savior; the enemy's hope has died and he is forgotten; they have died in the copious waters; we extol Him who raises up, and performs majestically.[5]

Some communities took note of Miriam's absence from the seder and strove to remember her with ritual. The following text from the tenth century refers to a custom by which Miriam was commemorated at the seder along with Moses and Aaron.

> They asked of the two foods placed on the seder table, and he responded that they symbolize the two messengers, Moses and Aaron, whom God sent to Egypt. There are those who place a third food on the seder table in memory of Miriam, as it says, "And I will send before you Moses and Aaron and Miriam"

(Micah 6:4). These three foods are fish, meat, and an egg, which correspond to the three types of foods Israel will eat in the world to come.[6]

Midrashic tradition associates Miriam with the well that followed the People of Israel in the desert, quenching their thirst in time of need. Miriam's well became a symbol of sustenance and healing for Jewish people of all times, and especially for women. A medieval encyclopedia of customs (fourteenth-century France) records the following practice:

> It is the custom that women draw water on Saturday night, as we find in the aggadah that the well of Miriam is located in the Sea of Tiberias. Every Saturday night this well taps into all the wells and springs of the world, and all who drink from this water, even if their entire body is full of boils, will be healed.[7]

As Miriam is remembered as a healer, she is also invoked as an intercessor. In the Yiddish *tkhines*—religious prayers of Ashkenazi women—the heavenly Miriam is called to plead on behalf of her sisters on earth:

> In the merit of Miriam the Prophetess, a well of water accompanied the Jews in the desert from the month of Iyar and on. Beloved God, remember us now in her merit, for she sang with the women when the Jews went out of the Red Sea, as it states, "Miriam the Prophetess, the sister of Aaron, took up the drum in her hand." Wake up, Miriam the Prophetess, wake up from your rest and stand in front of the King of all Kings, the Holy One, and beg him to have pity on us in this month of Iyar![8]

As we strive to increase women's involvement in Jewish spiritual life, we can look to Chasidic thought for inspiration. Rabbi Kalonomous Epstein (nineteenth century) interprets Miriam's dance on the banks of the sea as a symbol of the equality men and women will enjoy in the world to come:

> In the future there will no longer be the categories of male and female. All will come to realize the divine light equally. This is

just like a circle dance, where every part of the circle's circumference is equidistant from the center. So will all absorb the clear light of divinity equally. This was the intention of the prophetess Miriam. She had all the women follow her and performed circle dances with them, in order to draw upon the supernal light from the place where the categories of male and female do not exist.[9]

—LISA SCHLAFF

# *Maggid*

**T**he words "haggadah" and *"maggid"* share the same He-brew root, which means "to tell." "Telling" is the defin-ing obligation of the Passover seder; we tell the story of our Exodus, our journey from slavery to freedom. There are other holidays during which we are specifically obligated to listen. On Purim, we are commanded to hear the reading of the Book of Esther. On Rosh Hashanah, we are required to hear the call of the shofar. But on Passover, we must open our mouths and speak; we are obligated to tell this story in our own voice.

*Maggid* has many different parts, and the nine chapters that follow each focus on one important portion of the telling. Suggestions for participatory *maggid* activities and discussions are included in this section and can be incorporated throughout the telling, which is explored in greater depth in the nine chapters that follow. Using these readings and activity suggestions to supplement or replace the text of the haggadah will allow you to involve participants in an active and dynamic way.

At women's seders, participants often bring personal sharing and discussion into *maggid*. Some communities invite women to relate personal experiences that speak to the holiday's themes of slavery, exile, exodus, and liberation, allowing seder participants to engage with the story of the Exodus in an intimate way. This gives the ancient, collective narrative new immediacy and relevance and, at the same time, places the personal stories that are told within a powerful framework of shared meaning and significance.

# Suggestions for Participatory *Maggid* Activities and Discussions

## Our Passover Stories

Tonight we are going to find ways to remember, tell, and share our own Passover stories. Please read over the list below and find a topic that is important to you. During the *maggid* section of the seder we will have a chance to share our memories and reflections. Tonight, these stories will be a part of our telling.

A Journey from Slavery to Liberation
A Time of Exile
Searching for *Chametz*
Shopping, Cleaning, or Cooking for Passover
Mother at the Seder Table
Preparing the Haggadah
Stories of the Family Matriarchs
My Favorite Childhood Passover Memory
Family Stories Passed Down Through My Mother or
    Grandmother
A Righteous Woman from My Life
Sayings of the Mothers
Advice from Mother to Daughter
Advice from Daughter to Mother

—HER SEDER OF AMERICAN JEWISH CONGRESS, PENNSYLVANIA REGION

## Bibliodrama at the Seder Table: An Alternative *Maggid*

It is considered praiseworthy to expand on the telling of the story of the Exodus. One option is to approach the *maggid* section of the seder through the technique of bibliodrama, in which participants speak as characters *within* the narrative, rather than talking *about* the story.

Here are a few suggestions for conducting a bibliodrama that will take approximately 30 to 40 minutes, depending on the number of participants and how involved they get. As leader, you have these responsibilities:

- Frame and welcome people into the bibliodramatic experience.
- Facilitate this method of gaining insight into our story of slavery and liberation by asking questions that will be inviting to your particular group.
- Gently move the exercise to a close.
- If desired and appropriate, give the group members a chance to talk about what they have heard and learned.

Following the guidelines below, you will find several scenarios you might consider and suggested questions for conducting your bibliodrama.

### Introduction

Let people know that they will be doing something a little different. Instead of reading or talking about the text of the haggadah, you will be inviting them to speak as characters within the text (of the haggadah or the Torah, whichever you have chosen). Explain that everyone will speak in the first person as figures in the story. For example, one participant might say, "I'm Miriam. When I put my brother into the basket, I whispered a prayer for his safety." Let the group know that you welcome everyone's participation, and that it is fine if some people wish merely to listen—their quiet attention will be an important part of the experience.

Be sure to give a bit of the background of your text or story in order to set the scene for where you want to go. For example, you might say, "You may remember that after the plagues ended, before the actual Exodus, there was a night of watching and attentiveness."

### Getting People into Role

After this brief introduction, you will begin to move people into the scene itself.

You might say, "I'd like you to take a moment now and imagine that you are not a participant in this seder around this table, but instead an Israelite slave in Egypt. If it helps you, close your eyes for a few seconds and imagine who you are, how old you are, and what kind of work you do." There are other ways of beginning this shift; for example, you can ask participants to imagine that they are sitting together with their families in slave quarters in Egypt. Invite them to look around and see their tent walls and the few possessions they own.

It is very important at all times to give clear signals to the participants about where they are and what they are doing, so they know how best to participate (e.g. "And as you go to bed tonight after working hard, what is your last thought before you fall asleep?"). Confusion brings people out of role and diffuses the power of the experience. Also, as you continue to address them in character as "you," indicating who they are, you reinforce the magic of the drama.

Some people will "get" how it works immediately and can easily play along, but it is common for some to revert to speaking as they normally do, out of forgetfulness or resistance: "They must have been terrified—even though they knew that the plagues were directed at the Egyptians, I think they probably hated to see their neighbors suffer," or "There is a midrash I once read about the Egyptian women and Israelite women." You will need to gently bring them back: "So—you are an Israelite slave. You're feeling terrified," or "I was wondering that too. You are an Israelite woman—what are your relationships with Egyptian women like?"

Sometimes people will persist in wanting to bring in their knowledge, talking about the story, or asking questions. Do your best to bring them (back) into their roles—or let them know directly that there will be time for discussion and questions later, but for now you invite them to participate in the drama if they wish.

## Hints for Encouraging Participation

Ask inviting, open-ended questions: "Everyone around says, 'We are waiting for a miracle.' What is that like for you?" Reward people for their participation so that they feel heard and part of the drama. You may do this by repeating or restating what a person has said, especially if it clarifies something for the group, emphasizes something that was muted but that you think was implied, or de-escalates something that is too hot or complex to adequately handle. (You don't need to do this after each and every person speaks—sometimes you can accomplish more with eye contact.) Some examples:

> Restatement with a spin:
> > Player: "I've lived my whole life as a slave; I don't know anything different."
> > You: "Slavery is everything I know. I can't even imagine what liberation means."
> Emphasize/draw out something muted:
> > Player (quietly): "It wasn't so horrible for me."
> > You: "You know, slavery has its upsides—steady work, a predictable routine—it's not all bad." (Make eye contact with the speaker at the end to make sure you've got it right.)
> De-escalate:
> > Player: "You want to talk about oppression? It wasn't just working for no pay, but they owned our bodies: I was raped more than once, and I know it happened to other women. No one talks about it, but everyone knows."
> > You: "It was especially bad for us women—in every sense, our bodies were not our own, and we suffered."

Of course, these ways of reinforcing participation can be powerful and helpful, but simply conversing in your own voice as interviewer—for example, "It sounds as if there was more to your experience of slavery than the Torah records"—can also be very effective.

Also, keep in mind that some topics are to be approached with caution. In a large group or one where people do not know each other well (or even in a small women's group), a topic like sexual assault can obviously be a profound and heavy one, even in a dramatic context.

Bibliodrama is primarily a method for gaining insights into the narrative, not for personal growth and healing (though people can experience both). You can both reward your participants and take care of them not by ignoring what they give you but by responding to it and/or channeling it appropriately. For example, you could continue by saying, "Thank you for telling us," in a sincere and meaningful way to the woman who spoke, then continue by asking, "How else was it different for you as women?"

Remember: Your main job is host and interlocutor. Think of yourself as a wise and kind talk show host, not only asking questions but also ensuring a certain flow. You will keep things moving with your thoughtful questions, your restatements, your active listening, and your gentle guidance from start to finish.

### Leaving Roles and "Post-Game Analysis"

About ten minutes before you want to move on to the next part of the seder (longer if you want to allow more time for discussion), you should begin to bring the bibliodrama to its end, providing a sense of closure for the experience.

You can accomplish this in several ways: "I'd like to invite you to offer one sentence about what you want future generations to know about your life in Egypt (your journey to freedom, etc.)." Solicit multiple contributions.

To finish off the scene and move into a brief discussion and period of reflection, you need to bring people back to "real time." Sometimes it is enough to thank them for their willingness to be spontaneous, then invite them to return to being themselves, at the seder table. Other times, depending on how deep you think the experience was, you will want to be more explicit and directive—asking people, for example, to get up and stretch, look around, and notice that they are no longer in Egypt but back in the living room or auditorium. Always thank the group for participating.

Take a few minutes to discuss the drama. Be careful not to let people get back into their roles—addressing them by name or asking a more cerebral question in present time usually does the trick. The drama is over.

### Suggested Scenes and Sample Questions

- *Avadim Hayinu*/We Were Slaves: Think back to the time of your slavery. What is life like for you? What is your job? What keeps you going? What is one thing about your life now that you never want to forget?
- *Leyl Shimmurim*/The Night of Watching: What does the scene in your house look like? Who is there? What are you doing, and what are you talking about? What are the two things you must bring with you as you pack for the journey to freedom, and why? What are you feeling? Do you have confidence in Moses? In God?
- *Kriat Yam Suf*/Crossing the Sea of Reeds: You are running toward the edge of the sea. What are you thinking as you approach the water? What do you see around you? Who is with you? How will you manage to cross to the other side? What makes you afraid? What gives you strength?

—SUSAN P. FENDRICK

## Topics for Discussion

Rather than tell the story of *maggid* in its traditional form, you might initiate a discussion that will allow those at the table to tell the story themselves. Choose one of the questions below and instead of, or in addition to, reading the story of the Exodus, ask everyone at the seder table to offer her or his own opinions and answers.

What was it like watching and waiting on the night of the last plague?

Does someone always have to drown for another to be liberated? Can we imagine a liberation that doesn't entail destruction?

Why do we do this every year?

At different points in the seder, we say, "Once we were slaves; now we are free" and "Now we are slaves; next year may we be free." How do we understand the relationship between these statements? Which do you identify with?

In the seder, we declare that "In every generation, every individual should feel as though he or she has actually been redeemed from Egypt." What does this mean?

Where were the women during the actual Exodus and time in the desert? What must it have been like for them?

What would be necessary to convince you to leave behind your home and everything that you know?

What do we make of the fact that God had to liberate us from our slavery, that we were not willing or able to liberate ourselves?

Another option is to select a reflection from one of the chapters in this book to use as the basis for a discussion. Many of the readings in the nine chapters that follow can be used to begin a conversation addressing the central themes of the telling.

## The Question I Wait For

*The reading below can serve as a point of departure for discussing the meaning and purpose of the telling we undertake during* maggid.

It happened again when I was in Jerusalem several years ago, at a seder that was lovingly prepared. There we were in our linen clothes, fresh and eager to participate in the evening's ritual, the festival of freedom. We were planning to do our part to bring a better world into being.

A young guest patiently listened to much talk of freedom and the end of slavery, and then voiced a question: "How can we sit here and celebrate our freedom when so many other people are now enslaved?" There was a silence. Then, tentatively, one by one, guests began trying to answer the question. And as the conversation haltingly continued, to my mind the real seder began.

This is the question I wait for every year. I have come to believe that the entire ritual of the seder is meant to evoke this question. We sit here together and extol and praise our freedom just so that we can ask how we dare to do so. How dare we spend the night singing to God about our freedom against the backdrop of an enslaved world?

The paradoxical answer to this question is at the crux of why I return to the seder table spring after spring. Precisely because the world is broken, because there is still suffering and injustice, we must sit here and dwell on the miracle of our freedom from slavery.

By telling our story together, we affirm that while not everyone is free, that while even we ourselves are not wholly free, there is still freedom in our world. We remember in a rush what freedom feels like. And together, over the course of the telling, we re-create a communal vision of a better world. We voice our desire that we be not only the recipients of freedom but its instigators as well—a people ready to birth freedom at a moment's notice. Through our ritual and in our readiness, we isolate freedom, we stake it out, we approach it.

It is like any other act of faith. We know that there is pain in our world. But on this night, we do not let that pain paralyze us. We quietly but unmistakably deny pain the right to define our life's work. Rather, on this night, we gather together in our homes to stare into the eyes of freedom. We throw our mighty hands and our outstretched arms around its neck and refuse to let it go.

—NOA RACHEL KUSHNER

## A Holiday of Retellings

Why do we retell the same story year after year? Because just as history is codified in the selective retelling of our actions, so too is personal identity. It is the meaning conferred upon our actions that defines us more than the actions themselves. The one who shapes the stories, therefore, controls the shaping of identity. Take away our stories, take away our memories, and we cease to exist.

"Memories," said Elie Wiesel, "are not just what we own, but who we are." Passover is the time when identities get recharged. For the first night or two, we gather to speak of our communal identity. Both act (seder) and content (haggadah) become part of our story. So, too, once a year, we should speak of our familial history. The Friday night that falls in the week of Passover can be dedicated to the telling of the family stories.

Here, too, we can have the seder (the act of retelling at this ritual meal) and the haggadah (the stories that we tell). Over the years, the retelling will become the family catechism taught to the children, the in-laws, the *mahatanim*. It will be embellished and fought over by the grandparents, aunts, and uncles. And even the disagreements will become part of the story. As the children grow and become adults, the paths of the story will diverge. Each branch of the family will have its own version. But they will always be joined at the roots and the trunk, as far back as we can remember, or discover.

"My grandmother was an immigrant from Bessarabia. She went up to Israel and sojourned in the city of Haifa for seven years, until she met my grandfather...." The story line might be sparse at first. But everyone around the table can add to it their bit of remembrances. This *maggid* section can then be recorded and shared with other members of the family, inviting them to add their memories to the family's haggadah. And over the years, the story will grow, both in the memories that are recalled and in the new chapters that are yet to unfold.

This idea, a wonderful custom for the intermediate Sabbath of Passover, can also be adapted for those celebrating at a women's seder. A women's seder can be a time to recall your own women's traditions. Many of us will not yet have traditions to share. We can do one of two things: homework or dreams. Homework can entail doing research in books or on the Internet about lost women's traditions, poems, or prayers, or talking to unsung women in your community who do possess a hidden tradition passed on by their mothers. Absent that, we can dream. What traditions, poems, customs, words, acts, and artifacts do we want to pass on to our children for them to incorporate into their celebrations years from now? What we already have, we should recover and pass on. What we don't, we must create.

Passover will be a holiday of retellings, both of a people and of a family. And the individuals sitting around the table will learn both who they are and whose they are.

—NINA BETH CARDIN

# *Ha Lachma Anya*

The recitation of *Ha lachma anya* opens *maggid*. *Ha lachma anya* begins with the words "This is the bread of affliction that our ancestors ate in Egypt," lending a sense of immediacy and urgency to our telling. As this declaration is recited, the leader of the seder uncovers and points to the matzah on the seder plate. The matzah establishes the intimacy of our connection to the ancient Israelites, whose story we are about to tell. We will eat the same bread that they ate; we will experience the taste and texture of their lives as slaves.

We are not meant to hold this story at a distance. Our collective memories demand something of us. "Let all who are hungry, come and eat. Let all who are in need, share in our Passover celebration." We retell the story of our own suffering not to dwell on the past but to use its lessons to make ourselves more sensitive and responsive to the needs of the stranger standing outside our door. Some of the authors in this chapter ask us to contemplate issues of inclusion and exclusion: Whom have we really welcomed to our seder? Who is still standing outside the door, waiting to be invited to the table? Other readings focus on what can and must be done to address the devastating poverty and economic injustice that persists in our own communities and around the world.

*Ha lachma anya* concludes by reminding us that our journey toward freedom is not yet over. "This year we are slaves; next year may we be free. This year we are here; next year may we be in the Land of Israel." At the seder, we are asked to see ourselves, simultaneously, as free and not-yet-free. We celebrate and give thanks for our deliverance from slavery even while recognizing that our redemption is incomplete. Some of the pieces in this chapter urge us to consider our longings and aspirations as Jewish women: Where are we now? In what ways are we still enslaved? In what ways are we free? "This year we are here." What steps will bring us all closer to the Promised Land?

## Flatbread of Feeble Times

Have you ever listened to the ironic power of our Passover pronouncement, *Ha lachma anya?* This is the bread of poverty that our ancestors ate. Let all who are hungry come and eat. Let all who have need come and share in Pesach.

What is it that we are offering? Not our overflowing wine or a scrumptious array of foods. It is not fullness or wealth that we offer, nor proud stories of how we have built ourselves up from nothing. We offer, rather, the meager matzah, the flatbread of feeble times, the reminder of our suffering. This is where we can meet and sit down with the world. It is the common bond of humanity. This is truly where our riches lie as a people. We return every year not to the smorgasbord of our successes but to this simple offering of our poverty.

*Ha lachma anya.* This prayer pronounces the paradox of our greatness as a people. Precisely because we have suffered so profoundly, we can speak to the human experience with the language of the heart. Precisely because we have been flattened so continuously, we can offer this, our bread of humility. With this we open ourselves and invite in the world.

—TIRZAH FIRESTONE

## The Bread of Affliction

This is the Bread of Affliction our foremothers baked as they fled the land of slavery. Gathering their children and their possessions, they embarked upon a journey in the wilderness, leading us to freedom.

This is the Bread of Affliction eaten by Hannah: a courageous mother who gave faith and comfort to her seven sons as they were tortured by Antiochus; a mother martyred along with her children; a heroine of the Maccabbean revolt against oppressors.

This is the Bread of Affliction baked by Beruriah, wife of the talmudic sage Rabbi Meir and a respected commentator in her own right.

This is the Bread of Affliction coveted in secret by Beatrice de Luna, a secret Jew who fled the Portuguese Inquisition to become Doña Gracia Mendes, the greatest patron and savior of fugitive *conversos*.

This is the Bread of Affliction for which Regina Jonas lived and died, the first woman rabbi, ordained in Germany in 1935, and later murdered by the Nazis in Theresienstadt.

This is the Bread of Affliction that came to symbolize freedom for Ida Nudel and other prisoners of conscience, the symbol of our people's journey to freedom forbidden by the Soviet oppressors, but never forgotten.

This is the Bread of Affliction prepared in sorrow by today's chained women, the *agunot*, trapped between ancient laws and modern realities, unable to sever past ties, unable to move forward.

Though many remain unnamed or forgotten, when we partake of the Bread of Affliction, we remember the sacrifices of our foremothers and honor their memory.

—MARLA J. FELDMAN

## God-Wrestlers

Tonight we speak of the people who left Egypt—the Israelites—whose name comes from the Hebrew word meaning "one who wrestles with God." In this sense, anyone who wrestles with God is an Israelite, regardless of the accident of ancestry, tribe, religion, or family of origin.

Tonight we recognize that the seder is not only about retelling the history of the Jewish people but also about taking time, through ritual and reflection, to remember what God does for each of us, when God leads us forth from the narrow place, from the house of bondage.

Let us welcome to our table all who hunger to be part of this ritual. Tonight we will each take seriously the essential Pesach question: How do we, individually and as a community, step out of *mitzrayim* —the narrow place—toward freedom, liberation of spirit, expansion of mind and soul?

—DEENA METZGER

## This Is the Gate of the Lord

When you are asked in the world to come, "What was your work?" and you answer, "I fed the hungry," you will be told, "This is the gate of the Lord; enter into it, you who have fed the hungry."[1]

That hunger exists throughout the world is clearly a reality but it need not be so. Hunger is not the result of scarcity—the world produces twenty percent more food than is necessary to feed every man, woman, and child on the planet.

For Jews, the issue is clear. The traditional obligations of *tzedakah* refer not to charity but to justice. We needn't look far to see the pain of people who do not know whether they will be able to feed themselves and their children. In our own land of abundance, hunger exists in shocking proportions. The United States Census Bureau figures for 2000 tell us that thirty-one million of our fellow Americans are hungry or "food insecure," including twelve million children. In a time and place of plenty, this is not merely a shame—it's an outrage.

According to America's Second Harvest, 40 percent of those families seeking help have at least one person in the household who is working. To work and still be forced to choose between buying food and paying rent or utilities is a scandal. Justice—*tzedakah*—requires that we invite all who are hungry to enter and eat.

While we each must do all we can, we as individuals cannot do all that is required without a safety net of benefits like food stamps and school lunch programs to enable poor and needy people to overcome the scourge of hunger. Our commitment must include not just feeding people today but demanding systemic changes that address the root causes of hunger. We can all be the voice of the voiceless. This advocacy, fueled by our outrage about the prevalence of hunger, will truly fulfill our obligations for *tzedakah* and *tikkun olam*.

—BARBARA H. BERGEN

## Breaking the Silence about Class

"Let all who are hungry come and eat." As we read the haggadah's instruction to welcome those in need to our seder table, we must reflect on the ways that those of us who focus on the transformation of Judaism as a religious tradition have virtually ignored issues of class.

Yet, class is deeply related to the difficulties feminists have had institutionalizing our gains and moving beyond equal access to change in the content of Jewish life. As Ma'yan's study of the deplorable absence of women from the boards of major Jewish organizations suggests, our inability to systematically incorporate the insights of feminism into Jewish curricula on every level, or to fund major feminist projects, is surely tied to the absence of women from halls of power. We cannot separate so-called religious issues from issues of the material base of Jewish communal life and class relations.

What has money meant within the Jewish community, and how do we address the loaded topic of Jews and money in our society? What is the relationship among our difficulty in getting our issues on the Jewish communal agenda, our lack of economic power, and the economic marginalization of women in the United States and globally? How do we address the growing poverty of women in the United States and worldwide, and do so as part of a Jewish feminist theological agenda?

As feminists, we have broken communal silence in talking about God, sexuality, domestic violence, and many other issues that make Jews uncomfortable. Can we also take the lead in talking about the even more difficult subject of money?

—JUDITH PLASKOW

## Somos Judios

Egypt, the center of our emotional geography, is about the rush into exile. The haggadah asks us to experience the Exodus as if we had actually been there. No leap of imagination is required for my mother and her family. In two generations, they went from Turkey and Greece, to Cuba, and then to America.

The truth is that there has never been enough time for the bread to rise. My grandparents locked the door of their Havana apartment and walked away forever with the key still in hand. For years it dangled on a key chain in America. On the kitchen table in Havana, my grandmother left instructions about which plates were for meat and which for dairy, and where the Passover dishes were stored. My grandfather scorched the bathtub burning the money he couldn't take with him. After all that, there was no time to knead dough for *bourekas,* for bread. No photos, no jewelry, not even a morsel of that bread of affliction.

Permanent wanderers that we are, we are forced over and over to abandon possessions, countries. Only the Jew in us is handed down. *Somos Judios.* A slogan, a chant that echoes through the generations.

My mother and aunt hold up the matzah that we are asked to believe is *el pan de la afliccion que comieron nuestros padres en tierra de Egipto*—the bread of affliction that our ancestors ate in the land of Egypt; the bread of affliction that we have eaten in Spain, Turkey, Greece, Cuba, and now America. The two sisters sing proudly, defiantly, to welcome the stranger, to acknowledge their hunger.

They sing for all those in need of a place in history, a need to share in family myth: Come and celebrate the Passover with us. For Passover is about searching for firmer ground, safer ground. It is about a *compromiso*—an obligation to our ancestors to remember their lives and times as if they were our own.

—JUDITH BOLTON-FASMAN

## A Wandering People

We are a wandering people, and throughout our history we have left many Egypts for better places. I am blessed to have experienced such a journey personally. When I was a child, my family left Iran—a metaphoric Egypt not so geographically distant from the original. While I take inspiration from the haggadah's redemptive vision of the Promised Land, I also always feel some sadness during the seder when I think of the places we, over time, have left behind.

Jeremiah famously advised the despondent Israelites, recently exiled to Babylon: "Build houses there, and dwell in them; and plant gardens and eat their fruit.... Seek out the peace of the city to which I have exiled you. Pray to God on her behalf, for in her peace you will have peace" (29:5–7). Throughout our history, we have done just as Jeremiah asked, building houses, planting trees, developing cultures, and making peace in the exiles in which we have found ourselves. Indeed, it is hard to imagine a tradition as rich and multicultural as ours emerging from a people that did not wander in exile.

But because of the way we have embraced living in exile, escape from even the cruelest places meant losing something precious. I lived in Egypt one summer and visited what is left of Maimonides' *beit midrash*. I was heartbroken to see a great seat of Jewish learning reduced to a pile of rubble in an obscure corner of Cairo. Amidst the filth, I saw an alley cat born just when I stepped into what might have been the main study hall. Maimonides famously struggled with the idea of living in Egypt. He went there because he had no choice, and life was hard for him there. And yet, who can deny that Judaism was enriched because he was exiled to this part of the Islamic world, where he learned from his neighbors and integrated their ideas into his own writings? And who can deny some sadness in knowing that only the faintest tracings of his presence survive in Egypt?

In tribute to the ways we practiced Judaism in exile, and in honor of the Jews who are still in unhappy exiles, I suggest a Persian Jewish ritual for *Ha lachma anya*. Take some time to let each person at the seder hold up the seder and matzah plates and recite individually the *Ha lachma anya*. Each person, whether host or guest, is able to assert that she owns part of this seder meal enough to invite others to partake in it.

—TALI FARIMAH FARHADIAN

## All Who Are Hungry

This is the bread of affliction which our ancestors ate in the land of *mitzrayim*.

This is the bread I have not allowed myself to eat. These are the tears I shed three times over: before eating, when I was terrified of my own hunger; while eating, when I dissected each bite on my plate; after eating, when I forced myself to run six miles in the bitter cold to absolve myself of the sin of nurturing my body. This is *mitzrayim*, the narrow place—my younger sister's jeans, which I squeezed around my waist until I was little more than a pile of bones; my hollow eyes peering through an emaciated frame. This is the bread of my affliction, and this is the narrow place I am fighting to leave.

All who are hungry, come enter and eat.

All who are dying to be thin, come celebrate life. All who count calories, come count the blessings that sustain us. All who are haunted by images of food pyramids, come build a future on a foundation of health and strength. All who have fasted, come feast.

All who are in need, come celebrate Pesach.

All who are starving for love and warmth, come join hands around this seder table. All who feel unworthy, invisible, and passed over, come let us rejoice in your presence. All who feel broken, come break bread together. All who know all too well what it means to feel empty, come partake in the fullness of this moment.

Now we are here, next year in the Land of Israel.

Now we are fighting a disorder; next year, we will find seder. Now we run and restrict; next year, we will recline at the table. Now we are afraid to ask for help; next year we will learn to stretch out our arms.

Now we deny our potential to give and to grow; next year, we will live up to our promise.

Now we are enslaved; next year we will be free.

Now we can only weep salt water tears; next year, we will enjoy the egg of rebirth and new life. Now we are afraid to partake of the *maror* and *charoset;* next year, we will learn to taste life's bitterness and sweetness. Now we can only feel *tzar* in *mitzrayim;* next year we will feel *shaleym* in *Yerushalayim.*

This is the bread of affliction. All who are hungry, come enter and eat.

—ILANA KURSHAN

## The New Colossus

Our ethical engagement requires that we consider the wrongs present in the world and take action to redress them. But, before we can recognize what is wrong, we must be able to envision an alternative to the existing situation. Emma Lazarus' poem, inscribed on the base of the Statue of Liberty, describes such an alternative. "The New Colossus" articulates a powerful vision of a better, even ideal, world, and expresses a bright faith that America, the New World, might one day fulfill that ideal.

As yet, it has not. But Lazarus' poem is a part of our American story. It records a piece of our history; the Statue of Liberty was, for so many immigrants, the first sight alerting their imminent arrival to a new home. "The New Colossus" also tells of our hopes for the future, for a nation open, always, to all those in need of refuge. It imagines an intersection of Jewish and American values at their most welcoming and kind.

Rabbinic legend recounts that only when Elijah comes to earth clad as a beggar and is treated with gracious hospitality will God deem the world ready for redemption. Emma Lazarus gives us a glimpse of what a world ready for redemption would look like, and she challenges us to live up to her words.

Not like the brazen giant of Greek fame,
With conquering limbs astride from land to land;
Here at our sea-washed, sunset gates shall stand
A mighty woman with a torch, whose flame
Is the imprisoned lightning, and her name
Mother of Exiles. From her beacon-hand
Glows world-wide welcome; her mild eyes command
The air-bridged harbor that twin cities frame.
"Keep, ancient lands, your storied pomp!" cries she
With silent lips. "Give me your tired, your poor,
Your huddled masses yearning to breathe free,
The wretched refuse of your teeming shore.
Send these, the homeless, tempest-tossed to me,
I lift my lamp beside the golden door!"

—EMMA LAZARUS, WITH AN INTRODUCTION BY RUTH KAPLAN

## All Who Hunger

In making space within our community, we declare whole-
    heartedly:
Let all who are hungry come and eat with us.
Let all who hunger for spiritual sustenance
come and share this celebration and
let us rediscover our heritage together.

But in a world that remains suspicious of difference, in which
    individuals protect themselves and their interests at all
    costs, do we really open our hearts to the stranger? Would
    we be willing to welcome those whom we are taught to
    fear the most?

This year we are oppressed.
We live in a world in which hatred abounds, and in which
too many stand silently by—out of complicity and out of
    greed.

Next year, may we be free. May we live in a community that is
quick to open rather than close its doors, a community that
    strives

to love and respect all humanity, a community that can
   celebrate
differences and find comfort in that which
holds us together.

*—ACROSS THE SEA: A HAGGADAH*

# The Four Questions

The Four Questions set the stage for the rest of *maggid*. The Talmud states that the telling of the story of our Exodus from Egypt cannot begin until at least one question has been asked. Our sages stress that the rote recitation of the Four Questions does not fulfill this requirement. A spirit of honest inquiry, curiosity, and reflection should infuse our seder ritual. What, then, is required to commence with our telling of the Passover story? Nothing more and nothing less than one real question.

Each of the Four Questions in the haggadah asks, "Why is this night different from all other nights?" and continues with specific references to the unusual practices of the evening: eating matzah and *maror*, dipping our food twice, and reclining at the table. Even these traditional Four Questions have changed over time, as different practices have evolved and inspired new questions.

In this spirit, many women's seders include a set of alternative questions that are particularly relevant to women's seders or feminist issues. Just as the Four Questions are used to distinguish seder evenings from all others, you may choose to use this opportunity to distinguish a women's seder from other seders. What questions do we as women bring to the seder table? How are we affected by hearing one another's questions, perhaps spoken aloud for the first time at the seder? What new tellings will our questions yield?

This is a time to emphasize for all participants—children and adults alike—the value that the seder places on the process of authentic questioning. Serious, even difficult and challenging questions are to be encouraged. In the words of an old Yiddish proverb: *Fun a kashe shtarbt man nisht.* From a question, no one has ever died. Indeed, the seder teaches that it is our questions that keep us alive.

## The Spirit of *Mah Nishtanah*

Seder night is designed to shake us out of our ordinary ways of thinking. The Mishnah, an ancient compilation of the Jewish oral tradition, gives us a glimpse into the origins of seder rituals, including the *mah nishtanah,* or "Why is this night different?" In the Mishnah's account (*Pesachim,* chapter 10), after the pouring of the second cup of wine, the children would begin asking questions, trying to make sense of the ways that seder night was different. Why are we eating bitter herbs? Where's the bread? The children would then eagerly await the response to their questions, creating an opening to discuss the messages of Passover.

The familiar text of *mah nishtanah,* which children memorize and recite at contemporary seders, was originally taught to them only if they did not know how to ask questions. In the spirit of the original *mah nishtanah,* may we allow ourselves to be shaken out of our ordinary ways of thinking by asking new questions and celebrating with one another how tonight is different from other nights.

—MELISSA KLEIN

## The Daughters' Four Questions

The four daughters questioned; the four mothers replied.

The first daughter asked, "Mother, why is this night different from all other nights? Why do we celebrate a women's seder?"

The second daughter asked, "Mother, why do we taste this bitterness and keep it fresh in our mouths?"

The third daughter asked, "Mother, why then do we taste both salt tears and sweet?"

The fourth daughter asked, "Mother, why do we find it so difficult to lean back and relax during this meal?"

—ADAPTED FROM *SAN DIEGO WOMEN'S HAGGADAH*

## Four Questions for a Women's Seder

Why, on this night, have the women from our community gathered together?

Why, on this night, are the women served, rather than serving others?

Why, on this night, is there an orange on the seder plate?

Why, on this night, do we place Miriam's Cup on our table?

—*YALE WOMEN'S HAGGADAH*

## Free to Answer Our Questions

Tonight, as free women, we will answer the four questions freely, from our own experiences.

Matzah. We eat matzah to remind ourselves that as women we were once less full—that our lives were flattened, limited in many ways, and yet we were able to continue even when there was little to nourish us.

*Maror*. We eat *maror* to remind us of the bitterness that has been in our lives. As we taste the bitter herb we think of our losses, our missed opportunities, and the rules and customs that have kept us small and less valued.

Dipping. We dip twice, once in salt water to remind us of our tears of sorrow, and once in *charoset* to remind us of the sweetness in life. For we have each experienced times of constriction and times of expansion. Life has been both hard and good to us.

Reclining. Tonight we recline as a symbol of our freedom to be still, to savor the precious leisure time we have to be ourselves and know ourselves. Tonight we are in service only to the Supreme One.

—JEWISH FAMILY SERVICE OF DELAWARE WOMEN'S SEDER

## Why Is This Night Different from All Other Seder Nights?

At all other seders, we hear the stories of our forefathers,
But the voices of our mothers are silent.
*Tonight they will be heard.*

At all other seders, the heroic deeds of our sisters
Miriam, Yocheved, Shifra, and Puah are kept hidden.
*Tonight we will celebrate their courage.*

At all other seders, we denounce the Pharaoh of the past.
*Tonight we will also examine the pharaohs of our own day.*

At all other seders we rejoice only in our liberation as a people.
*Tonight we also celebrate our empowerment as Jewish women.*

—ELAINE MOISE AND REBECCA SCHWARTZ

## On Questioning at the Seder

The Four Questions asked at the Passover seder are understood as a celebration of children's curiosity and a manifestation of our tradition's esteem of the act of questioning. Tonight, we ask ourselves how many real questions these scripted questions, and the seder itself, allow us to ask.

The ability to honestly question the status quo is one of the defining elements of freedom. Indeed, the danger of patriarchy—or of other oppressive social hierarchies—is not only its overt violence and dehumanization but also that it threatens to make the inequality on which it is based a part of each individual's consciousness. Oppression is victorious when it becomes so taken for granted that criticism does not need to be actively suppressed. No one even thinks of asking "why" or "how" or "who benefits from this arrangement" or "are there other ways in which we can live?"

Ritual, it seems to me, is one of the most effective and widespread means of enlisting the allegiance and cooperation of all members of society, even those who have little to gain from the perpetuation of the status quo. The power of ritual lies in its ability to evoke strong sentiments rather than rational questioning, to distract attention from large ideological problems through the systematic focusing of attention on the minutiae of ceremonial detail, and to draw individuals into a communal script that is presumed to be natural and God-given.

The Passover seder (literally, order), one of the most highly ritualized events in Jewish life, presents a fine opportunity for examining the processes and meanings of the "taken for grantedness" of our lives and culture. Every aspect of the seder—the food, the style of seating, the songs, and even the questions that are asked—is structured and ceremonial. While the traditional haggadah includes excerpts from the intellectual tradition of rabbinic debate and commentary, the power of the seder for many of us lies in the evocative smell of matzah ball soup, the sight of a beautiful seder plate or of a matzah cover hand-painted by a young family member, rousing melodies such as *Dayeinu*, the special taste of horseradish and *charoset*, and distinctive tactile experiences like dipping one's finger into a glass of wine. The annual repetition of these embodied acts re-creates a sense of order, of structure, of cosmic "rightness." Even the questioning that takes place at the seder is ritualized. Children memorize and recite questions composed centuries ago, often not understanding what they ask or, alternatively, already knowing the answers.

Feminist seders and feminist haggadahs can be important tools for resisting the seductive pull of custom, for questioning the naturalness of the traditional order. Yet, women's seders, like other rituals, run the risk of themselves becoming arenas for creating the uncritical warm and fuzzy feeling of tradition rather than remaining sites in which we permit, encourage, or perhaps even force ourselves to ask fundamental questions about our own lives, our culture, and our world.

Tonight, we add four such questions to our Passover seder. When we luxuriate in the evocative sensory experience of Passover customs, do we suspend our critical faculties, forgetting that slavery—formal and informal—still exists in the world today? When we proclaim "Once we were slaves but now we are free," are we speaking from our own true life experiences, or are we reciting a cultural script crafted by others for purposes that may or may not be beneficial for us? When we focus—some would even say obsess—on ceremonial details, do we distract ourselves from questioning the ethics of a freedom narrative that divides humankind into good guys (us) and bad guys (them)? And do we have the courage to ask our questions not only at special women's seders but also at family and community seder tables?

—SUSAN SERED

## A Passover Prayer to Speak Out for Children

On Passover, we celebrate freedom from oppression.
*On this Passover, let us think of the children oppressed by poverty.*

On Passover, we celebrate the promise of a free people.
*On this Passover, let us recognize the promise within all children.*

On Passover, we welcome the stranger into our homes.
*On this Passover, let us think of those children who have no place
to call home.*

On Passover, we dip the herbs in salt water to remind us of
the tears shed by our ancestors.
*On this Passover, let us think of all the children whose tears must
be dried.*

On Passover, the breaking of the matzah represents the bread
of affliction.
*On this Passover, let us place a fourth piece of matzah and
remember those children who have no more than crumbs
to eat.*

On Passover, we spill wine to represent the ten plagues visited
upon the Egyptians.
*On this Passover, let us think of the hunger, homelessness, poverty,
and abuse plaguing so many children's lives.*

On Passover, the children recite the four questions.
*On this Passover, let us resolve to speak out and act for the children who have no voice.*

—NATIONAL COUNCIL OF JEWISH WOMEN

# Avadim Hayinu

**A**vadim hayinu comes as a response to the Four Questions. The central question of the seder has been posed: *mah nishtanah?* "Why is this night different from all other nights?" Now, the haggadah responds: "We were slaves to Pharaoh in Egypt, and the Lord brought us out from there with a strong hand and an outstretched arm." The answer is unexpectedly straightforward. The whole story of the Exodus, the entire narrative of redemption, is reduced to this one sentence. Perhaps the brevity of the response is meant to teach us something: It is important to be able to articulate the essence of things.

We are reminded of the story of a heathen who asks the sage Hillel to teach him the whole Torah while standing on one foot. Hillel replies: "Do not do to another what is hateful to yourself. The rest is commentary. *Zil g'mor,* go and learn."

The haggadah, like Hillel, teaches us the value of being able to speak clearly about what is essential, what is foundational, what defines us. Yet, the haggadah, like Hillel, reminds us that this is valuable only if it is a way of opening, rather than closing, the door to further learning and discussion.

Indeed, Hillel's parting words—"Go and learn"—are the same words used in the haggadah for the continuation of *maggid*.[1] While *Avadim hayinu* begins by articulating the essence of the Passover story, it ends by emphatically acknowledging the importance of continued exploration: "Whoever elaborates upon the story of the Exodus is worthy of praise."

This closing statement has inspired many women to create ritual and textual innovations for their women's seders. Incorporating the stories of our foremothers into the Passover seder is praiseworthy; it is part of the elaboration that is prescribed. The new questions, insights, and perspectives that we as women bring to the seder table enhance the Passover experience for all Jews. Similarly, many of the authors in this chapter discuss the contemporary political issues affecting women, Jews, and the greater global community. Although we, today, are free, we must not forget others' ongoing struggles for freedom even while celebrating our own liberation.

This passage of the haggadah raises other questions as well. Why do we tell this story in the first person plural? What does it mean to say that we—not they—were slaves to Pharaoh in Egypt? How do we define slavery and freedom? Are we really free? Dare we say that we are not, when so many people still suffer under conditions of harsh poverty and oppression? To what, or whom, do we attribute the freedom we enjoy? What do we mean when we say that "God brought us out" of the house of bondage? What was and is the role of human beings in bringing an end to slavery and injustice? Remembering our historical experience of slavery and liberation, how—in our own time—shall we respond to others' struggles for freedom? The pieces in this section challenge us to address these urgent questions with empathy and action.

## Getting Egypt Out of Us

The Torah devotes fewer than ten chapters to recounting the Jews' leaving of Egypt. The rest of the Torah is not about getting out of Egypt. It is about getting Egypt out of us. Once, at a women's liberation workshop, I heard a woman who had never read the Bible say,

"If all sexist practices ended today, we would still carry sexism inside of us for forty years." I smiled at this unexpected echo of the Israelites' forty-year sojourn in the desert.

Our ancestors crossed the desert with God taking care of their every need. Food was coming from the sky, and a well traveled with them. According to midrash, their clothes did not fade, the children's shoes grew with their feet, no one ever needed a bathroom, and the sand rose and sank to flatten any hills or mountains so that they would walk a flat plain. Yet, coddled as they were, they still lived in constant fear and worry. They still sent spies to Israel to test that it was safe, and their mission failed before it started because they saw themselves as grasshoppers.

Internalized sexism, a contemporary version of "slave mentality," is so much a part of us that sometimes we do not even know it is there. It clouds our thoughts and actions daily.

Our mothers and grandmothers were heroines in what they accomplished in paving the way for the liberation of all women. But the work is not done until we purge the effects of the oppression from inside of us. The right to vote, the pay we earn, the education and jobs we acquire—all these leave us still thinking our worth is conditional. Slavery leaves a profound emotional legacy: It makes us feel like grasshoppers facing giants. Accepting God's love for us is the ultimate and final blow to any oppression. It is the key to the Promised Land.

—ELA THIER

## Ma'aseh B'Rebbe Eliezer

Ma'aseh B'Rebbe Eliezer *is a passage in the haggadah that describes a seder conducted by five Rabbis during the Roman occupation. Their seder lasted all night until their students entered to call them for the morning* shema. *The story of these Rabbis is included in the haggadah to model, for us, the act of elaborating on the story that the seder prescribes. The Rabbis' own process of elaboration is reflected in both the length of their seder and, as the reflection below discusses, the content of their conversation.*

This story of Rebbe Eliezer and his colleagues, related in the traditional haggadah, contains details that sanction the act of bringing contemporary political concerns to the seder—an act in which we are engaged tonight.

Tradition asks many questions about the peculiarities of this story: If this ritual emphasizes the teaching of the Passover story, why weren't the students sitting with their Rabbis at the seder? How could the greatest teachers of the day tell the *maggid* without inviting students to learn from them? And how could these sages be so careless about the time to say the morning *shema* that they needed their students to remind them? Did they not see the light of daybreak as a reminder?

We know from the Mishnah that the Rabbis named here were leaders of the Bar Kochva rebellion that rose against the tyranny of Roman rule in 132–135 C.E. Some have suggested that they were plotting that very rebellion during their seder. They did not notice that the sun had risen because they held their seder in a cave to ensure secrecy. The students were not present at the seder because they were stationed on watch at the mouth of the cave.

Some say that the notion of a women's seder, a mix of traditional ritual with contemporary social or political issues, is inappropriate. This story challenges such a claim, demonstrating that our wisest sages understood that ritual loses meaning if it occurs in a vacuum. They understood the living issues of the haggadah—liberation, self-determination of a people—and actively engaged them.

Tonight we do the same.

—JUDITH ROSENBAUM

## The Battle of the Women of the Wall

*Avadim hayinu l'Pharaoh b'Mitzrayim.* We were slaves to Pharaoh in Egypt. As I read these words, I think of the connections between our slavery in Egypt and the current legal and political status of Women of the Wall.

Women of the Wall is a courageous group of Jewish women who meet every Rosh Chodesh to pray at the Western Wall in Jerusalem, the

Kotel. For this act they have endured harassment and attacks, and they continue to fight a difficult legal battle to ensure their right to pray together at our holy site.

As the legal liaison between the International Committee for Women of the Wall and our attorneys in Israel, I witness the injustices perpetrated against these brave women by those in the highest Israeli judiciary and political circles. I can imagine in some small way the desperation of our people in Egypt and understand how their suffering led them to cry out for God's help.

In our own battle for freedom, the Women of the Wall filed a lawsuit in the Israeli Supreme Court. This suit sought to secure the right of women to pray aloud, in groups, with Torah and *tallit,* in the women's section at the Kotel. Although a 1994 decision ruled in our favor, the government has failed to carry out this decision, and the court has not forced them to do so.

Until we achieve victory, the Women of the Wall will continue to pray each Rosh Chodesh at the Kotel despite the threats and harassment they face. To comply with the court's directives, they must conduct parts of the service in muted voices and then retreat, exiled, away from the Kotel for the Torah service. If the group fails to comply, the women face a penalty of up to six months in prison or a heavy fine. Furthermore, legislation has been introduced in the Knesset to increase this penalty.

We read in the haggadah, "We were slaves to Pharaoh in *mitzrayim,* but Adonai our God brought us forth with a mighty hand and with an outstretched arm. And if the Holy One, praised be God, had not taken our ancestors out of *mitzrayim,* then we, and our children, and our children's children, would still be enslaved to Pharaoh in *mitzrayim.*"

We learn from this passage that conditions of slavery and injustice are not irreversible. Despite the travesty of justice now afflicting the Women of the Wall, I imagine the day when justice will prevail, when the Israeli legal and political systems will cease their capitulation to *haredi* (ultra-Orthodox) violence or threat of violence, and when

Women of the Wall will be able to pray the full service at the Kotel, not in exile.

—MIRIAM BENSON

## The Measure of Our Success

Sweatshops are a part of our heritage as American Jews. Women, children, and men, mostly from Eastern Europe, spent countless hours, morning and night, sweating away at irons and cutting boards in the tenement buildings of New York and other large cities. Eventually, they organized unions and won victories for themselves and future generations of workers. Today, a new generation of immigrant women and children toil in sweatshops that have sprouted up all over America's cities as a response to the new global economy. They are black and brown; they come from El Salvador, Cambodia, and Mexico.

The workers are women like Aracely, who has worked in contracting shops in Los Angeles for thirteen years, ever since she came from Mexico. She works seven days a week, more than twelve hours a day. She has had no time to learn English, though her children are fluent. She earns about $80 a week as a presser, working on her feet all day with an industrial iron. Once, she burned herself; she now has large purple scars because her employer didn't give her proper treatment. She has no holidays and no health coverage.

Our tradition teaches us clearly that, as is written in Deuteronomy 24:14, "You shall not oppress a hired laborer that is poor and needy, whether he—or she—be of your people or of the strangers that are in the land within your gates."

Historically, the American Jewish community has heeded this command and played a truly important and valiant role in eradicating the sweatshops of an earlier era. When Eastern European Jewish immigrants toiled in the sweatshops, courageous Jewish women activists fought on their behalf. Reformers like Lillian Wald from the Women's Trade Union League joined female trade union heroines like Clara Lemlich, Rose Schneiderman, Bessie Hillman, and Rose Pesotta. The fact is that a significant portion of American Jewish history is about building the United States' union movement, with women playing pivotal roles.

In the United States today, Jews are, in aggregate numbers, doing well economically. If we measure success in numbers, then we've made it. But I would like to suggest that we not measure success solely by how "we" as a community make it, but rather by how we treat the strangers among us—how we interact with those who don't enjoy the economic benefits of today's fast-changing world.

The notion of recalling our own slavery in Egypt and caring for the strangers among us seems to me to be the heart and soul of who we must be as a people and as a community. This evening as we reflect on the oppression of the Jewish people, our sense of responsibility must lie with those who suffer in sweatshops today.

—JO-ANN MORT

## We Cannot Go Back

In 1963, a decade before *Roe* v. *Wade* made the news, I was working on Wall Street while putting my husband through law school. I became friendly with a woman colleague who told me that she was very much in love with her beau. Their relationship was a difficult one, however, and became more difficult when she became pregnant. She very much wanted to have the child with her "boyfriend," but he threw $300 at her and told her to "take care of it."

It was only when she returned to work after being out of the office for about two weeks that she shared her story with me. She described the "dirty back-alley" abortion she had had, the fever and bleeding that developed, the fear that she would never again be able to bear a child, the terror that her family would find out, and the ice-cold reaction of the child's father, who had sent her off by herself, never to talk to her again.

I was stunned. At twenty-one I was a pretty sheltered person, but I tried hard to lend her courage and strength and shore up her self-esteem. I have never forgotten her story.

An amazing thing happened in 1992. My one-time colleague showed up at my Senate victory party in Washington, D.C. I hadn't seen her since the early '60s, but I had never forgotten her and the hell she went through because abortion was illegal. I don't remember too many acquaintances from those days, but I could never forget her. When we saw each other after all those years, we looked into each other's eyes but did not speak of the secret we shared. Remembering her fears, I was relieved to hear that she was a proud parent.

On this night of remembrance, when we reflect on the bitterness of past slavery and the miracle of liberation, let us not forget the suffering endured by women who were denied reproductive freedom, nor the important strides taken to protect their rights. Together, we reaffirm our commitment to the continuing struggle for a woman's right to choose. We cannot go back to the days of darkness again—no matter what obstacles we face and no matter how much energy it takes.

—BARBARA BOXER

## We Were Slaves

In Egypt they stole our voices.
We would open our mouths to refuse them,
But no sound came from our throats.
Like a dream where you try with all your strength to run
And cannot walk a step,
We would shout and scream and argue
Until our bodies shook with the noise
That could not escape from our heads.

In Egypt they outlawed "no," killed "stop"
And decreed silence to be "yes."
Muted and chained, our anger sounded to us
Like defiance.
But they heard nothing
And called us slaves.

In Egypt we were slaves.
But we chose each morning to eat and continue.

Within the tiny volume of our choices
We shouted muted rage.
We were silently resisting.

Today we celebrate our freedom
And sing so everyone will hear us.
But for the one who screams in her head—
For the silenced one whose denials no one can hear—
For the one who lives in a world stripped of "no"—
For the muted one who cannot deny or affirm—
We understand, and we pray.
We, too, were slaves.

—REBECCA L. DAVIS

## She Who Saves a Single Life

The recurrent exhortation of the Passover service is to remember that
we were strangers in Egypt and to help those who are, in our own time,
the strangers. Today, this injunction requires that we give our attention
to those known as refugees or internally displaced persons.

Refugees—both those who have fled across national boundaries
and those uprooted from their homes and forced into areas in their
own countries where they are treated as political prisoners—number,
today, between twenty million and eighty million persons, depending
on which definition is used.

Today's refugees are sometimes fleeing natural disasters. More
often, they are escaping political upheaval that puts their very lives at
risk. They leave their homes and escape with their lives, but not much
else. Traumatized by their experiences, they are living in a twenty-
first-century desert, in camps or tent cities, with limited access to food
and easy exposure to disease. There are almost always more people in
the camp than there are adequate facilities, so families are crowded
together in situations where tensions and dysfunctions mount. The
burden of these refugees and refugee camps on the host countries is
usually huge, which is a source of additional political and social tension and hostility.

It is incumbent on us, during our seders, to think of people who have recently escaped a natural disaster or who are victims of political oppression. While we cannot expect ourselves to solve the problems of the millions of others who need our help, we must not retreat to the convenience of being overwhelmed. We must feel compassion and act on it. We must find ways to make a difference in one refugee camp or for one refugee family or even one refugee child. As our tradition teaches, she who saves a single life, it is as if she had saved the world. It is not for us to complete the task, but neither are we free to desist from it.

—RUTH W. MESSINGER

## Let My People Go

When Israel was in Egypt land
Let my people go

Jews are not the only group to find profound meaning in the story of the Exodus. Enslaved African Americans recognized themselves in the toiling Hebrews.

Oppressed so hard they could not stand
Let my people go

The story of slavery ended happily for the Israelites, who at last attained freedom and then the Promised Land. For African Americans, literal freedom from slavery was quickly constrained by new and debilitating forms of oppression: legal segregation, economic and social discrimination, racial violence, and bigotry.

Go down, Moses
Way down to Egypt land

While legal, visible forms of discrimination have now eased, more subtle barriers to equal opportunity and full citizenship remain. From the criminal justice system to the frayed safety net, from the conditions of ghetto poverty to the old-boys' club, from redlining and zoning to hiring and promotion practices, from inadequate health care to racial stereotyping, African Americans too often remain victims of persistent, if extralegal, inequality. Jews, who are mostly white, often do not recognize these structural impediments, and this lies at the heart of Black-Jewish tensions.

> Tell old Pharaoh
> Let my people go.

Jews value dialogue; African Americans need action. Jews seek to change hearts; African Americans seek to change structures of opportunity.

> My Lord delivered Daniel from the lion's den,
> Jonah from the belly of the whale,
> And the Hebrew children from the fiery furnace;
> And why not every man?

For the Exodus to speak to the Jewish desire for universal freedom and justice, we must be mindful of others' Exodus stories as well as our own. We must help everyone reach the Promised Land.

> Oh brothers, don't get weary
> Oh sisters, don't get weary
> We'll land on Canaan's shore.

—CHERYL GREENBERG

## Witness to Survival

The story and traditions of Passover have special significance for me because of my personal family history. Both my parents survived the terrors of the Nazi regime—my mother was literally taken from her home during the seder. Telling the story each year of God freeing the Jews from the hands of ruthless tyranny recalls not only the memory of our ancestors who fled Egypt but also my own family's liberation and exodus after World War II. The lessons of freedom, tolerance, and justice that are central to the Passover story were instilled in me from childhood.

When my husband was selected to be the Democratic vice-presidential candidate, Al Gore asked me to speak at the announcement. As I took the stage that day in Nashville, I felt as if I was standing in front of the world, a witness to survival, immigration, and the blessings of freedom, representing so many of us who fled distant places and difficult circumstances. I shared with the audience the words I had shared with the vice president at dinner the evening before. "Thank you," I said. "I never would have dreamt I would be sitting here, the daughter of Holocaust survivors—an immigrant—and now the wife of the vice-presidential nominee. I thank you for this great honor."

The time I spent on the campaign trail strengthened my belief in the connection between our ancestors fleeing Pharaoh and the struggles for liberation in modern times. In the haggadah, we read the story of four sons who inquire about the Exodus from Egypt. It is the wicked son who asks, "What does this ritual mean to you?" The traditional haggadah sees him as wicked because he separates himself from his people. But any time we separate ourselves from the struggles of others, failing to understand that our story is bound up with theirs, we reenact the transgression of the wicked child. Everywhere I went on the campaign trail, I witnessed firsthand the universal struggle to overcome hardship and rebuild life among immigrants and refugees. In every corner of this country, I met people of all races, religions, and ethnicities, liberated from persecution and intolerance, trying to build a life of opportunity and freedom for themselves.

The haggadah recalls how God took us out of slavery in Egypt and sustained us for forty years in the desert until we reached the Promised Land. We know all too well how long and arduous the journey can be. As individuals called to act in the image of God, we must give of ourselves to help sustain the less fortunate as they struggle to cross the desert to freedom.

—HADASSAH LIEBERMAN

# The Four Children

I n the middle of the biblical narrative of the Exodus—just before a description of the dramatic final plague, the horrible slaying of the firstborn Egyptian children—we find a surprising interruption. Suddenly, there is a pause in the telling of the story, and the text shifts to a description of the laws of the Passover holiday. Remarkably, the Torah describes the requirements for our observance of the Passover festival before recounting the Exodus itself. This unusual structure suggests that the history of the Exodus cannot be separated from the meaning that it bears for us and for our children.

The Bible anticipates that future generations of children will have questions about the meaning of this story: "And when your children ask you, 'What do you mean by this rite?' you shall say, 'It is the Passover sacrifice to God, Who passed over the houses of the Israelites in Egypt and smote the Egyptians, but saved our houses'" (Exodus 12:26–27). The haggadah takes the questions laid out in the biblical text here and elsewhere and puts them in the mouths of four children with different temperaments, qualities, and abilities.

This passage has become one of the most richly developed parts of women's seders. Traditionally imagined as Four Sons, these children appear in many women's haggadahs as Four Children or Four Daughters.

Contemporary feminists have imagined the questions that we, as daughters, might bring to the seder table, and the responses that we, as mothers, might offer. How would these voices change the nature of the dialogue?

Alternatively, many contemporary commentaries urge us to see these children not as four distinct types of people but as different aspects of ourselves. This can raise powerful and provocative questions. In what ways do we experience ourselves as wise, wicked, simple, and silent? How do we seek to respond to the questions that arise from the disparate parts of ourselves?

ᔐ

## Where Are the Women?
## The Question Our Daughters Ask

Jewish tradition requires that the telling of the Passover story be initiated by the questions of our children. In addition to the Four Questions, the compilers of the haggadah included questions from four types of sons, teaching us that we must tailor our responses—the way in which we tell the story—to the different needs of each one who asks. More liberal haggadahs, to be more inclusive, change "sons" to "children," leaving the questions themselves the same. Here, we have questions from four types of daughters, each seeking to learn about the role of women in the Passover story, as their stories have been omitted in the traditional telling.

The wise daughter asks, "What does Judaism demand of me? I cannot accept the secondary role that our tradition has assigned to women. There must be more. What is the real place of women in Judaism? What is my role at the seder?"

The wicked daughter, who excludes herself, asks, "Where have women always been during the seder? Preparing the meals, making sure the seder plate is full, and spending most of the time in the kitchen. Women have not been at the table, asking questions. This seder has no meaning for me. I can only ask the men, what does this seder mean to you?"

The naïve daughter asks, "Why are the stories in the haggadah only about men? Where are the women of the Passover story? Surely, women must have had a role. Is our history about only men? I don't understand what is going on here."

The daughter who does not know how to ask simply says, "It all seems so foreign to me. I feel so far removed from Jewish tradition. I don't even know where to begin."

The four daughters, each coming from a different place, are asking essentially the same question: Where are the women in this fundamental story of the Jewish people? We can respond to all their questions by telling them about the righteous women of Passover. Although their stories are not included in the haggadah itself, they are in the Bible and in the midrash, the rabbinic expositions of biblical texts. Rabbi Akiba taught in the Talmud, "Israel's deliverance was in reward for the righteous women."[1] Indeed, it was the women who took the first daring steps of defiance that led to our redemption from Egypt.

—RENNI S. ALTMAN

*Renni Altman continues to answer the daughters' questions through her telling of the righteous women of the Exodus in the next chapter (pp. 126–29).*

## The Song of Questions

Mother, asks the clever daughter,
who are our mothers?
who are our ancestors?
what is our history?
Give us our name. Name our genealogy.

Mother, asks the wicked daughter,
if I learn my history, will I not be angry?
Will I not be bitter as Miriam
who was deprived of her prophecy?

Mother, asks the simple daughter,
if Miriam lies buried in sand,

why must we dig up those bones?
Why must we remove her from the sun
    and stone
where she belongs?

The one who knows not how to question,
she has no past, she has no present, she
    can have no future
without knowing her mothers,
without knowing her angers,
without knowing her questions.

—E. M. BRONER AND NAOMI NIMROD

## Each Wants to Ask Her Questions

The traditional haggadah tells of four sons—one wise, one wicked, one simple, one who doesn't know how to ask. Throughout our history, these four voices have been recognized as parts of each of us. The questions of these "four sons" are questions we return to throughout our lives.

### A Wise Woman

Long ago, it seems another lifetime now, I was earnest, devoted to the pursuit of holiness with every part of my being. My mouth, my tongue, my fingers, my eyes, my intellect, my heart—all wanted nothing more than the knowledge of how to be holy. When do I bow, when do I cover my eyes, how do I hold the *etrog* when I make the blessing. Tell me the way it's supposed to be done, the approved way, the time-honored way for a Jew to be holy. I will hear and I will obey.

### A Wicked Woman

Not so long ago were days when I praised myself for simply getting out of bed in the morning, getting dressed, going about the business of the day. Sometimes the pain of life is so great you marvel that you are still on your feet. At that time, a friend said that what got her through the experiences of abyss was prayer—did I pray to God? "God," I spat back at her, "God??" And then I spoke terrible words, I blasphemed. Those were days of anger and pain. I didn't need to be told, "Had you been there you would not have been redeemed." I could see that for myself.

### A Simple Woman

Sometimes I say, explain it to me as if I were a child. This body of knowledge is complex, it embarrasses me because it seems that an intelligent adult should know this, yet, I don't. I've heard it many times, but it never quite makes sense. This is the place where I get lost, my eyes glaze over, and my mind wanders. These are the hardest questions, the simple questions. I am ashamed to still be asking these questions, the questions that make me feel simple.

### A Woman Who Does Not Even Know How to Ask a Question

The morning after arriving in this foreign country, this strange new place, I unpacked and reordered the rented apartment, ventured out to the corner store for milk, bread, mangoes, and yogurt. Finally it was time. Map in hand, ten-year-old daughter and seven-year-old son in tow, I took the bus downtown. I turned the map 'round and 'round; I turned myself 'round and 'round. A sympathetic stranger approached. "Can I help you?" he asked. I responded, "I am too lost to ask a question." Then I knew. I put the map back in my bag, I began looking, walking, smelling, tasting. The terror of being overwhelmed gave way to the joy of being overwhelmed. "O children," the tears welling up, "we are really here! We are in Jerusalem!"

### All

I sit at this seder and what you see is my festive dress, my clean shining hair; if you look closer you will see the face and hands and ankles that bear the weight of my seder work. What you can also see is that once I was pious, once I blasphemed, once I was ignorant, and once I was so lost that I needed to put away the map. All these women are a part of me. All of them are here at the seder. Each wants to be here, each wants a place at the table. Each wants to share, to celebrate, to experience. Each wants to ask her questions.

—MERLE FELD

## The Four Girls Within All of Us

### *Wise Girls*

At times, we are wise girls: strong and confident in what we know and who we are, curious and eager to learn more, seeing clearly through tangled and complex dilemmas, and able to make wise and appropriate decisions for ourselves and on behalf of others. Yet, as wise girls we risk growing complacent in our knowledge, smug in the "superior" wisdom of the status quo, and so caught up in the pursuit of learning and producing that we neglect others around us and our own well-being.

### *Wicked Girls*

At other times, we are wicked girls: angry, rebellious, critical, and negative. We set ourselves apart from our community, feeling, perhaps, that we don't belong and not understanding that it is we, not others, who place ourselves on the outside. Yet, it is as wicked girls that we are able to see our world from another perspective, to see that sometimes the emperor wears no clothes and to speak up and criticize what is wrong and what is unjust.

### *Simple Girls*

At times, we are simple girls: relaxed and playful, enjoying life without questioning, analyzing, or examining deeply; loving others with passion that cannot be expressed in words; being loved in return without any logic or reason. Yet, as simple girls we risk missing the color and texture of our complex universe, and we may forfeit the opportunity to contribute to *tikkun olam,* the repair and healing of the world.

### *Girls Who Don't Know How to Ask*

At other times, we are girls who don't know how to ask; we don't understand; we find that we cannot speak the language of the people in our company; we are struck dumb by a profound or strange new experience; or we are fearful because nothing like this has ever happened to us before. If we can remain silent, and tolerate our fear and our inability to speak for a while, we may discover worlds of riches we couldn't possibly have imagined. But if our fear paralyzes us, if we lose confidence and withdraw from the world, or if it is fear of others that silences us, we truly need to be brought out from our slavery "by a mighty hand and an outstretched arm."

Each girl within us needs the other girls. The wise girl needs the forcefulness of the wicked, the playfulness of the simple, and the sense of wonder of the speechless one. The wicked needs the erudition of the wise, the self-acceptance of the simple, and the contemplative spirit of the speechless. The simple needs the diligence of the wise, the clear vision of the wicked, and the confusion of the speechless. And the one who is struck dumb needs the words of the wise, the shout of the wicked, and the song of the simple.

At different times, each of our girls appears. We are, in turn, interested and curious, frustrated and angry, calm and contented, sad and fearful. It is easy to praise the wise, scold the wicked, smile with the simple, and rescue the speechless. It is far more difficult to challenge the wise, to love and appreciate the wicked, to prod the simple, and to allow the dumbstruck to struggle with confusion. We must learn how to encourage each girl's special gifts and discourage destructive tendencies.

All of these exist within us, sometimes in harmony and other times in cacophony. Our personal liberation depends upon understanding and balancing all of the very different parts of ourselves. May we come to know and accept the four girls within all of us so that we can grow closer to wholeness and freedom this year.

—RUTH BERGER GOLDSTON

## Our Continuing Survival

*This piece is taken from the* Survivors' Haggadah, *written for incest survivors and survivors of sexual abuse, who may still be struggling out of bondage and out of pain, out of the narrow places in their minds.*

Our sages speak of the four kinds of children who view the seder and wonder about it in different ways. There are several ways for us to think about what happened to us.

The intellectual survivor asks: What does it all mean? We suggest that this person read the literature and scholarship about sexual abuse and study to come to one kind of understanding.

The survivor still in denial asks: What does this mean to you? She or he does not say "us" but "you." It is hard to know how to answer. The denial isolates her or him from the support of those with similar experiences and from the truth of her or his own life.

The survivor still in confusion and pain asks: What is this? We can answer that we are remembering the experiences of long ago, to help us remember that we are free now, we are safe now, we can help ourselves now move toward and appreciate our freedom.

To the survivor who is too overwhelmed to ask, we can offer our patience and the example of our continuing survival.

—EVELYN GERSHON

## The Fifth Child

In the traditional Passover haggadah, the wise son asks, "What are the meanings of the laws and customs associated with Passover?" He embraces the Jewish tradition while trying to learn more about it. When the wicked son asks, "What is the meaning of this seder to you?" he separates himself from the seder experience, demanding to know what it means to others. The first son is wise because he asserts his desire to learn about the Jewish tradition and be a part of the community. The second son is wicked because, filled with disdain, he separates himself from the community.

In Hebrew, the language of these two questions is identical. The difference between how they are interpreted lies in a subtle distinction in tone. Similarly, within each of us, the questions of the wise and wicked children are often intertwined.

When I first struggled to define Judaism for myself, I became the wise child. I asked what all these rituals and beliefs have meant to the Jewish community in order to understand what they could mean to me. But as I learned more about my tradition, I became uncomfortable with the aspects of Judaism that made me feel excluded or secondary as a woman. The distance from Judaism that the wicked child's question provides allowed me the space to negotiate between my growing love for the Jewish tradition and my commitment to feminism.

And so I asked the questions of both the wise child and the wicked child and became a fifth child: a feminist child. For the feminist child, the combination of these questions prompts an altogether new question: How do I remain faithful to my tradition without compromising my feminist values? The feminist children all around us—authors, historians, poets, friends, teachers, and family members—have each asked this question in different forms and come up with their own answers, offering wisdom that can guide others in their exploration.

The feminist child steps back and calls into question what she sees without disrespect or disregard. She does not blindly follow one source of information; her Jewish identity and practice grows out of an awareness of traditional texts as well as contemporary feminist thought. Her integration of her commitment to both Judaism and feminism enriches and shapes the tradition of which we are all a part.

—RACHEL R. CYMROT

## A Daughter's Question

Tonight, we have heard the questions of the four children, but for many of us the most important questions are the ones our own children will ask. What does the teenaged daughter ask? She asks, "Why do I have to be here every year listening to the same boring story when I could be out having fun with my friends?"

Her mother patiently explains, "My beautiful daughter, the story of our people's Exodus from slavery in Egypt is one of the most exciting adventure stories ever written, and it's about your relatives. Try to imagine what it might have been like for young women like you. They were not only escaping slavery, not only leaving a place where there were frogs and vermin, locusts and wild beasts, but they also had to find a new recipe for bread-on-the-run, and it turned out to be flat.

"During our Passover seder, you should think not only about them but also about the Jewish women and girls who followed their example, struggling to keep their families safe, educated, fed, and proud in the times of the Spanish Inquisition, pogroms in Russia, and even the Holocaust. Tonight, we should think about girls like Anne Frank, who also would have preferred to just be with her friends.

"I like to think that our family has also contributed to the ongoing Passover story. Many of us have worked on behalf of people who are discriminated against and marginalized in our society. Along with many other women, I have struggled to protect and increase women's rights. When I do this work, I believe I am acting in the same tradition as those women who had the courage and faith to defy Pharaoh.

"You must remember that the Passover story continues today. There are women and girls, millions of them in all corners of the globe, who are enslaved. Millions of them are living in families where they are beaten and abused, in countries where they can't go to school or work or even leave the house alone. Millions of girls are forced to have part of their genitals cut off in a coming-of-age ritual, and millions more are trapped by such poverty that we can't even imagine it. Even in the United States, there are hardly any women leading major businesses. There are only thirteen women in the United States Senate out of a hundred members, and there has never been a woman president or vice president. Women still earn only seventy-nine cents for every dollar that men earn, and many more women than men live in poverty.

"I know that you are a very loving person. I know you are nice to everyone you know. But I hope that you will also learn to care about people you may never meet. Even today, in this country where we enjoy so much freedom, people are facing painful, sometimes brutal discrimination because of their color, their religion, their gender, their sexual orientation, their disability—just because they are different in some way. Sometimes they are even murdered because they are different. This same discrimination plagued the Jews, who were forced to live as slaves in Egypt.

"You are here tonight, reading the haggadah so that you can figure out how to write your own chapter in the Passover story. In your own way, you could be a modern-day Moses and lead people to a Promised Land, where they are free from fear and hunger and have the opportunity to gather in peace with their friends."

—JAN SCHAKOWSKY

# Go Forth and Learn

This is the heart of the telling, the account of the Exodus—our Exodus—from Egypt. Significantly, the opening words of this passage point to the revolutionary meaning of what we do at the seder: Go forth—*tzei*—has the same root as *yetziah,* the word used to describe the Exodus from Egypt. Even as we retell the story we are urged to go forth anew.

At the seder, our going forth does not involve physical travel but rather intellectual and spiritual movement. This *yetziah* is about learning. It is about leaving behind a narrowness of mind and heart. Our liberation is tied to asking and answering questions, to telling the story over and over again without ever assuming that we already fully know it. At the seder, we are all learners; if we learn nothing new, we have not gone forth.

What do we learn when the story is told by women? This is one of the defining questions at a women's seder. Voices of women, long silent, now speak. How does this transform our telling? What do we see in the story that we did not see before? *Who* do we see that we did not see before?

Strikingly, the Exodus narrative is one of the few biblical texts that is exceedingly rich in female characters. Shifra and Puah, Yocheved, Miriam, Pharaoh's daughter, and Tziporah are all active and important players in the story of our people's liberation from slavery. Many women's seders include traditional and contemporary commentaries that focus on these women and explore what they have to teach us about courage, resistance, and freedom itself.

## *Maggid*

With *maggid* we tell the story,
The exodus
From degradation to dignity,
*M'g'nut l'shevach,*
From slavery to freedom.

Each of us is to tell this story
and we who do so at length
are surely to be praised.

But this collective story
of the journey from slavery to freedom
is not the entirety of the tale.

Each of us bears our own
stories which relate our journeys,
our paths to freedom.

If each of us must relate our people's story
all the more so
should we be praised
for continuing the story
adding the individual strands
which make our identity,
which explain our journeys.

To journey is
to prepare,
to leave,
to travel,
to wander and wonder.

To journey is
to arrive,
to accustom,
to question,
to change,
to remain as we were,
yet touched by the journey.

What are our journeys
from slavery to liberation
from alienation to community
from afar to within
from foreign to familiar
from anxiety to comfort
from narrow spaces to expanse?

As we answer,
We continue *maggid*.
We tell our stories.

—LISA S. GREENE

## The Telling

Ima, *Mother, tell me a story.*

Yocheved looks down over her bulging belly at the little daughter tugging at her hem. This is her Miriam, full of whys and whens and how comes. A story? Yocheved, sitting at her loom, has only one story to tell—one she fears her daughter is too young to hear. But Miriam will not be hushed, and so Yocheved, weary from the mud and the cloth and the stove, begins....

*Once there was a people enslaved by an evil king. They worked day and night, but he was never satisfied. This king, Miriam, wanted more, wanted everything the people could give. And he took everything from them, down to their lives, down to their sons.*

Miriam, bored of the story she has heard so many times, puts her hand on her mother's belly.

Ima, *will I have a brother?*

*Yes.*

*And* Ima, *will the bad king take my brother?*

*No. This time, the bad king cannot have everything he wishes. The voices of slavery will call out and be answered; through the strength of the few, all will be saved. Do you understand, my daughter? Only through courage will the bad king be overcome. Ahh, Miriam, I am a slave, but my children, they will be free...you hold the power to make them free.*

*Tell me a story,* whispers Shifra to Puah as they wait, tense, in the darkness. Another baby will soon be born, but on this night, the angel of death will be forced away. *Puah, I am afraid,* and Shifra reaches for her hand.

*Do not be afraid, my sister, my friend.* Puah's voice does not shake. *We are the givers of life, and the power of life is strong, stronger than Pharaoh and his gods, stronger than law. Remember the force of life, within us all, in this birth tent, in this women's camp, and you will not be afraid.*

*And what story can you tell me?* whispers Pharaoh's daughter to the baby in the basket, his cries already slowing. She holds him to her breast. *What else can you be to me but a gift, a little treasure? A child for a woman who is barren, and when I am old you will tell my stories for me.* Pharaoh's daughter knows the origin of this gift, so often prayed for, but holds her silence. She walks calmly into her father's house. *Father, I have brought you our future, my son,* she says.

*I have sent my husband Moses back to You,* Tziporah tells the darkening sky outside her tent. *I found him aimless in the desert, but I know he belongs to You, and to his people. He will have a hard time of it, I know; he hates crowds and says he doesn't speak well. I have a child on the way, and he said he wouldn't leave me, but I saw Your voice in his eyes and so I have sent him...may he go with visions for the future and return with the faces of his past. What stories, then, will he have for our child?*

The women have dropped their tambourines in exhaustion; the sun is beginning to set. *Miriam, Miriam, sing to us, they cry. Miriam, tell us a story.* And Miriam, the child of slavery, hears the voice of her mother. And Miriam, the prophetess of freedom, begins to tell the story....

—ARIELLE DERBY

## *Mesorah* and Kabbalah

Teaching and learning, *mesorah* and kabbalah: They form the core of the seder experience. The halakhah instructs that even if one celebrates the feast of matzot alone in one's house, the tale of the Exodus must still be told. The night's obligations cannot be filled without transmission, absorption, renewal. We all shine as teachers at the seder as we endlessly explore new ways to engage our children and ourselves. The chain of *mesorah* is kept strong all year long by our teachers.

A part of this chain, Jewish women have long held the keys to Jewish knowledge and tradition. In our homes, we have carefully molded Jewish identity for our children as we passed down the intricate ways of our mothers. At times we could not even write the *alef-bet*, but we shared our wealth of knowledge, from mouths to ears. Women, along with men, are responsible for the education of their children, as the verse says: "Listen, my sons to the *musar* of your father; do not stray from the Torah of your mother." Outside our homes, too, we have steadily shown our faces as teachers and models of Torah. In ancient times, Miriam, Devorah, and Chana lit the torch for the public teaching of Torah. Today, we reclaim that early flame. Female Torah giants of our times, like Nehama Leibowitz and Sarah Schenirer, have left indelible marks on the ways we read Torah. They did not emerge from an unlit path. The *firzogen,* or female prayer leaders, of Ashkenazi synagogues were the forebears of our teachers.

We have only begun to witness the impact of female teachers on the whole of our community. As more and more women are trained in Torah study and are afforded the opportunity to share their knowledge, our community will be transformed. As the haggadah says, the more we teach, the more we shall be praised.

—TAMMY JACOBOWITZ

## In Reward for the Righteous Women

*The following reading should be read responsively. The seder leader reads the stories of the women of Exodus, and participants respond, together, with the italicized refrain.*

The name of Moses is not mentioned in the haggadah in order to underscore the notion that it was divine, not human, action that redeemed the Israelites from slavery in Egypt. Nonetheless, one can say that God had "human hands," partners in enabling the deliverance of our ancestors from slavery. In the biblical account, Moses dominates the story as the leader of the Israelites and God's primary partner. Too often overlooked in the story, however, is the crucial role that several women played in ensuring that Moses would, in fact, survive and rise to the position that enabled him to lead his people to freedom. The courage of these women, who risked their own lives, was noted by the great Rabbi Akiba, who taught that "Israel's deliverance was in reward for the righteous women."[1]

The story begins with Pharaoh's decree to kill all male Israelite babies. Pharaoh attempted to conceal his responsibility for this genocidal plan by acting through intermediaries, two midwives, so that the deaths would appear to be natural. The midwives, Shifra and Puah, whose lives were dedicated to supporting life, defiantly refused to kill the babies: "But the midwives feared God and did not do as the King of Egypt had told them, but kept the infants alive" (Exodus 1:17).

Shifra and Puah did not allow Pharaoh to escape the consequences of his acts. Their moral courage is a model of responsible, ethical behavior.

*We were redeemed for the sake of the righteous midwives, Shifra and Puah, who defiantly saved life at the risk of their own lives.*

Once the midwives refused to kill the babies, Pharaoh came up with another plan: All male Israelite children were to be cast into the Nile. In defiance, one woman hid her infant in her home rather than send him off to certain death. But, "when she could hide him no longer, she made a wicker basket for him and caulked it with bitumen and pitch. She put the child into it and placed it among the reeds by the bank of the Nile" (Exodus 2:3). Yocheved could not allow her son to be simply cast into the river to die, and tried to provide him with the means to reach safety. Yocheved opposed Pharaoh's decree, risking not only her son's life but also the lives of her whole family. She thereby saved her son, the eventual savior of her people.

*We were redeemed for the sake of the righteousness of Yocheved, moth-er of Moses, who had the courage to save her son by giving him to another.*

Yocheved saved her son for the first three months of his life, but it was another who was responsible for him after that: "And his sister stationed herself at a distance, to learn what would befall him" (Exodus 2:4). Miriam watched over Moses and dared to approach the Egypt-ian princess to suggest a Hebrew nursemaid for the babe—none other than the child's natural mother, Yocheved.

Miriam appears at various points throughout the biblical narrative as a leader, a woman of conviction, with the courage to stand up for her beliefs. She led the women in joyous song and dance after the miracu-lous crossing of the Reed Sea. She dared to speak against Moses when she believed that he was wrong, and she suffered for her words with the affliction of leprosy. She was banished from the camp for seven days while she healed, but the Israelites honored her and awaited her return before moving on. According to rabbinic tradition, because of the mer-its of Miriam, the Israelites received a well of water that sustained them and accompanied them throughout their journey in the desert. When Miriam died shortly before they entered the Promised Land, the well suddenly disappeared.[2]

*We were redeemed for the sake of the righteousness of Miriam, coura-geous child and leader of the Israelites in the desert, a source of redemption for her people.*

A non-Israelite woman also played a crucial role in the Exodus story. Had the Egyptian princess not had compassion on the Hebrew baby, he might never have lived. Rabbinic tradition provides two leg-ends to explain how the princess suddenly brought a babe home to the palace. In one version, she pretended that she was pregnant for some time before having the baby fetched from Yocheved's home. In that way, she ensured that Moses would receive the treatment usually afforded a prince.[3] According to the second legend, the princess sim-ply told her father, "I have brought up a child, who is divine in form and of an excellent mind, as I have received him through the bounty of the river in a wonderful way, I have thought it proper to adopt him as my son and as the heir of thy kingdom." Pharaoh welcomed the baby into his home. Jewish tradition strongly approves of the Egyptian heroine and applauds her courage. A rabbinic commentary relates that God spoke directly to the princess, saying: "Moses was not your child; yet, you treated him as such. For this, I will call you my daughter, though you are not my daughter." Therefore the princess, Pharaoh's daughter, bore the name Batya, "the daughter of God."[4]

*We were redeemed for the sake of the righteousness of an Egyptian woman, Batya, "daughter of God," daughter of Pharaoh, who rescued one not her own.*

These are the righteous women of the Exodus story, because of whose strengths we were delivered from Egypt. Their stories, like those of other women in our tradition, are not often told. Our foremothers remain in the shadows of our forefathers. As we celebrate our freedom at this Passover seder, may we also pray and strive for the freedom of women everywhere. We look toward the day when the lives of women will no longer be hidden in the shadows of the lives of men, but when the two shall stand side by side, as both are created in the image of the Divine.

—RENNI S. ALTMAN

## Leaving Egypt

The night is so dark
and I am afraid.
I see nothing, smell nothing,
the only reality—
I am holding my mother's hand.

And as we walk
I hear the sounds of
a multitude in motion—
in front, behind,

all around,
a multitude in motion.

I have no thought of tomorrow—
now, in the darkness,
there is only motion
and my mother's hand.

—MERLE FELD

## Who Were Our Mothers?

*According to the* Mishnah Pesachim, *rabbinic commentary on Deuteronomy 26:5–8 constitutes the core of the haggadah. Many of the questions we ask tonight have been asked by the Rabbis before us. Their midrashim, or rabbinic legends, tell the story of the women of Exodus but are not traditionally included in the haggadah.*

*"My father was a wandering Aramean"* (Deuteronomy 26:5).

Who were our mothers? Why are their stories untold?

*"He went down to Egypt with meager numbers and sojourned there"* (Deuteronomy 26:5).

Serach bat Asher went down to Egypt with the rest of Jacob's family. Without her, the Children of Israel might never have left Canaan. From the time of Isaac, there was a tradition that the one who would redeem Israel from slavery in Egypt would say a certain phrase, signaling that he was the true redeemer. By the time of Moses and Aaron, the phrase had been forgotten by everyone—except Serach bat Asher.

"It was transmitted from Isaac to Jacob, and from Jacob to Joseph, and from Joseph to his brothers that God said to the Children of Israel, *'pakod yifkod'* ('God will surely redeem you'). And Asher, son of Jacob, transmitted the secret of the redemption to Serach his daughter. Years later, in Egypt, Moses and Aaron came to the elders of Israel and performed wonders before them. The elders then went to Serach bat Asher and said to her, 'A man came to us and performed wonders before us.' She asked them, 'Was there nothing distinctive in these signs?' The elders answered, 'He said *"pakod pakadti"* ("I will redeem you").' Whereupon Serach bat Asher said to them, 'This is the man who has come to redeem Israel, for this is how I heard it described to my father, that God's messenger would say, *"pakod pakadti."'* Immediately after hearing of this, the elders of Israel believed in Moses."[5]

*"But there he became a great and very populous nation. The Egyptians dealt harshly with us and oppressed us; they imposed heavy labor upon us"* (Deuteronomy 26:5–6).

Were there no righteous people among the Egyptians, none who resisted the oppression of the Israelites?

Some say that the midwives Shifra and Puah were righteous Egyptian women who feared God more than they did Pharaoh. Hence, when Pharaoh commanded that the firstborn Israelite males be killed, they refused. As it is written: "They kept the men-children alive" (Exodus 1:17).

"Not only did the midwives not do what Pharaoh told them, they even dared to do deeds of kindness for the children they saved. On behalf of poor mothers, the midwives would go to the house of rich mothers and collect water and food, which they gave to the poor mothers and thus kept their children alive."[6]

What of Pharaoh's daughter, who violated her own father's decree and rescued Moses from the waters of the Nile?

"The daughter of Pharaoh repudiated idolatry, as it is written: 'And the daughter of Pharaoh went down to bathe by the river' (Exodus 2:5). Rabbi Yochanan said in explanation of this verse: That she went down to cleanse herself from the idolatry of her father's house."[7]

"When her handmaids saw that Pharaoh's daughter wished to save Moses, they said to her, 'Our lady, it is the world's practice that when a king issues a decree, even if the whole world does not obey it, his own children and the members of his household do obey it. Yet you would violate your father's decree!' At that, Gabriel came down and smote them to the ground [leaving the princess but one handmaid]."[8]

*"We cried out to the Lord, the God of our fathers, and the Lord heard our plea and saw our plight, our misery, and our oppression"* (Deuteronomy 26:7).

How did our mothers sustain hope in the midst of such dark times? Our sages teach that Miriam, sister of Moses and Aaron, was a prophetess.

"Before Moses was born, she prophesied, saying: 'In the future my mother will bear a son who will save Israel.' When Moses was born, the entire house filled with light. Whereupon, her father rose and kissed her on the head and said to her: 'My daughter, your prophecy has been fulfilled.' However, when pursuant to Pharaoh's decree they cast Moses into the river, her father rose and struck her on her head and said to her: 'My daughter, where is your prophecy now?'

"Therefore it is written: 'And his sister stood herself at a distance to know,' which is interpreted to mean: To know what will be with the end of her prophecy."[9]

Miriam was unwilling to give up hope that her brother would survive and her prophecy of liberation would ultimately be fulfilled.

How did the mothers of Israel know that the Blessed Holy One had heard their pleas?

"At that time the Holy One said to the ministering angels: 'Descend from My Presence and look at the children of My beloved Abraham, Isaac, and Jacob being thrown into the river.' The ministering angels rushed headlong down from the Holy One's Presence and, standing up to their knees in the water, caught the Children of Israel in their arms and set them upon rocks. Then out of each rock the Holy One brought forth nipples, which suckled the Israelite children."[10]

*"And the Eternal One freed us from Egypt by a mighty hand, by an outstretched arm, and awesome power, and by signs, and wonders"* (Deuteronomy 26:8).

By a mighty hand and an outstretched arm?

Consider the mighty hands of the midwives Shifra and Puah, who caught the Children of Israel as they were born and protected them from Pharaoh's decree. As it is written: "They did not do as Pharaoh the king of Egypt had commanded them, and they kept the children alive" (Exodus 1:17).

Consider the outstretched arm of Pharaoh's daughter that reached forth to bring Moses from the waters of the Nile.

The arm of Pharaoh's daughter is compared to the golden scepter of King Ahashuerus, which was miraculously extended to welcome Queen Esther into the king's private chambers, when she came before him to save the Jewish people from destruction.

"Some say that the king's scepter was originally two *amot* long and an angel made it twelve *amot* long.... Elsewhere it was taught: It was stretched to sixty *amot*. Similarly you find with the arm of Pharaoh's daughter, that it miraculously stretched to sixty *amot* when she extended her hand to reach for the baby Moses as he lay in a basket in the Nile River."[11]

The strong hands and the outstretched arms of our foremothers ensured our survival. As it is written, "In reward for the righteous women in that generation, Israel was redeemed from Egypt."[12] Tonight, as we recite the familiar words "My father was a wandering Aramean," we also remember the journeys of our mothers and their part in our people's liberation.

—SHARON COHEN ANISFELD

## Until All of Us Are Free

Go forth and learn. All who have been oppressed can also oppress.

Sarah, our mother, oppressed her Egyptian maidservant Hagar. Sarah was barren and she wanted a child. She gave Hagar, her Egyptian maidservant, to Abraham as a wife. When Hagar conceived and became pregnant Sarah grew lesser in her eyes. So Sarah oppressed her and Hagar ran away, as it says:

*"V'ta'aneiha Sarai va'tivrach mipaneyha"* (Genesis 16:6).[13]

Go forth and learn: Pharaoh the Egyptian oppressed our people when they dwelled in Egypt.

The Israelites descended to Egypt and lived there. When they became a nation—great, mighty and numerous—Pharaoh feared that the Egyptians would be overcome by the great multitudes of Israelites, so he decreed that every male child born to an Israelite woman be thrown into the Nile. And the Egyptians treated us harshly and oppressed us: They imposed hard labor on us, as it says:

"*Vayarei'u otanu hamitzrim va'y'anunu va'yitnu aleinu avoda kasha*" (Deuteronomy 26:6).[14]

This you should never forget: The same word used for Hagar's oppression at the hands of Sarah is used for the Israelite's oppression at the hands of the Egyptians.

This too you should never forget: The Children of Israel were saved through the brave and righteous acts of two women—one Hebrew and one Egyptian, Miriam and the daughter of Pharaoh.

Go forth and learn: It is easier to oppress than it is to be free. "Until all of us are free none of us is free" (Emma Lazarus, "Epistle to the Hebrews").

—TAMARA COHEN

## preparing for passover

doors flung open
bread tossed to the birds
we shop for the matzoh the bitter
herbs the honey the eggs
the wine the brisket
the onions the potatoes
the escape the memory
of the escape

from what
to what
for what

promise

we remember blood midnight

so much blood smeared
and then and then

we were like sheep running

we had no knowledge
only fear
the dust in a haze
along our track
away from the cities
the man like a great dog
the flame pillar
the cloud pillar
terrifying
our baaing

when we saw the chariots
we started stampeding
toward the sea my god
you swept us
there you
hurled us across
like a wind raised
cliffs of water
far above us
oh yes we ran
track over track in mud
we got over
then the engorged water
folded like a scroll
over our enemies
when we understood how they were dead
how we laughed how we danced

because you chose us you loved us
with our frightened sheep eyes
hysterical bleating
you watched us from
your fiery whirl
preparing laws to
change us from slaves
make us a free
nation your
instrument

you did not understand we were animals

now you drive us through the desert in circles
you send this man who herds us
you speak to him mouth to mouth
you do not speak to us
or you speak in riddles
though we beg you
though we dance
and sing for you

freedom

how it has to come from suffering

—ALICIA SUSKIN OSTRIKER

# Readings on the Women of Exodus

## Yocheved Works

*to build an ark*

of loam, slime
papyrus and pitch
weaving it watertight

*to set a son*

unnamed, adrift
in reeds, a wail
beneath her prayer

*to nurse an infant*

whisper, hold
let go toward
history

*to save a child*

*to mold a man*

*to be a mother.*

—DAVI WALDERS

## Miriam

My brother and I
were God's witnesses
in the desert.
He inscribed life
on the rocks,
and I played at imagining
water on the sand,
bitter and dark.

My brother was the chosen one
he received the gift of language.
His demeanor and
courage pleased God.

Angered over my desire
to be a pilgrim just like my people,
God covered my skin
with scales of dead fish.

Amid the most opaque darkness
I remained in a dungeon
and in the pure light of the garden,
of the whole desert,
the women waited for me
singing my name.

Suddenly
I realized
that only my brother
wrote
amid the rocks the dictations of God,
that God who had left me so silent and alone
in the vast solitude of the Sinai.

I stayed behind
with my women
without names,
without history,
without God.

My name is Miriam,
I sing,
I grant words.

—MARJORIE AGOSIN, TRANSLATED BY MONICA BRUNO GALMOZZI

## Pharaoh's Daughter

A nameless virgin wanders through the desert sand
The men turn into mortar, hard red backs,
Naked, bend.

Breath heavy now, hungry eyes
Turn quickly to the cold wet Nile.
Willows scrape hard rushing calves

And leave a scar.
And maybe someone, hiding in the willows, watches, waiting.
She wades in,
Sighs, before she hears the cry
Of one whose birth was not
Allowed.

Floating, alone.
The small red fists reach
For a mother's breast not there.

She wades in deeper
    Staring into dark new eyes,
        She lifts the infant to firm breasts.
            He cries harder.

—DAPHNA RENAN

## In Honor of Batya

I once bought my children a copy of the story of the three little pigs as told from the wolf's point of view. This simple children's book reminded me that there are many ways to perceive the same story. It is with this in mind that I revisit the story of Batya, Pharaoh's daughter.

If the story is told from Batya's point of view, we can assume that she saw herself as Moses' mother because, after all, she scooped him out of the Nile, saved his life, and brought him home to raise him. Surely she thought he would grow up to be an Egyptian prince, following all the customs and religious practices of her people.

As a mother of both an adopted child and a biological child, I can relate to this perspective. In my mind there is absolutely no difference in how I view my two daughters—they are both my children. This is not to say, however, that they view their birth histories as inconsequential. As a three-year-old, my adopted daughter took my breath away when she asked, "Mommy, if I was that beautiful, wonderful baby that you said I was, why didn't my other mother want me?" I muddled through an appropriate response for a child not yet four. Later, she began asking questions like, "Why do I have to be Jewish when I wasn't born Jewish?"

I always told our adopted daughter that she was "stuck" being Jewish because her father and I were raising her as a Jew. We were Jewish and because she was our daughter, so was she. In our house, that was to be the end of the discussion. She would occasionally balk at the idea of this religion being forced upon her, but Judaism was a way of life in our home. It provided a sacred sense of roots and connectedness to a heritage that I hoped she would someday embrace. It was so important to me that I insisted she go to Sunday school and become a bat mitzvah. I was vindicated and rewarded shortly after her bat mitzvah service when she reflected back on it, saying, "This was the best day of my life, and I am so glad I am Jewish." I am not sure how or when the transformation occurred, but as a Jewish parent I was filled with relief and unmitigated joy.

But what if Batya had acted as I did and had imposed her religious values on her adopted son, Moses? What if Moses had not been allowed to return to his biological roots? Where would our Passover story be today? We are grateful to Batya for saving Moses, but I, as the mother of an adopted child, admire her. I can imagine the pain she must have felt in losing her child, Moses. Tonight, we must remember the story from Batya's vantage point, and honor her valor and her grief.

—BETH GOMBERG-HIRSCH

# The Ten Plagues

**W**e are taught that God delivered us from Egypt with "great signs and wonders" (Deuteronomy 26:8). This is an explicit recognition that liberation is not achieved easily, that resistance to change—particularly from the Egyptian oppressors but also on the part of the Israelite slaves—is profound. God says to Moses, "Yet I know that the king of Egypt will let you go only because of a greater might. So I will stretch out My hand and smite Egypt with various wonders which I will work upon them; after that, he shall let you go" (Exodus 3:19–20).

The Ten Plagues visited on the Egyptians are a dramatic manifestation of this "greater might." After each plague, Pharaoh refuses Moses' demand: *"Sh'lach et ami."* "Let my people go." With each plague, there is a moment of opportunity, a possibility that Pharaoh will reconsider and relent. Yet, after the initial horror of each plague has passed, Pharaoh resumes his unyielding position. Following each of the first five plagues, we are told that Pharaoh "hardened his heart" and turned Moses away. After that, Pharaoh no longer hardened his own heart; instead, the text tells us, God "hardened the heart" of the Egyptian king.

The recitation of the Ten Plagues at the seder is often accompanied by a ritual that reflects our ambivalence about this aspect of the

Passover story. As each plague is recited we spill a drop of wine from our glasses: We cannot rejoice fully, we cannot drink from an overflowing cup knowing that such great suffering and loss of life on the part of the Egyptian people accompanied our liberation. At most women's seders, the tension between our own celebration and the troubling memory of the plagues is expressed even more strongly. Many communities explore the profound theological and moral questions raised by the violence with which our liberation was achieved.

Other seders choose to name contemporary plagues, inflicted not by God but by humanity, that diminish our joy and force us to consider just how painful and arduous the path to freedom can be.

## Wrought by Humankind

Tonight we acknowledge contemporary plagues. None are dealt by God; instead, they are committed by humankind. As we read, we dip into our wine glasses and spill one drop of wine for each plague we recite:

Apathy
Envy of others
Intolerance
Persecution
Injustice
Poverty
Violence
War
Exploitation of others
Deafness to cries of help

—*JEWISH FAMILY SERVICE WOMEN'S SEDER: A SEDER BY AND FOR
THE JEWISH COMMUNITY OF DURHAM / CHAPEL HILL*

## The Ten Plagues

Maybe old Egypt was lucky after all
so what if the Nile stank of blood for a week?

year after year our rivers
run excrement, effluent,
    profit and poison

the Egyptians scratched lice
and slapped at gnats
and when locusts devoured the crops
they netted the critters and
fried 'em for dinner
we're fool enough to poison the bugs
the birds that eat them
and our wheat as well
their cattle died and frogs overran
the land; our cattle overgraze
we burn down the forests to feed them

we've developed chemicals
that eat the sky and kill
all the pretty little amphibians
our frogs are rarer than princes

they had boils and we have AIDS
they had hailstorms but
everyone gets some bad weather

we could bear the blows
of heaven and earth
even endure a child's death
bear all evils but the two
that cause most misery:
human greed
and human cruelty.

—MARTHA SHELLEY

## Our Hardened Hearts

In 1998, the most recent year for which we have statistics, 3,792 American children and teenagers died by gunfire in murders, suicides, and unintentional shootings.[1] As we think of the Ten Plagues and the unfathomable devastation, terror, and loss they brought to Egypt, perhaps they can help us reflect on this violence in our own country.

After each of the plagues struck the Egyptians, Pharaoh was given an opportunity to free the Jewish slaves and end the misery afflicting his own people. However we understand Pharaoh's hard heart, it defies our imagination that a leader could stubbornly refuse to see that change was so desperately needed. How could he continue to make choices that were so clearly wreaking havoc in the lives of his own people?

As we ask ourselves this difficult question, we are reminded of the fear and the pain that so many in our country endure today. Although new gun control laws could help keep guns away from our children and out of their schools, we have been unwilling or unable to make the changes that would help prevent school shootings.

On February 2, 1996, two students and one teacher were killed, and one student was wounded, when a fourteen-year-old student shot at his algebra class in Moses Lake, Washington.

On October 1, 1997, two students were killed and seven were wounded in Pearl, Mississippi, when a sixteen-year-old student shot them. He was also accused of killing his mother.

*How long will we harden our hearts to the violence around us?*

On December 1, 1997, three students were killed and five were wounded while participating in a prayer circle at school in West Paducah, Kentucky, when a fourteen-year-old student shot them.

On March 24, 1998, four students and one teacher were killed and eleven others were wounded at a middle school in Jonesboro, Arkansas. Two students, aged thirteen and eleven, shot them.

*Have we done everything we can to bring an end to the suffering?*

On May 21, 1998, two students were killed and twenty-two were wounded when a fifteen-year-old shot them in his high school cafeteria in Springfield, Oregon. His parents were later found dead in their home.

On April 20, 1999, in Littleton, Colorado, fourteen students and one teacher were killed and twenty-three others were wounded, when two students, aged eighteen and seventeen, shot them.

*Have we, like Pharaoh, opened ourselves temporarily to the need for change after each tragedy, only to become indifferent when the losses feel more distant?*

On February 29, 2000, a six-year-old girl was shot and killed by a six-year-old boy at an elementary school in Mount Morris Township, Michigan.

On March 5, 2001, two students were killed and thirteen were wounded in Santee, California, when a fifteen-year-old student shot them.

*Have we mourned each of these losses but failed to take action until the violence invades our own community?*

—CATHERINE SPECTOR

## We Will Walk Beside You

Battered women and their children live under a domestic reign of terror and can only dream of the Promised Land of freedom. Even for those who dare to flee, with Pharaoh right behind them, the desert is wide and often dangerous.

Let us recite together and spill one drop of wine for the women and girls who have experienced:

Wrongful blame
Shame
Incest
Humiliation
Stalking
Nightmares
Threats
Rape
Beatings

*Tonight we say the following words together:* We say tonight to every battered woman—We hear you, we believe you, and we will walk beside you through the desert. Together we can make the road less desolate so that those bound by domestic abuse will come to know the taste of liberation, the meaning of redemption, and the experience of shalom.

—BASED ON A READING CREATED BY *SHALOM BAYIT:* BAY AREA
JEWISH WOMEN WORKING TO END DOMESTIC VIOLENCE

## God Works, Naturally

What do we make of God's role in the plagues that devastated Egypt, and how do we understand the hardening of Pharaoh's heart?

God works,
naturally,
with materials at hand:
water and silt,
hysteria, guilt.

In the bloodred river
fish die
that would have eaten
clear foam of frogs' eggs,
and raucous armies of
frogs invade
path and hearth.

It must have been like that:
small variations in pattern.

A few degrees of heat and wind
bringing all of Africa's locusts,
ravenous, in
dark waves of whirring wings,
as God, sovereign weaver,
tugs the strands slightly,
loosening and tightening
the living fabric.

Pharaoh builds with
brick and stone,
enduring but inflexible.
And all God has to do

to harden Pharaoh's heart
is let the god of Egypt
be. Immutable.

—RONNIE M. HORN

## A Healing Ritual for the Earth at Passover Time

In our recitation of the Ten Plagues, we explain how God used the natural world to punish the hardhearted ancient Egyptians for their crimes of oppression. The Ten Plagues are part of the fun of a child's Passover —frogs, insects, wild beasts! And yet, far from overrunning the land, these creatures, and thousands more, are vanishing from the earth. Humans, like those ancient Passover plagues, are devouring the habitat of every living creature at an alarming rate. Calling frogs, insects, and wild beasts plagues, when so many species of these animals are at risk of extinction, is in dissonance with the fundamental values of Passover, the holy day of liberation.

How can we truly celebrate human liberation without liberating the natural world from human domination? The extent to which we restore the health of the earth's ecosystems will determine our future and the future of our children. A healthy abundance of species filling the earth will be the final measure of our humanity. As it is written: "The Creator extends tender mercies upon all creatures." As we are called to act in the image of God, we are obligated to respect all life.

The Ten Plagues are a kind of accumulating natural disaster. The interconnection of all life means that when one aspect of life suffers, soon a disastrous chain of events is unleashed, and death can spread like a cancer. As we remove the drops of wine from our cups, let us pray for the healing of each of these ten parts of the earth.

House made of water, frogs, insects, and four-leggeds
House made of animals, soil, locusts, and hail,
House of dark skies, house made of children
We pray for your healing
We acknowledge our greed
We remember our kinship with you.

Let my heart tremble with the waters.
The voice of the waters is my voice.

Bless the waters, the flood plains, creeks, rivulets, arroyos,
Streams, hidden springs, aquifers, waterfalls, and the mighty
    rivers and the vastness of the sea
And all that lives therein.

Frogs form the bridge of life from water to land.
Our long-tongued ancestors enter each other's bodies as they
    sing in the spring.
From fish to frog, from frog to lizard, from lizard to bird and
    warm-blooded beings.
Let my heart tremble with the frogs. The voice of frogs is my
    voice.
Bless the jelly eggs, tadpoles, frogs, lizards, toads, snakes, ser-
    pents, dragons,
And all amphibian and reptile beings.

Insects and flowers are born together.
Pollen entices the dance of spring.
Let my heart tremble with insects and flowers.
The voice of insects is my voice.
Bless spiders, flies, beetles, ants, snails, moths, butterflies,
    wasps,
bees, dragonflies,
And all manner of flying and crawling beings.

—LYNN GOTTLIEB

## Ten Plagues/Ten "Blows"

Not all were guilty; not all were oppressors. Yet, the misery of the
Israelites was not only inflicted by individuals. It took systemic dehumanization—a culture of slaves and slavemasters—to hold them
down. The nation inflicted, and stood by; and the nation suffered—a
result of both actions and the failure to act.

To think that we could really understand the reasons, the "whys,"
for the Ten Plagues or for each plague would be theological chutz-
pah. But we can imagine what the experience of living through each

plague signified for the Egyptians and what observing them signified for the Israelites.

Let us remember with equal measures of relief and horror.

*Dam* (Blood): From impossibly difficult work, their hands cracked and bled. The river has turned to blood, and in your hearts, you know why.

*Tzefardeya* (Frogs): When you cracked the whip, they jumped—not at play, but in fear. Now your land is covered with jumping creatures, and you are afraid.

*Kinim* (Lice): You treated them like detestable pests; now you know what it is like to be overrun with true vermin.

*Arov* (Swarms of insects): You feared their numbers; now you drown in more bugs than you can count.

*Dever* (Cattle plague): These people were your beasts of burden. Even your animals, dying by the thousands, can't take orders from you now.

*Shechin* (Boils): Their skin, marked with scars from their labors and their lashings; your skin, aflame.

*Barad* (Hail): You looked to the heavens that the gods might bless your ruthless pursuit of wealth and domination; now you live under the skies' curse.

*Arbeh* (Locusts): Your animals are already dead, and these creatures decimate your plants and trees; creation undone.

*Choshech* (Darkness): You failed to see the Israelites; their individual faces, their humanity, did not register. Now, all is dark, and you cannot see a thing: not your neighbors, not your own children—not even your own face in the mirror.

*Makat bechorot* (Death of the firstborn): Israelite baby boys came into this world subject to a sentence of immediate death; Pharaoh ordered and was obeyed. You who banded together to murder innocents—now you come together to mourn. The mingled cries of all the children, whose lives ended before they'd begun, ring in your ears: No more! No more!

—SUSAN P. FENDRICK

# Dayeinu

At this point in the seder, we sing *Dayeinu,* the well-known Passover song that recounts the fifteen great deeds God performed for the Israelites on their journey to freedom. As we sing about each of these steps from Egypt to the Promised Land, we affirm that, had God bestowed no further kindness, performed no further miracle, *Dayeinu*—it would have been enough. While it may not literally be true that any one step of the journey would have been enough, the song reminds us to contemplate and value each miracle God performed. In this way, *Dayeinu* both expresses and cultivates our sense of gratitude, teaching us to find joy in the small blessings in our lives.

Some women's seders maintain the spirit of the traditional song, while revising its content to focus on Jewish women or feminist concerns. They affirm, for example, that had we been given any one of our Jewish heroines, it would have been enough for us.

But how many women could whole-heartedly say *Dayeinu* if the fifteen steps of the song recounted our feminist journey? What feelings emerge as we imagine declaring, "If we had been given an education but not been permitted to use it in the work force, *Dayeinu.* If we had been permitted to go to work but not to control our bodies...."

Thinking about the rights and opportunities that women have been denied, it is difficult to say *Dayeinu*.

Consequently, few women's seders consider this moment of the seder to be simply an exercise in gratitude. As participants gather with the shared understanding that our tradition has excluded and marginalized the voices of women, many women's seders find it too difficult to say *Dayeinu*. Instead, many communities contemplate the future, articulating realities that must change before we can truly say "it has sufficed us." At other women's seders, texts for *Dayeinu* discuss past injustices, and participants affirm that only if they had not been perpetrated would we be able to say *Dayeinu*.

*Dayeinu*, the playful song that seems so simple when sung around the family seder table, has become much more complex at women's seders. The question of what it means to say *Dayeinu* crystallizes the tensions between celebrating our progress and remembering the work yet to be done, offering gratitude and expressing anger, accepting and critiquing the tradition passed on to us, thanking God for our blessings and sending our prayers for justice and freedom up to heaven.

## Cultivating Gratitude

Just let this baby be born healthy and whole. That's all I ask.

I said this over and over when I was pregnant with my first child, as if I didn't know how briefly I would savor the relief when the time came, God willing, as if I didn't know how quickly and greedily I would begin to come up with new anxieties, new requests, new demands.

How easy it is to live in constant anticipation, promising God and ourselves that we will be satisfied and grateful, if only...but there is always something else. This is part of what makes us human.

When we say *Dayeinu*, on one level we are lying. We say, "It would have been enough." But we know that this is not true. No single step of our journey out of slavery would have been sufficient.

Yet, we tell this lie in order to cultivate our capacity for gratitude.

We exercise our thanking muscles, trying at least for a moment to appreciate each and every small gift as if we really believed it was enough.

Of course we want more. We have hopes and dreams for ourselves and for our children. But for their sakes, and for our own, we must also be able to stop and say *Dayeinu:* "This is enough for us, thank God." For a moment, to feel that we have everything we need—that is what it means to say *Dayeinu.*

—SHARON COHEN ANISFELD

## It Would Have Been Enough

It would have been enough for God to take us out of Egypt.
It would have been enough to bring us through the Red Sea,
   enough to give us the Torah and Shabbat, enough to bring
   us into the land of Israel.
While we count each of these blessings as if it would have
   been enough on its own, we know that more was given,
   and more is promised.
From singing *Dayeinu* we learn to celebrate each landmark on
   our people's journey.
Yet, we must never confuse these way stations with the
   redemptive destination.
Because there is still so much to do in our work of repairing
   the world.
If we speak truthfully about the pain, joys, and contradictions
   of our lives,
If we listen to others with sensitivity and compassion,
If we challenge the absence of women in traditional texts, in
   chronicles of Jewish history, and in the leadership of our
   institutions, *Dayeinu.*
If we continue to organize, march, and vote to affirm our
   values,
If we fight economic injustice, sexism, racism, and homo-
   phobia,
If we volunteer our time and money, *Dayeinu.*
If we break the silence about violence against women and

children in the Jewish community and everywhere,
If we teach our students and children to pursue justice with
all their strength,
If we care for the earth and its future as responsibly as we care
for those we love,
If we create art, music, dance, and literature, *Dayeinu.*
If we realize our power to effect change,
If we bring holiness into our lives, homes, and communities,
If we honor our visions more than our fears, *Dayeinu.*

—TAMARA COHEN

## Smallest Blessings Enough

When you have cancer, you choose between option A and option B, neither of which you want. After a while, you get pretty good at downplaying your condition. When I was first diagnosed with breast cancer, I told myself, "At least I don't have ovarian cancer," and when the breast cancer metastasized to my skull, I was glad it wasn't in my brain. Finally, when my condition became far worse even than that of other survivors I knew, I embraced my doctor's advice about not comparing cancers: They are all different.

I have never found solace in "terminal uniqueness"—the idea that we're all unique in our suffering. That kind of mentality only leads to loneliness and alienation. Some relatives and friends, God bless them, share stories about other people's misfortunes in an attempt to comfort me. But all this does is force me to go back to the game of comparing war stories, as if someone else's trouble is my gain.

I'm not the competitive type, so this misery-loves-company strategy fails to boost my morale. What I need is another kind of solace. Something less combative and more poetic. Something having to do with the cup being half full rather than half empty.

Every Passover we recite a humbling prayer called *Dayeinu.* In my view, the prayer is one way we thank God for the small favors that mean everything. The point is that every step of the way, there's a blessed "thank you" given that God made it all possible. To me, *Dayeinu* means something like, "It's enough already! Any more would tip our full cup over." But God keeps pouring and pouring, and people continue to be surprised by the bounty.

I like the whole idea of *Dayeinu*. I don't expect a lot, so I'm always surprised. After ten years of metastatic breast cancer, I am still alive. Frankly, I hadn't expected to come this far. Had tamoxifen only kept at bay for three years the cancer that spread to my bones: *Dayeinu*. Had the newly discovered abdominal injection, Arimidex, only checked the cancer that had spread to my hip and shoulder: *Dayeinu*. Had Taxol chemotherapy only stopped the cancer after it had spread to my other hip and my skull: *Dayeinu*. Will God's mercy never end?

Today, after years of battling an incurable disease, I am miraculously healthy. During this creative period, I've met and married a wonderful man. I lived to see my daughter give birth to two grandchildren. I have an adorable convertible, and best of all, the current treatment allows me to keep my hair—blowing in the wind. It's enough to say: *Dayeinu*.

—CATHY SMITH

## If

If my aunts, sisters, grandmothers, mother, or her friends had
  told me often, you are wonderful, my dear, you are so
  independent—in the same breath,
If my aunts, sisters, grandmothers, mother, or her friends,
  who kissed me often, had taught me as I grew up that kiss-
  ing is good only when it feels right to me and not when it
  doesn't,
If the guidelines on short skirts and other adolescent instances
  of self-discovery and power-learning had been tempered by
  humor, understanding, and room to grow into power,
  instead of disapproving glances and condemnatory tones,
And if these women who raised me had ever discussed with
  me the what and why of setting boundaries and, most
  important, the how,
*Dayeinu*.

If, years later, when a boyfriend pushed me farther than I
wanted to go, I had had the presence of mind to say to him
Stop! Remember our conversations,

If, afterwards, I hadn't felt like I was more bonded to him
now than before,

If, afterwards, I had understood that my power was challenged, and in turn hadn't lost the sense of my independent self or my self-reliance,

If, once the deed was done, I had been able to call it by
name,

*Dayeinu.*

If, years later, when I confronted this former boyfriend and
told him what I knew to be true, he had rejected the face
in the mirror I held up to him, and said, I don't want to be
that man,

If, when we spoke years later, he had apologized,

If, when we spoke years later, he hadn't said, I thought you
were playing a game when you said no,

And if, now, I could forgive myself for having made bad
choices,

*Dayeinu.*

If, when my cousin was raped by a friend's friend, she hadn't
stayed silent about it, out of shame and youth,

If, when my cousin stayed silent, I knew how to read the
signs,

If I knew how to read the signs, and I could help her heal
herself,

If I knew how to help my cousin, and, in turn, to protect and
help myself,

*Dayeinu.*

If, after my friend was attacked by a high school chum, she
told me about it,

If she told me about it and I in turn told her the real story of
my experience,

If, after we shared our stories, we drew strength from one
another,

And if we said, we've lived through this, and acknowledged

that reflection gives our experience meaning,
*Dayeinu*.

If my neighbor hadn't said to me, It's not so bad that I'm
   afraid for my life, but I can't afford to raise my daughter on
   my own,
If, instead, my neighbor had said to me, I know fear and I
   don't want to live like this any longer,
If, with the hotline and divorce lawyer's phone numbers in
   hand, my neighbor had picked up the phone to call,
And if her husband had understood that you cannot make
   love in fear and you cannot force love by tyranny,
*Dayeinu*.

If we, as women, as men, as sentient beings, say Not Any
   More,
If we, as mothers, aunts, sisters, daughters, and friends, say, I
   will look out for you,
If we, as mothers, grandmothers, aunts, and sisters say, We
   will raise our boys to be different,
If, this year and every year, each of us says, we will not let it
   happen again,
*Dayeinu*.

—SARAH ANNE MINKIN

## Scallions and *Dayeinu*

It is getting late, and the children at the seder are getting sleepy at the
table. My father reads from the haggadah in thickly accented Hebrew
that I never hear when I am away from home. His voice spreads serenity over the table. I am the first to notice that *Dayeinu* is approaching.
The rush of adrenalin gets me excited. I know that in a few moments,
the children will no longer be sleepy and my father's voice will be difficult to detect. In a few moments, there will be no serenity at our
Pesach table.

I scan the items on the table and notice that the stack of scallions
on the silver tray has been placed far from my reach, unfortunately.
These scallions are the weapons with which we reenact the whippings

that our ancestors received from their slave masters in Egypt. During *Dayeinu,* everyone but my father runs around the table and sometimes into the adjacent rooms in order to whip every single family member. My father, who remains sitting at the table in order to read the poetic verses of the song is, therefore, an easy target.

Other people notice my insidious smile and realize that the moment is approaching. Even before my father starts singing the verses of *Dayeinu,* we all reach for the scallions—we are armed and ready to go.

*To incorporate this Persian Jewish custom into your seder, include a plate of scallions on your seder table. When you reach the chorus of* Dayeinu, *everyone should get up to "whip" the other guests around the seder table with a scallion. The most plausible explanation for this ritual is that Persian Jews were so influenced by the Shi'ite society (in which self-flagellation plays a large role in religious ritual) that they developed a flagellation ritual of their own.*

—SHERRY FARZAN

## Are We There Yet?

Do women have enough power today?

Look at the place where you go to school, the place where you work, the companies in your town, the companies you own stock in. Are they run by women? Are half the top officers women? Do women hold half the board seats? Look at the government: at Congress, at City Hall, and at Capitol Hill.

Are we there yet? Is it enough?

*Dayeinu?* Not yet.

How hard is it to balance work and family? Are employers welcoming women back in their forties, after they've raised their children? Are they giving men and women time off and flexibility in their twenties and thirties, when they need it? Is this the best we can do?

*Dayeinu?* Not yet.

Women have fought long and hard for freedom. We have much to be thankful for. We are free to dream. And we should.

What would the world be like if women really did wield half the power? What would it be like to grow up as a girl for whom everything really was wide open?

Is this really the best we can do?

*Dayeinu?* Not yet.

Freedom is an incredible gift. Use it.

Raise your sights. Raise your hand. Raise your voice. Time enough to compromise later. That will come. But not yet.

Now is the time to dream big, take a risk, reach out a hand, remember the blessing that our lives are, the energy that comes from action, the cosmic payoff of good politics.

*Shehecheyanu, v'keeyimanu, v'heegiyanu....*

Bless the Lord who has gotten us here, with some help from powerful women along the way.

And let us take the mantle, use our freedom, each of us in her own way, taking that extra step, dreaming the bigger dream, seeing the blessing in believing in ourselves and the joy of giving a younger woman a helping hand.

Let us help each other across the lines of who has what (husband, job, kids) that divide women and undercut our strength.

Let us say: I have value, I will not be done in, I can change the world, and I will. Let us say that, remember that, the next time someone says no to you.

Let us use our freedom well, so that our daughters and sons will have more of it.

And let us not say enough.

*Dayeinu?* Not yet.

—SUSAN ESTRICH

# The Three Symbols

A s we reach the end of the *maggid* section of the seder, we
read a talmudic passage quoting Rabban Gamliel, who
established a minimum requirement for our seder observance: "Rabban Gamliel would say, 'Whoever does not
discuss the meaning of the following three symbols of the seder on
Passover evening has not fulfilled her obligation. The three are the
Pesach lamb, the matzah, and the *maror.*'"

By this point in the seder, we have elaborated extensively on the
Passover story and on the meanings of Exodus and liberation in our
own lives. We have added our own questions to those of the haggadah;
we have investigated both traditional commentaries and contemporary
concerns. But in this passage, Rabban Gamliel reminds us that if we
have not come to some basic understanding of what the Pesach, matzah,
and *maror* represent, we cannot conclude the telling of our seder.

And so, at the end of *maggid,* we return to the three symbols at the
center of our story and ask, Have we told that which is essential to
tell? Have we gotten to the heart of the matter? By drawing our attention to the Pesach, the matzah, and the *maror,* the haggadah brings
back into focus the fundamentals of the Exodus story.

The traditional text continues with an explanation of each of these
three symbols. Rabban Gamliel lived in the period after the destruction

of the Temple, when our ritualized telling and these three symbols had to fulfill the role of the actual paschal sacrifice. In this context, the act of speaking about the Pesach, matzah, and *maror* takes on particular poignancy and importance. The destruction of the Temple and the exile from Jerusalem were a devastating loss for our people, but they did not destroy us. Speaking, studying, remembering, telling, and retelling have allowed us to survive.

Many women's seders choose simply to read the traditional text of this passage. Some omit this part of the seder altogether, exploring the meaning of these symbols at other points in the ritual. Other communities use alternative readings, such as those included in this chapter, to elaborate on their significance.

If you include this passage in your seder, the leader should lift the matzah and *maror,* holding them up as she explains their meaning. We do not lift or point to the shankbone, because we no longer make the paschal sacrifice. Some vegetarians follow an alternative custom mentioned in the Talmud and substitute a beet for the shankbone.

## How Far Would We Go?

Rabban Gamliel said: "Whoever does not discuss the meaning of the following three symbols of the seder on Passover evening has not fulfilled his duty": Pesach, matzah, and *maror.*

Pesach: What sacrifices would we make for freedom today? What would we leave behind? How far would we go? How deeply would we look within ourselves?

Matzah: Our ancestors had no time to wait for their bread to rise. Yet, we, who have that time—what do we do to be worthy of our precious inheritance?

*Maror:* We were slaves in Egypt, but now we are free. How easy it is for us to relive the days of our historical bondage as we sit in the warmth and comfort of our seder. How much harder to relieve the pain of those who live in bitterness and oppression today.

—SHARON L. SOBEL

## The Three Symbols

Pesach: This roasted shankbone or beet symbolizes the lamb's blood that marked the doorposts of our homes in Egypt. The blood protected us from the Angel of Death as it passed over our houses and killed the firstborn of the Egyptians. We lift this symbol and celebrate life-giving and life-saving blood.

Matzah: We think of all the world's homeless and hungry to whom this simple matzah would be a full meal. Mahatma Gandhi once said, "There are people in the world so hungry that God cannot appear to them except in the form of bread."

*Maror: Maror* leads us into memories of bitterness—the bitterness of Egypt, bitter waters, bitter words, enslavement, the bitter cold of the desert night and the bitter heat of the desert sun, the bitterness of wandering, and the bitterness of exile. Yet, even as we remember the bitterness of slavery, we know that no bitterness is without end.

—STEPHANIE AARON

## What Lies Before Us

In the words of Rabban Gamliel, "Whoever does not mention these three things on Pesach has not fulfilled her obligation." And these are they: Pesach, matzah, *maror*.

*The seder plate lies before you on the table. Look, and speak about what you see.*

The search for the *afikomen* at the seder playfully reminds us that we live in a world where there is much hidden, much we cannot see. But the words of Rabban Gamliel remind us of another truth: there is also much that lies before us, readily seen if only we open our eyes and take notice.

Could it be that, with all our words and blessings and stories this evening, we still have not seen and spoken about that which is most important to us, that which we need to learn *this year*, as we go forth from Egypt yet again?

Pesach: Memories of a night thousands of years ago, when our ancestors marked their doorposts with lamb's blood, and then waited in fear and anticipation while death struck all around them. In the Egyptian houses, the firstborn children died that night; the Jewish homes were spared. How dare we give thanks? How dare we not? By morning, our ancestors had begun their flight from Egypt.

Ancient echoes. For generations, the Pesach sacrifice was offered up at the holy temple in Jerusalem to commemorate that night. Tonight, an echo of an echo, the shankbone lies on our seder plate.

Matzah: There is not enough time; there never has been. Not enough time for any of the important things: making bread, making love, redemption. Our people was born in a hurry. After an interminable night of waiting—actually, it was hundreds of years—freedom came suddenly. Unexpectedly. Unpredictably. We were not ready; we never are. We leave in a hurry but are slow to arrive. We wander. But we have a great recipe for flat bread.

*Maror:* Words fail. The story of bitterness is the most difficult to tell, perhaps because it is not really a story after all. It is a taste in the mouth. The taste of sharp words—unspoken—dissolving on the tongue. The taste of swallowed anger. Heart burn. It is useful to eat as big a chunk of these bitter herbs as one can bear. If there is hope, it lies in the tears that well up in the eyes and the clear headedness that comes after.

—SHARON COHEN ANISFELD

## Symbols of Our Foremothers

Rabban Gamliel said, "Whoever fails to mention these three things on Pesach has not fulfilled her or his obligation. And these are they."

*Point to the shankbone or beet:* Why did our ancestors eat the Pesach offering at their seder?

As a reminder that God passed over the houses marked with lamb's blood, as it is written, "And you shall say, 'It is the Passover offering for God, who passed over the houses of the Israelites in Egypt, and killed the Egyptians but saved our homes'" (Exodus 12:27).

Traditionally, the shankbone has represented the paschal offering brought to the Temple in ancient times. It has also symbolized the outstretched arm of God as the Almighty led the Jews out of Egypt into the Promised Land.

The shankbone can also represent the outstretched arms of Yocheved as she placed her baby, Moses, in the wicker basket she made to carry him into the arms of another woman; the outstretched arms of Batya as she gathered the child to her breast; the outstretched arms of Miriam as she carried her brother back to Yocheved to be nursed; the outstretched arm of Tziporah as she reached for a piece of flint to circumcise her son.

*Point to the plate of matzah:* This matzah, why do we eat it?

To remind us that the Israelite women attempted to provide food for their loved ones, even under the most dire of circumstances. Even though there was no time for the bread to rise, the Israelites had matzah to eat along their difficult journey. As it is written, "And they baked the dough which they brought from Egypt into matzot" (Exodus 12:39).

Our ancestors baked the matzah quickly as they fled from Pharaoh's armies. It is a reminder that although our people have been uprooted suddenly at times throughout our existence, God has always provided sustenance for our journey—wherever it might lead.

The matzah can also symbolize the haste with which Yocheved wove her son's reed basket to save him from Pharaoh's decree, the race Miriam ran with the current to keep pace with her baby brother's cradle on the rushing waters of the Nile, the quickened beating of Batya's heart as it awakened to the love of a child, the speed with which Tziporah circumcised her son to spare him from death.

*Point to the bitter herb:* The *maror,* why do we eat it?

As a reminder that we learned from our experience in Egypt that the life of slavery is a bitter one, as it is written, "And they embittered their lives with hard labor in mortar and bricks, with every servitude of the field, with torment" (Exodus 1:14).

The *maror* reminds us of our obligation to work toward the end of slavery of any kind, wherever it exists.

The *maror* can also symbolize the bitterness of Yocheved and her husband when they chose to separate rather than have more children who would almost certainly be murdered by Pharaoh, Miriam's bitterness as she struggled to reunite her parents, Batya's sorrow caused by her own inability to give birth, Tziporah's agony at having to abandon her parents' home when she married Moses and joined the Israelites.

—NANCY GAD-HARF AND MARLA J. FELDMAN

## A Passover Triptych

Rabban Gamliel said: "Whoever has not spoken of the following three matters on Passover has not fulfilled the obligation of the holiday. They are Pesach [the paschal lamb], matzah, and *maror* [the bitter herb]."

Miriam is usually associated with water. When she is not around, the waters either disappear or turn bitter. I associate Moses with the matzah, which is broken into two parts at the beginning of the seder. Half of the matzah is hidden away for the *afikomen*—just as Moses was hidden for part of his life. Aaron is the first priest, and his duties are those of bloody sacrifice. These three siblings are mentioned together, by the prophet Micah, in the context of redemption from Egypt: "My people! What wrong have I done you? What hardship have I caused you? Testify against Me. In fact, I brought you up from the land of Egypt, I redeemed you from the house of bondage, and I sent before you Moses, Aaron, and Miriam" (Micah 6:3–4).

Miriam the Bitter
*"Maror"*

She stands apart.
One of three.
Separate, different.
Sister to a priest.
Midwife (they say)
To the Leader.

The waters broke.
With song and delicacy
She pulled *him* out
And sweet water
From hard rocks.

As a child I knew
Blood, fear
Endless crying—
He was in my power.

I gave my all.

My reward:
*He* has turned God against me,
Whiteness of skin,
Shielded from sun and friends
With no one to listen
To my prophecy.


Moses the Leader
*"Matzah"*

Ill tempered, Hitter of rocks,
Breaker of tablets, parter of
Waves, wrecker of homelife. He
Gets his Way—no diplomat he.

Leprosy makes his point. Pitiless
Provider of plagues.

He casts his rod and parts the Reed
Sea.

*She* stands by his side with her
Timbrels and musical instruments.

Duet: Sing a song of sea, oh!
Moment of glory, togetherness.

The waters broke. She saved him
And brought him sweet water from
Hard rocks.

Home wrecker: jealousy—three
Leaders—only one is chosen.
Abandon ship: women first (wife,
Sister), then the brother.

From heavy tongue to eloquence:
*Eyl na, refa na lah* (Please god,
Heal *her*). *She* puts music to his
Words. They wait.

Aaron the Priest
*"Pesach"*

Bowed down by sacrifice,
Bleating of lambs,
Mewing of cows, blood spewed.

Wash, blood, wash, blood,
Wash...the heady rhythm of drums
In background—prayer forgotten,
Sons neglected.

Always a spokesman, never a
Leader—except for one golden
Moment. Sacrificial calf
Transformed to idol. Heady stuff
To be worshipped, chosen by
People, never by God.

*He* was on the mountain
Dialoguing with God; *she* was
Busy with song and healing.

The people needed someone, some
Thing. He fashioned a golden
Symbol; it was rejected—caused
Chaos and death. His sons!
Punishment for arrogance.

Impatience is a family trait.

Pontifical remnants: Priests,
Penitence, Prayer. Sacrifice is
Always accepted.

—NAOMI GRAETZ

# B'chol Dor Vador

The Exodus experience transcends history. We are asked not only to tell this story but also to tell it as if it were our own. "In every generation, each person is obligated to see herself as if she had personally gone forth from Egypt." For women, who have often experienced Passover from the periphery of the seder table—or from the kitchen—this moment of the seder can be particularly resonant. *B'chol dor vador* invites us, even requires us, to reject our own marginalization and see ourselves as active participants in the ongoing story of our people.

To remember our departure from Egypt is, first of all, to remember Egypt. It is to remember what it was like to be a slave, a stranger in a strange land. The primary lesson that emerges out of this memory is empathy: "You shall not oppress the stranger, for you know the feelings of the stranger, having yourselves been strangers in the land of Egypt" (Exodus 23:9). Many of the authors in this chapter reflect on the deep connection between our people's experience of oppression and our special responsibility—as Jews and as Jewish women—to work toward ending injustice in all its forms.

To remember the departure from Egypt is also to remember the very birth of our people, the movement of thousands of slaves in the night. It is to know that even the most powerful forms of oppression can be overcome, that there is no such thing as an utterly hopeless situation.

The sense of hope and possibility that we can draw from the Passover story is relevant not only to the challenges we face as a people but to our private struggles as well. *B'chol dor vador* urges us to take seriously the possibility of liberation and transformation in our own lives and hearts. As Rabbi Nachman of Bratslav taught: "The Exodus from Egypt occurs in every human being, in every era, in every year, and even in every day."

The act of remembering our departure from Egypt binds us to generations of Jewish women, both past and future. *B'chol dor vador* provides an opportunity to honor those who have "gone forth" before us—those whose struggles have yielded so many of the important freedoms that we now enjoy. It also offers a time to consider the legacy we will leave for those who will continue to "go forth" after us—those who will leave behind the narrow places that still restrict and constrict us for expanses that we have not yet begun to imagine.

## To Trace My Life

In every generation we are obligated to see ourselves as if we, personally, had come out of Egypt. As if we had been slaves. But in our freedom, can we possibly know slavery? Our homes are well stocked; can we possibly know hunger? Do we presume to understand need when we live with abundance?

The haggadah instructs us, and we are obligated. It is not enough to read about our ancestors. It is not enough to try to understand their hunger, their sore backs, their despair. We are told to experience those lives from the inside, to go there, to feel the bricks on our backs, the fine herbs crushed between our fingers. We are asked to feel our bellies swell with life, only to be faced with sacrifice and death.

How does a woman travel through time to a distant land, an

unknown home? How does a woman feel the desert wind blowing when she lives in the city?

How does a woman find her voice, a history that refracts her life, a story that mirrors her dreams in a story of liberation—in fact, the quintessential story of freedom—when she cannot even recognize herself in the printed words?

It is both the act of understanding the other—trying to taste the desert heat, the scarcity, the fear—and the act of finding ourselves— decoding the text, bringing fresh insight to its rich texture—that come together through this Pesach seder.

We must get close enough to smell the stench of slavery, to taste the bitterness of the narrow place. Perhaps Leah's eyes will help us see a mother handing off her child. Sarah's laughter will ripple in my chest as I release sounds of joy and abandon.

I look for myself in the words I read. Not because I believe that my story is everywhere, but because I want to trace my life, to root it in the stories of women before me, to sugar their blood, to mingle our voices, to tie my history—sparse and fleeting as it is—to another time, a place of womanhood where I can go both in my days' dreams and in the night's darkness.

—SUSAN BERRIN

## Telling Our Stories of Liberation

*It can be very meaningful to have participants share personal stories of liberation at the seder. One way to do this is to invite all participants to bring objects that symbolize their personal liberation. Collect these objects in a tambourine and, after reading the "In Every Generation" passage of the haggadah, pass the tambourine around, inviting each guest to share the significance of his or her object. You may wish to use the following reading to introduce this ritual at your seder.*

We are told that in every generation each of us must feel as though we ourselves had been taken out of Egypt. To this end, I have asked everyone at the seder to bring an object, a symbol of his or her personal liberation. I have gathered these in a tambourine to remind us that after crossing the Sea of Reeds, Miriam took her timbrel and led the women in song and dance. Let us now share what each of us has brought, and tell our freedom stories. May all our difficult journeys bring us to a place of celebration.

—MATIA RANIA ANGELOU

## We Will All Remember

Tradition dictates: "Pass the story down from father to son, from generation to generation."

Tonight we proclaim: "We will *all* remember the story of our Exodus, and we will *all* pass the story down to our children, from generation to generation."

Tradition dictates: "God is the God of our fathers, of Abraham, Isaac, and Jacob."

Tonight we proclaim: "God is the God of *all* our ancestors, Abraham and Sarah, Isaac and Rebecca, Jacob, Rachel, and Leah."

Tradition dictates: "Better to burn the Torah than to let a woman read from it."

Tonight we proclaim: "We will *all* read together, pray together, remember together."

—*HER SEDER OF AMERICAN JEWISH CONGRESS, PENNSYLVANIA REGION*

## To Her Grandchild

You asked me about the sea;
you want to know about that day we crossed the sea....
Why talk about that place, it's so quiet here.
Plenty of water, grass for the animals
cooling shade in the afternoon.
Perhaps we'll stay a while,
I'm so tired of wandering about.
But you asked me about the sea. Yes,
I remember, though I try to forget,
it was so terrible.

In the mouths of our storytellers
the sea crossing has become a miracle.
It was a nightmare.
Dead Egyptians,
hundreds of them in the water,
I still see them at night sometimes
when I close my eyes,
when the wind blows in a certain way.
Moses promised us a wonderful thing,
that day by the sea, but it was terrible.
We have a good place here;
the animals seem content, the children safe.
The children were screaming *that* day;
the wind so strong, the mud so thick
we could scarcely walk.
The smaller animals stumbled, could not get up;
men were screaming at their women,
everyone was straining to help the children,
keep the animals moving.
We knew the Egyptians were behind us,
but the sand was in our eyes
the wind roaring, pounding us,
then—it stopped.
For a moment there was nothing;
everything was still.
Then a trickling, a rushing of water
and then we heard them, Egyptian voices.
They were children's cries.
We saw nothing, sand was heavy in the air
but we heard them;
heard the water, the horses neighing.
Our children began to wail again
and as the sand settled we saw them in the water,
drowned, caught in the reeds.
They *were* children!
young boys, their uniforms wrapped around
their pale, frightened faces.
My neighbor saw her owner's son

and I, a palace guard who helped me pack
and gave me food for the journey.
Everyone saw a face they knew
and such wailing then! It went on and on
we were so tired, so frightened.
Where was Moses, when would he take us home?
Then gradually, through the crying,
Miriam's thin sweet voice—
trembling, her tune spun in the air
and floated over us.
It was a quieting song,
one we used to sing to our animals in Egypt,
and now she sang it to us
like a shepherd to her frightened goats.
As our fear left us, we began to sing with her;
then Moses took up the song
and the men began to chant of victory
and the death of the mighty Pharaoh.
Well, you know that song, child,
we sing it today, but it has changed some
since that time at the sea.
This is a calm, quiet place,
so green, such lovely shade.
If only we could stay here longer.
It's so much like Egypt.

—JANET BERKENFIELD

## Remembering Feminist Struggles

As we remember our liberation from Egypt, it is also important to remember the thirty years of collective effort through which Jewish women have gained the possibility of full participation in so many areas of Jewish life, including the possibility of celebrating Passover together as women. Why should we reflect on our marginalization and our struggle at a time of relative freedom? I can think of three reasons.

First, our gains have been and will again be undermined. Many generations of women have had to reinvent the wheel, creating from scratch arguments for full enfranchisement. How many of us know that in 1918, Puah Rakowski called for a national Jewish women's organization with branches throughout Poland? How many of us know that Regina Jonas, not Sally Priesand, was the first woman to be ordained a rabbi?

Second, remembering the past helps us understand the roots of the present. Many girls growing up in liberal congregations say that they still feel distanced from Jewish life, as if the learning and synagogue ritual offered them is not for them. The source of this sense of alienation can be difficult to identify until women realize that in gaining equal access to many aspects of Jewish learning and leadership, we have gained equal access to a male Judaism. Educated in traditional texts and liturgies that our mothers had little direct hand in creating, we are being offered entry into a tradition that simultaneously is and is not ours. It is only as we name this exclusion that we become able to reshape the Jewish tradition and our relationship to it.

Third, knowing our history provides models for continuing resistance. The achievements of the past thirty years did not come without struggle. They were fought for by a loosely organized, but nonetheless highly self-conscious, social and religious movement. Through their speaking, writing, organizing, demanding, and disrupting, Jewish feminists have gained many freedoms for ourselves and for those who come after us. These do not constitute an ultimate victory, however, but first steps that need to be consolidated, expanded, and shaped anew by every generation.

—JUDITH PLASKOW

## While We Sit Content

In 1973, the Supreme Court held in the landmark case of *Roe* v. *Wade* that the choice to terminate a pregnancy is among women's fundamental rights. In 1992, the Supreme Court held in *Planned Parenthood of Southern Pennsylvania* v. *Casey* that states may restrict a woman's right to abortion at any stage of pregnancy, as long as the restrictions do not place an "undue burden" on her decision to terminate her pregnancy.

In 2001, on the twenty-eighth anniversary of *Roe,* President George W. Bush reinstated the global gag rule, limiting federal aid to international organizations that use their own funds to campaign for reproductive rights.

In every generation, there are threats to women's rights, autonomy, and reproductive freedom. Previous generations of women fought for and won many rights and freedoms for us. We should respect the feminism and passion that brought us to where we are, and we must sustain that legacy. But many of us have become complacent, confident that our rights and privileges will not be taken away. Today's political realities tell us that this is not true.

Worldwide, an estimated seventy-eight thousand women die each year as a result of unsafe abortions.[1] As we sit quietly, content with our own opportunities, our government is considering laws that would severely limit reproductive freedom both in our own country and abroad: parental notification laws, mandatory delay and biased counseling laws, and funding restrictions.

Here, celebrating our freedom as Jews and as women together, we can reflect on the generations of women who came before us and those who will follow. Regardless of the particular decisions we have made, or will make, about our own lives and bodies, we cannot allow the work of the women who came before us to be eroded. We must work proactively to protect our reproductive rights so that we can pass them on to another generation.

—SARA BUCHDAHL LEVINE

## Bearing Memory

In June 1982, using the pretext of an assassination attempt on the Israeli ambassador to England, Israel invaded Lebanon and unleashed a war on the Palestinians. I volunteered to go to Beirut to work as a nurse to show that not all Jews supported Israel's actions.

When I arrived in August, the scene in and around the West Beirut camps was startling and surreal. Many-storied buildings were reduced to crumpled fragments of brick and wire. All around were displays of the ammunition that had been used to do these deeds. Many of the shells and casings were labeled "Made in USA." The worst part was the human toll. In hospital bed after hospital bed lay a once-whole person. What remained were blinded, limbless humans clinging to life.

I was assigned to a hospital in the Sabra camp. I was there during the massacre that occurred between September 16th and 18th, during Rosh Hashanah. The Israel Defense Forces (IDF), commanded by Ariel Sharon, allowed and aided a Lebanese militia hostile to the Palestinians to enter the unprotected camps. The IDF were in control of the camps. They became aware of some of the atrocities being committed, and they did nothing to stop them. Approximately one thousand men, women, and children were slaughtered by the Lebanese militia.

As the occupying force in Beirut, the IDF was responsible for the safety of the population. The IDF opened the refugee camps to a militia with a history of hatred and indiscriminate violence against Palestinians. It sealed off the refugee camps. It refused to allow terrified, pleading camp residents to escape through the exits of the camps. The IDF supplied the flares that lit the way for the murderers; it provided a bulldozer to help bury bodies in a mass grave and hide it with earth. And no Israeli official intervened when it became clear that innocent lives were being taken.

When I heard that the government of Israel was establishing a commission of inquiry into the massacre and inviting witnesses to testify, I knew that the Palestinians and Lebanese who had survived would not go to Jerusalem to testify. They were frightened. I remembered what I had learned as a child growing up during the Holocaust: Someone needed to speak for those who could not; one must not be silent in the face of an injustice; one must speak out for those who cannot, to be their voice.

I went to Israel to testify before the Commission of Inquiry into the Events at the Refugee Camps in Beirut. In 1983, the commission concluded that Sharon, as the minister of defense, bore personal and indirect responsibility for the massacre. Yet, he has never served time in prison for his actions; on the contrary, he became head of the Jewish state.

The passage of time has not diminished the significance of the event or the emotions it raises. The images of bloated bodies, the grotesque scenes of mutilated children and of people slaughtered in the most barbaric ways are now a permanent part of history. The survivors live with both physical pain and psychological scars. Their losses, and their memories of what happened in those hours, have remained with them, have become part of their daily consciousness. Most remain in the camps in Beirut, where they know they are never safe. All of them still live in fear.

In every generation, it is our duty to ensure that nations and leaders be held accountable for human rights abuses. Violations must be documented, and violators must be punished. Justice must be done for all.

—ELLEN SIEGEL

## An Echo of Home

What is it, when we hear a story of injustice—a genocide in Rwanda, the lack of medical care for millions dying of AIDS in Africa, a fight against military occupation in Chiapas—that makes some of us identify instinctively with the victims? What makes others immediately reach for a way to blame the oppressed for the injustices committed against them, to say that they were asking for it, were lazy, were not fully human? And what makes so many more shake their heads and conclude that the problem is just too big, that activism is ineffectual, vaguely absurd?

Political disengagement is as strange to me as activism seems to so many others. *Tikkun olam* isn't a righteous choice; it's an involuntary reflex, a habit. It's an impulse inside me, and I think these stories of oppression and injustice that we tell and retell around tables like this one are what planted it there.

Once a year, we symbolically taste the tears of our ancestors. We recreate the heavy bricks that crushed their spines, confine ourselves to the unleavened food of their long desert flight, and even mourn for the spilled blood of their sadistic masters.

What does this strange ritual look like to non-Jews? Self-pity? Wallowing? Does it seem that we Jews enjoy nursing ancient grudges? That we like the taste of thousand-year-old wounds? Today, Jews are among the most powerful and wealthy people in the world. So why do we always gather to tell one another stories about a time when we were weakened, broken, and enslaved?

"To remember," our parents and grandparents tell us. They give the same reason for our Holocaust education, for why we visit all the memorials and museums. Remembering grievances committed against us in the distant and not-so-distant past—through telling, retelling, enshrining, memorializing, videotaping, dramatizing—is, in many ways, how we learn what it means to be Jewish.

But what does it mean to have this activity at the heart of Jewish life? What effect does all this have on our collective identity? I believe that it depends on how we learn to remember; it depends on the tone in which our parents say to us, "Never again!" Is it a sacred promise or a grudge? Is it said with an open heart or through clenched teeth?

There are as many ways of remembering as there are Jews. Remembering can make us small, paranoid, isolationist, aggressive. And it can make us expand, transforming the seder into a ritual about the ongoing struggle against oppression—even for those of us who have never been hungry, never lacked for a home, never faced the hatred in a killer's eyes.

My own family incorporated this ritual of retelling into my privileged childhood, expanding it to include not just stories about Egypt and Germany but also stories closer to home: about a grandfather blacklisted for union organizing, a father exiled for protesting the Vietnam war, a mother ostracized for refusing to give up her career. These narratives—wrenching, thrilling, gripping—were the soundtracks of long car trips, the glue of family reunions.

Over hundreds of years, our borrowed memories of oppression and the struggle for freedom have become a part of us. Activism isn't only a choice; it's also an echo of home.

—NAOMI KLEIN

## Freedom as a Practice

In every generation, each person must regard himself (herself) as if (s)he had come out of Egypt, as it is said: "And thou shalt relate it to thy son (daughter) in that day, saying, this is done on account of that which the Lord did unto *me*, when I came forth out of Egypt" (Exodus 13:8).

I have always loved Passover—from the extensive house cleaning to preparing multicourse meals and chicken soup with matzah balls to the ritual of group readings from the haggadah and the communal singing of passages and prayers. And I particularly love the cited passage, which accents the fact that we retell the story of our ancestors in the first person to emphasize the point that it is not "their" story but our own. This section explicitly speaks to individual responsibility and accountability for projecting oneself into the immediacy of history, complementing Bob Marley's reproach of those without memory: "If you knew your history, you would know where you were coming from and you wouldn't have to ask me."[2]

The celebration of Passover enables a comforting and comfortable union between the histories of my peoples in diaspora: the Jewish people and people of African descent. The themes of slavery, oppression, resistance, and survival, woven subtly throughout the text, allow me to remember the lives of my ancient relatives.

The rituals of eating the matzah, which signifies both the rapid escape to freedom and the bread of poverty, and eating the *maror,* which recalls our bitter life under slavery, compel us to struggle with historical and contemporary issues of exploitation, injustice, and inequality.

Passover forces us to think about the relationship between God and individual agency. References to "the Lord" do not, for me, diminish the import of human action in transforming one's circumstances. Instead, the haggadah invites us to consider liberation and exodus as radical transitions in which (wo)man does not act in isolation: "And the Lord brought us forth out of Egypt with a mighty hand and with an outstretched arm; with great terror and with signs and with wonders."

At our seder, by tradition, we spill a drop of wine from our glass as we recite each plague—an act against gloating over the defeat of our enemies. And yet, as a black and Jewish woman, this "great terror" invariably reminds me of Malcolm X: liberation "by any means necessary."

Emancipation is not merely the result of an individual human's actions, whether one interprets this as the tangible intervening hand of God, as my Orthodox friends believe, or an aggregate commitment to working against evils fostered by human fallibility. The value of physical liberation is measured in relation to emancipation of the mind; being free is a *practice*. And so the celebration of Passover obligates us *both* to remember the past and to be grounded in the material world, where our freedom is qualified as long as there is political, economic, and social injustice.

—KATYA GIBEL AZOULAY

## Passover Prayer for a Daughter

May my daughter always see a perfect orange
on her family's seder plate
and feel the pride of her womanhood overflow
like water from Miriam's Cup.

May my daughter always recline in comfort knowing
that she is equal to all those who gather
in the presence of *Shekhinah*
to recall our Exodus from *mitzrayim*.

May my daughter never feel
as if her people abandoned her in the wilderness
when the history of *B'nai Yisrael*
was written down by our forefathers.

May my daughter's search for meaning
be as full as the pearl moon
cyclical in wonder and endless in being
providing her with a life of endless journeys.

—LISA LIDOR

## Women of Wisdom

*Eight women should be asked to hold the corners of two large tallitot. The leader of the seder calls up everyone present who is over sixty years old, and they stand under the tallitot. She then says a special blessing while the women are under the tallitot.*

Sovereign of the Universe, our most compassionate, loving God, we ask for Your blessing and for the vast protection of the *Shekhinah's* wings for these wonderful women. These are women, O God, who have seen tragedy and losses in their lives and who have had great triumphs.

As I look into their eyes, I see a deep understanding of life and love, illness and perseverance, as well as the wisdom that comes as a result of their experiences. We know that people tend to discount the many gifts our elders possess, so we ask that their wisdom, Great Healer, be honored and treasured for the wealth and depth it provides to our lives. We ask that You help those around them to realize that their value far exceeds rubies, for they are, indeed, Women of Valor and Women of Wisdom. We ask that they may experience a healing of the body and of spirit, a healing of the soul, the essence of each of these dear women. And we ask that they may experience Your greatest gift: a healing that is filled with peace. We say together: Amen.

—MARILYN J. LADIN

## Justice, Justice Shalt Thou Pursue

*As we recite "In every generation, each of us is obligated to see herself as if she had personally gone forth from Egypt," we think of the many gener-ations of Jews who have undertaken this task before us. The following read-ing prompts us to consider what we can learn from the experience, wisdom, and example of our foremothers. In it, Justice Ruth Bader Ginsburg reflects on the Jewish women who have inspired and sustained her.*

On the walls of my chambers, I have posted the command from Deuteronomy: *Tzedek, tzedek tirdof,* "Justice, justice shalt thou pur-sue." These words are an ever-present reminder of what judges must do "that they may thrive."

There is an age-old connection between social justice and Jewish tradition. As a judge, I find this connection extremely meaningful. The humanity and bravery of Jewish women, in particular, sustain and encourage me when my spirits need lifting. I will mention just three examples.

High on my list of inspirers is Emma Lazarus. Emma Lazarus was a Zionist before that word came into vogue. Her love for humankind, and especially for her people, is evident in all her writings. She wrote constantly, from her first volume of poetry published in 1866 at age seventeen until her tragic death from cancer at age thirty-eight. Her poem "The New Colossus," etched on the base of the Statue of Liberty, has welcomed legions of immigrants to the United States. In it are these inspiring words:

> "Keep, ancient lands, your storied pomp!" cries she
> With silent lips. "Give me your tired, your poor,
> Your huddled masses yearning to breathe free,
> The wretched refuse of your teeming shore.
> Send these, the homeless, tempest-tossed to me,
> I lift my lamp beside the golden door!"

I draw strength, too, from a diary entry penned decades ago by a girl barely fifteen. These are her words:

> One of the many questions that have often bothered me is why women have been, and still are, thought to be so inferior to men. It's easy to say it's unfair, but that's not enough for me; I'd really like to know the reason for this great injustice!
>
> Men presumably dominated women from the very beginning because of their greater physical strength; it's men who earn a living, beget children, [and] do as they please.... Until recently, women silently went along with this, which was stupid, since the longer it's kept up, the more deeply entrenched it becomes. Fortunately, education, work and progress have opened women's eyes. In many countries they've been granted equal rights; many people, mainly women, but also men, now realize how wrong it was to tolerate this state of affairs for so long....
>
> Yours,
> Anne M. Frank

This insightful comment was one of the last made in her diary. Anne Frank was born in the Netherlands in July 1929. She died in 1945, while imprisoned at Bergen-Belsen, three months short of her sixteenth birthday.

My third example comes from Hadassah founder Henrietta Szold, who had seven sisters but no brother. When Henrietta's mother died, Haym Peretz offered to say the kaddish that, according to ancient custom, could be recited only by men. Henrietta responded in a letter dated September 16, 1916:

> It is impossible for me to find words in which to tell you how deeply I was touched by your offer to act as "Kaddish" for my dear mother.... What you have offered to do is [beautiful beyond thanks]—I shall never forget it....
>
> [Y]et I cannot ask you to say Kaddish after my mother. The Kaddish means to me that the survivor publicly...manifests his... intention to assume the relation to the Jewish community which his parent had, [so that] the chain of tradition remains unbroken from generation to generation, each adding its own link. You can do that for the generations of your family, I must do that for the generations of my family....
>
> When my father died, my mother would not permit others to take her daughters' place in saying the Kaddish and so I am sure I am acting in her spirit when I am moved to decline your offer. But beautiful your offer remains nevertheless, and, I repeat, I know full well that it is much more in consonance with the generally accepted Jewish tradition than is my or my family's conception. You understand me, don't you?

Szold's plea for understanding, for celebration of our common heritage while tolerating—even appreciating—the differences among us on matters of religious practice, is captivating.

Each of these Jewish women informs my understanding of justice. I am a judge, born, raised, and proud of being a Jew. The demand for justice runs through the entirety of Jewish history and Jewish tradition. I hope, in all the years I have the good fortune to serve on the bench of the Supreme Court of the United States, I will have the strength and courage to remain steadfast in the service of that demand.

—RUTH BADER GINSBURG

## Memory

Standing on the corner of 72nd and
Amsterdam, a flag in one hand
A sheaf of flyers in the other,
Hollering for workers' rights to unionize,
I wonder if my grandmother
My great-grandmother
Ever stood on this spot, this exact spot in New York City
On her way somewhere
If she paused and looked up

What did she see?

She sees important offices she will
Never enter, nice, well-furnished homes she will never keep,
    perhaps
She sees nothing—after a twelve-hour day basting seams in a
Sweatshop, who looks up at the sky?

But does she see me,
Her American girl-child crystallized in her bones,
Imbued in her blood, biding my time
Waiting to redeem her
To grow up comfortably,
Never sleep hungry, go to college,
Lose all her stories and her Yiddish behind my clumsy Ameri-
    can tongue,
Peppering my speech with the occasional *oy* or *genug*

Standing on this street corner

She stands for a moment's respite
Between the shirtwaist factory
And the withered cabbage and potatoes at home, waiting to
    be chopped
She doesn't look up

*This is because of what the Lord my God did for me when I was*
    *a slave*
In the land of Egypt, when I worked for five dollars a week in
    a Lower East Side sweatshop

I hand out flyers on a crowded street full of people with other
    things on
Their minds, my desperation

To make myself worthy of you

—JENNY AISENBERG

# *Rochtzah*

**R**ochtzah is the second handwashing of the seder. The first washing, *ur'chatz*, was conducted in silence. Now, as we prepare to eat the matzah, we wash our hands, and this time we recite the customary handwashing blessing.

This ritual act is described in the blessing as *netilat yadayim*, literally, "the lifting of hands." These words suggest that we wash our hands not simply to cleanse them but to uplift them, elevate them, dedicate them to our sacred work in the world.

On Passover, we are reminded that this work includes the ongoing task of *tikkun olam*, repairing the world. Reflecting on the idea that God delivered us from slavery with a "strong hand and an outstretched arm," we might contemplate what it would mean to act in God's image by using our own strong hands and outstretched arms to bring an end to the suffering of others. Alternatively, this can be an opportunity to reflect on what it means to sanctify and cleanse our hands. Additional information on the ritual handwashing can be found in the chapter on *ur'chatz*.

Following *rochtzah*, it is customary to remain silent until the *motzi* is recited and the matzah is eaten. This is done so that the washing of hands and the breaking of bread are experienced as one continuous, holy act.

## To Make Our Hands Holy

Before eating, we wash our hands, thanking God for the commandment that impels us to mindfulness. Why wash hands and not, for instance, feet, as our Middle Eastern ancestors did? Not only because it's impractical for seder guests to doff shoes, but also because hands are the instruments with which we work in the world. It is hands that plant and write, that caress and create—but also hands that strike in anger and hatred, that do violence and harm.

We wash our hands not to absolve ourselves of responsibility but to affirm the need to make our hands holy. We sanctify our hands to remind ourselves that *tikkun olam* is the task to which we, and our hands, are called.

At this season of freedom and rebirth, we consecrate our hands to the task of building freedom for all who suffer.

—RACHEL BARENBLAT

## In One Another's Hands

As we prepare to eat the matzah, the simplest of breads, we turn our thoughts toward the source of our food, the source of life. Traditionally, we wash our hands before eating bread, purifying ourselves as the priests used to do each day in the Temple. Doing so, we bring to mind the awesome power that brings forth bread from the earth.

Tonight, we remind ourselves that our closest connection with the source of life is through one another—all of us created in the image of what is most holy. Let us purify ourselves this night not in water but through the cleansing touch of one another's hands. With this act, we elevate ourselves and our meal and feel among us the presence of the Divine.

*Turn to the woman sitting next to you. If you are on the right, take her hands between yours. Massage them gently, like water flowing. Now, turn to the woman on your other side, and let her do the same for you.*

With this symbolic cleansing, we are prepared to begin our seder meal.

—JORDANA SCHUSTER

## Handwashing Before the Meal

Washing the hands, we call to mind
the holiness of body.

נְטִילַת יָדַיִם לִפְנֵי הָאֲרוּחָה

תִּזְכֹּר נַפְשֵׁנוּ אֶת קְדֻשַׁת הַגּוּף
בִּנְטִילַת יָדַיִם.

—MARCIA FALK

## Blessing for Handwashing with Feminine God Language

בְּרוּכָה אַתְּ יָהּ אֱלֹהֵינוּ רוּחַ הָעוֹלָם
אֲשֶׁר קִדְּשַׁתְנוּ בְּמִצְוֹתֶיהָ וְצִוַּתְנוּ
עַל נְטִילַת יָדָיִם.

*B'rucha at yah eloheinu ruach ha'olam asher kidshatnu b'mitzvoteha v'tzivatnu al n'tilat yadayim.*

You are Blessed, Our God, Spirit of the World, who makes us holy with *mitzvot* and commands us to wash our hands.

—*THE JOURNEY CONTINUES: THE MA'YAN PASSOVER HAGGADAH*

# *Motzi* Matzah

One of the traditional names for the Passover holiday is *Hag Hamatzot,* or the Festival of Matzah. Of all the ritual foods arrayed before us on the seder table, the matzah stands out as the defining symbol of Passover. Although flat and meager in its physical appearance, the matzah is anything but one-dimensional in its symbolic importance. This modest piece of unleavened bread yields a vast range of associations and interpretations.

The commandment to eat unleavened bread on Passover comes from the Book of Exodus: "Seven days you shall eat unleavened bread; on the very first day you shall remove leaven from your houses" (Exodus 12:15). The matzah reminds us that our ancestors left Egypt so quickly that there was not enough time for their bread to rise. It is a symbol of our rush to freedom, of movement, urgency, unpredictability, and possibility. Because it is associated with the night of our deliverance from Egypt, matzah is known in some traditional texts as *maych'la d'mhaymenuta,* or the "bread of faith."

Yet, matzah is also described in the haggadah as *lechem oni,* the "bread of poverty" or "bread of affliction." "This is the bread that our ancestors ate"—not only during their rushed journey out of Egypt but during the long years of slavery as well, endless days and nights when their spirits were flattened and brittle like the matzah itself.

Two blessings are recited over the matzah. First, we say the *motzi*, the blessing recited over all kinds of bread. Then we add a blessing—*"al achilat matzah"*—that focuses on our special obligation to eat the unleavened bread of the Passover festival. And finally, we recline as we prepare to taste both slavery and redemption in a single bite.

## Half-Baked Bread

As our people hurried to flee from Egypt they took with them half-baked bread, pulled from the ovens before it was really ready. The bread was incomplete, unfinished—as it is in our world. Here we live, in a universe that is still a work in progress, still in need of completion. Here we live in a world that is, like matzah, still broken, in need of wholeness and repair.

Rabbi Tarphon once said: "The day is short, and the work is great; the workers are sluggish.... You are not required to finish the work, but neither are you free to desist from it."

As we bless this unfinished bread we make a commitment to *tikkun olam*—the repair of the world. We set for ourselves the task of helping to bring about the perfection of the universe and all that is in us.

—*HER SEDER OF THE AMERICAN JEWISH CONGRESS, PENNSYLVANIA REGION*

## To Movement

For the times when we do not know which way to go, but
    move forward anyway;
For the times when immediate action is required, and we are
    able to act swiftly;
For the times when immediate action is the easy answer,
    and we wait and let the truth ripen;
For the times when we do not know enough to make a
    decision, but we must decide, and so we do;

For the times when we have a hunch, a flash, a knowing that
    comes to us without our knowledge,
    and we use these things to guide us;
For our half-thought dreams, our visions, the farthest reaches
    of what we think we can become;
For movement, despite our fears,
    despite their obstacles and delays,
    in times when movement means growth and life;
To all these times, to action, movement, dreaming, we dedi-
    cate this matzah.

—JUDITH STEIN

## Meditations on Matzah

the matzah that our foremothers baked feverishly, in the last
    moments of slavery, as they rushed to pack the all-important
    picnic lunches, God forbid they should be without some-
    thing on which to make *hamotzi;*

the matzah baked lovingly by *bubbes* in the kitchen with the
    eighteen-minute egg timers, kneading and poking and
    shaping and pulling it out of the oven dimpled and bubbly
    and surprisingly soft;

the matzah whose wheat we supervise so carefully, not letting
    a drop of water fall on it lest it rise too soon, planting the
    seeds for the eternal Jewish *mishegas* about time: "don't-
    let-that-overcook: you-see-what-you-made-me-do?";

the matzah, just flour and water; not egg matzah, that deca-
    dent imitation, so rich with apple juice that we adults sneak
    tastes, not understanding whether or why it's forbidden;

the matzah from which we abstain for a month before Pesach,
    so our first taste, tonight at the seder, can be new to our
    tongues, surprisingly liberating from the bloat of bread;

the matzah, in all colors and flavors like all of us; machine or
    handmade; round or square; whole wheat, white, and even

spelt for those poor allergic folks; pieces sporting fragile, broken corners;

the matzah that we cram down our throats with the enthusiasm of a child, chewing the mammoth portion required by tradition with only wine to lubricate;

the matzah, one remaining box sitting unopened in our pantry for the next eleven months, until we begin shopping for next year and, disoriented, find it, laughing to discover it is actually stale;

the matzah, symbol of Jewish-American consumer food culture, the supermarket shelves overflowing with the bounty of Manischewitz and Streit's and Rokeach, displayed in April and then again in December for Chanukah, those silly clerks;

the matzah, as sandwiches toted by schoolchildren in their Pesach lunchboxes, made into *matzah brei* and muffins by creative chefs during those food-feeble last days of Yom Tov, fed to the ducks in May;

the matzah, cheap food, poor food, open-to-everyone food, able-to-fill-you-up food, diluting the eye-watering *maror* with its reassuring blandness, strengthening our spines for the demands of freedom;

the matzah, bread of affliction, crisp and crumby and torturous for the next eight days, but which tonight we taste sweet and full of promise like those ancestral picnic-basket women tasting manna in the desert for the first time.

—SARA MEIROWITZ

## Rising Out of History

Matzah, unleavened bread, has great significance in Judaism. It represents humility and simplicity. Matzah is the symbol most strongly associated with Pesach. Tonight we eat unleavened bread because our foremothers baked in haste. They were responsible for taking their families and possessions out of Egypt as quickly as possible, and there was no time for the bread to rise. We also remember that the stories of our foremothers have been flat—they were given no character, no voice. They were one-dimensional images: daughters, mothers, and wives. Tonight they rise out of history and into our imaginations, full-bodied.

—ELAINE MOISE AND REBECCA SCHWARTZ

## On Women and Poverty

In the haggadah, matzah is described as *lechem oni,* the bread of poverty. As we taste the matzah tonight we call to mind those women living in poverty in our country.

The feminization of poverty is a tragic reality in the United States today, where poor single mothers make up the largest proportion of people in poverty. Despite this, most Americans know very little about the daily obstacles these women face.

Poor single mothers face overwhelming barriers to obtaining work and maintaining stable employment. Many employers are afraid to hire them, and the women often lack the experience to qualify for the jobs that would allow them to support themselves.

Even when they do find employment, these women face incredible obstacles. If trouble hits, they must fend for themselves while continuing to support their families. Missing a day of work to contend with a housing crisis, a sick child, or a cancellation of childcare means missing a day of wages. If this happens more than once or twice, these women may be fired.

Furthermore, because it is impossible to support a family on one minimum-wage income, these women rely on promised childcare subsidies, transportation stipends, rent assistance, and food stamps to become economically self-sufficient. Frequent mistakes plague the system that provides these services, and the women who depend on these benefits are often left without them. The system intended to support them creates a situation in which poor women cannot keep their jobs. They are trapped.

But we can help make important changes that will improve poor women's lives. We can fight alongside these women to provide the support they need in negotiating with a system of empty promises. Indeed, many of the problems these women face are not difficult to resolve. For example, until recently, a center serving a Vietnamese neighborhood in New York City had no Vietnamese-speaking translators or caseworkers on staff. This language barrier caused confusion and delays. But when angry clients and a large group of their supporters publicly confronted the center, it agreed to hire several translators. This single change, brought about by individuals who simply saw a problem and identified a solution, dramatically improved the lives of hundreds of women struggling in poverty.

To support poor women in the battles they fight, we must take up their cause, voicing our protest and educating one another about the problems they face. As we eat the bread of poverty at our seder tonight, we commit ourselves to stand alongside women in poverty, who need our help to become free from the bonds of a system that cannot help them.

—CELINE MIZRAHI

## Bread of Faith, Bread of Healing

The *Zohar* teaches that matzah has many meanings. On the first night, it is the bread of faith, *maych'la d'mhaymenuta*. Before we bless the matzah, we ask ourselves: In this world, at this time, what do I genuinely have faith in? In the power of our communities, our acts of *tikkun olam* and lovingkindness, in the Great Mystery? The *Zohar* teaches that as we bite into the matzah and feed ourselves, our faith, our *emunah*, in the redemptive powers in the world is strengthened and increased.

On the second night, matzah becomes the bread of healing, *maych'la d'asuta*. On this night we begin to count the *omer*, connecting ourselves with the outpouring of God's *chesed*, lovingkindness. So before we bite in, we consider where the healing in our lives is most needed. We bring to mind our friends who need strengthening and healing; we reflect on the places in our families where repair must be made; and finally, we think of the areas in the world that are so broken that only God's grace can heal them. As we bite in, we allow the matzah of the second night to grace us and the areas of our concern.

—TIRZAH FIRESTONE

## Blessing Before the Meal

Let us bless the source of life
that brings forth bread from the earth.

הַמּוֹצִיאָה

נְבָרֵךְ אֶת עֵין הַחַיִּים
הַמּוֹצִיאָה לֶחֶם מִן הָאָרֶץ.

—MARCIA FALK

## Eating the Matzah

As we eat the matzah,
may we enter the spirit
of our liberation.

אֲכִילַת מַצָּה

יִתְרוֹמֵם לִבֵּנוּ,
תְּשׁוֹבַב נַפְשֵׁנוּ
בַּאֲכִילַת מַצָּה.

—MARCIA FALK

## Blessings Over the Matzah with Feminine God Language

בְּרוּכָה אַתְּ יָה אֱלֹהֵינוּ רוּחַ הָעוֹלָם
הַמּוֹצִיאָה לֶחֶם מִן הָאָרֶץ.

*B'rucha at yah eloheinu ruach ha'olam hamotzi'a
lechem min ha'aretz.*

You are Blessed, Our God, Spirit of the World, who
brings forth bread from the earth.

בְּרוּכָה אַתְּ יָה אֱלֹהֵינוּ רוּחַ הָעוֹלָם
אֲשֶׁר קִדְּשַׁתְנוּ בְּמִצְוֹתֶיהָ וְצִוַּתְנוּ
עַל אֲכִילַת מַצָּה.

*B'rucha at yah eloheinu ruach ha'olam asher kidshatnu
b'mitzvoteha v'tzivatnu al achilat matzah.*

You are Blessed, Our God, Spirit of the World, who
makes us holy with *mitzvot* and commands us to eat
matzah.

—*THE JOURNEY CONTINUES: THE MA'YAN PASSOVER HAGGADAH*

# *Maror*

**M**aror derives its name from the Hebrew word for bitterness. In the Book of Exodus, another form of the same word is used to describe the lives of our ancestors in Egypt: "The Egyptians ruthlessly imposed upon the Israelites the various labors that they made them perform. Ruthlessly they made life bitter for them with harsh labor at mortar and bricks and with all sorts of tasks in the field" (Exodus 1:13–14).

The bitter herbs that we eat at the seder are meant to evoke the memory of slavery in Egypt. Perhaps, if we eat a large enough chunk of horseradish, we will be able to imagine, for a moment, the sting of a cruelty sharp enough to bring tears to the eyes.

At many women's seders, *maror* is associated not only with the suffering our ancestors endured as slaves in Egypt but also with the harsh oppression still experienced by women—and men and children—all over the world today. Several of the readings in this chapter challenge us to experience their suffering with the same sense of immediacy and grief that we feel as we recall our own people's bondage in Egypt.

*Maror* can also provide us with an important opportunity to reflect upon the nature of bitterness itself. What is bitterness? It is used to describe food—but what does it taste like? It is used to describe people—but what does it feel like? Women, in particular, are frequently disparaged for being bitter. Why? What do we mean when we call someone bitter? What does it say about her—and what does it say about us? Can the *maror* teach us something about how to experience bitterness without becoming embittered ourselves?

The *maror* is dipped in *charoset,* a sweet mixture of fruit and nuts, and eaten after the traditional blessing is recited. We do not recline while eating the *maror;* when we recall the bitterness of slavery, we relinquish the luxurious posture of freedom.

## This Is the Way to Experience Bitterness

This is the way to experience bitterness: Take a big chunk of raw horseradish; let the burning turn your face all red.

This is the way to experience bitterness: Dig back to a time of raw wounds; remember how it felt before the healing began, years or months or days ago.

This is the way to experience bitterness: Hold the hand of a friend in pain, listen to her story, remember Naomi who renamed herself Mara, bitterness, because she "went away full but God brought [her] back empty" (Ruth 1:21).

This is the way to experience bitterness: Recall the pain of exclusion that is part of the legacy of Jewish women. Listen to the words of Bertha Pappenheim, founder of the German Jewish feminist movement, who said, "No continuing education can repair how the souls of Jewish women, and thus Judaism in its entirety, have been sinned against...."

Or the words of Henrietta Szold, founder of Hadassah, who wrote, "But do not speak to me of the progressiveness of Judaism! Why isn't there one prayer in all the books to fit my modern case—not one to raise up the spirit of the so-called emancipated woman?"

How big a piece of *maror* must we eat to reexperience this bitterness?

And what if I've known enough pain this year already? And what if exclusion is not just a memory for me?

And what if I eat the whole root and my tongue catches on fire and my ears burn? Then will I know slavery?

—TAMARA COHEN

## Beyond Bitterness

Why do we eat the bitter herb tonight? The standard answer is that we must be reminded that we were once slaves in Egypt. But why must we remember our slavery? What is the meaning of memory's bitter stranglehold on Jewish life? Do we dwell too much on the pain—vowing to "never forget"—at the expense of healing, of moving forward, of becoming free?

There is a danger in clinging to a victim mentality—in insisting that we always have been, and continue to be, an oppressed people. Excessive attachment to the past can prevent us from seeing our potential, from growing into greatness. Worse, envisioning ourselves as slaves can also enable us to become the master without even noticing the change. When we're not conscious of the power we hold, we risk abusing it. And, at times, we have.

After the first taste of horseradish burns, there are tears of sorrow—and cleansing. Before we can be truly free from enslavement, we must first look deeply at it—to feel the horror, the sadness, the anger.

But when we have done this, rather than cling to our pain, let us begin to let it go. Let us try to surrender some measure of our pain, and stretch ourselves to a new understanding of our power. As we do this we become free people, with all of the joy and responsibility that brings.

—DANYA RUTTENBERG

## For Equity and Dignity

*Maror* takes its place on our seder plate because the Egyptians embittered the lives of the Israelites as they built with mortar and bricks. We continue to build—families, communities, careers—and we still suffer the bitterness of inequitable treatment in our places of work.

As we taste this bitter herb, we commit ourselves to the struggle of working women everywhere for equity and dignity in their labors.

—LISA S. GREENE

## Us

*As Jews we are commanded to taste the* maror *each year in order to experience the bitterness of our slavery in Egypt. Tonight, we read the following reflection by playwright Eve Ensler, and ask ourselves to taste and feel, with the same grief and understanding, the pain of those who are not our people. Tonight, we refuse to separate ourselves from the millions who are suffering around the world; instead we stand with them and taste their suffering.*

We make decisions all the time. Decisions about them. Them is always different from us. Them has no face. Them is a little bit deserving of all the bad that happens to them. Them is used to violence—it's in their blood.

There are rules about them. We keep them over there, out of sight, conceptual. We do not get close enough to touch or smell or know them. We do not want to see how easily we could become them—how quickly violence arrives, how swiftly people turn, embracing racist hate. We do not want to know or touch the parts of ourselves that are capable of behaving like them.

Sometimes, if we are lucky, an image, a poem, an invitation to a foreign place pierces our perception. We suddenly stare down at a photograph on the cover of *Newsday*—six young Bosnian girls just returned from a rape camp. Their faces are beautiful and young and destroyed. We see their utter incomprehension and terror. We feel their shame.

We are compelled. We go and meet them—young, old, Muslim, Croatian, Serbian, Haitian, Rwandan, Afghan, Chechen. We sit in dusty barracks, makeshift refugee camps, peeling centers. We hold the strong, earthbound hands of the farmers longing for their land, we walk through beet fields with the woman with strawberry stains as she describes the execution of her parents, we sit in a hot room in a crowded refugee hotel with a mother and six children and one son who lies suspended in a bed, mute from three months in a concentration camp. We watch woman after woman shake, pace, smoke, choke, weep as they describe the gang rapes, the public rapes, the rapes of mothers, sisters, and grandmothers. We see how they have lost their homes and identities. That they do not eat or can't stop eating. We hear how they did not expect this or want this and our secure usness, our little usness, begins to unravel. It is dangerous.

—EVE ENSLER

*As we taste this maror, we taste the suffering of women victims of war. May we commit ourselves, in the coming year, to dissolving whatever barriers we have erected between these brave women and ourselves. May we strive to keep the taste of their pain fresh in our own mouths, and may it rouse us to work for peace and to act on their behalf.*

## A Bitter Plight

As we gather to celebrate the Passover seder, we are given the opportunity to reflect not only on the past, on the experiences of the Jews in Egypt, but also on the present and even the future. To ensure that we keep the messages and meanings of Passover fresh for each new generation, we must apply the story's lessons to the critical issues we face today.

In an increasingly interdependent world, global flows of information, products, and people offer the potential for radical improvements in human development. Yet, despite the progress that has been made in recent decades, enormous gaps still exist in the quality of human existence around the world. In the developing world, nearly one billion people are illiterate. Forty million suffer the plague of HIV/AIDS,[1] and millions lack basic sanitation.

As we taste the *maror* tonight, we remember the bitterness of their plight. The Passover seder calls on us to rededicate ourselves to alleviating the suffering of our fellow humans, whether it is from hunger, disease, oppression, or strife. While we are thankful for the bounty we are able to enjoy at this table tonight, we are also mindful of those who do not enjoy such privilege.

—ZOE BAIRD

## Cries of the Oppressed

The *maror* is a potent reminder of the slavery our ancestors endured in Egypt. Tonight, we taste the bitterness of their hard labor and call to mind those who suffer working in harsh conditions today.

When our ancestors toiled as slaves in Egypt, they cried out to God, and their cries were heard: "And we cried unto the God of our ancestors, and the Eternal heard our voices, saw our affliction, our sorrow, and our oppression."

It was not simply work that made us cry out. Jewish tradition has great respect for work and for workers. In *Avot d'Rabbi Natan* (chapter 2), it is written, "Love work: What is that? This teaches that a person should love work and that no one should hate work. For even as the Torah was given as a covenant, so was work given as a covenant; as it is said, 'Six days shall you labor, and do all your work; but the seventh day is a sabbath to the Lord your God' (Exodus 20:9)." It was the abusive nature of the work that broke our families and made us weep as we returned daily to work that was beyond our strength.

As we strive to act in God's image we must be conscious of our own capacity to repeat the sins of the Egyptians, of our own complicity in oppressing workers. In the Book of Malachi we are told that the transgression of oppressing workers is comparable not only to that of oppressing widows and orphans but also to the sin of faithlessness against God:

> I will come near you to judgment and I will be a swift witness against the sorcerers, and against the adulterers, and against the false swearers, and against those who oppress the hireling in his wages, the widow, and the fatherless; and against those who turn aside the stranger from his right; against all those who do not fear me, says the Lord of hosts (Malachi 3:5).

Support for workers' rights to organize against unacceptable working conditions, inadequate pay, or degrading treatment by employers is present in our Jewish texts and tradition. Indeed, the responsibility to respect and protect workers is fundamental to Judaism. It is our obligation as the people who were brought out of Egypt to serve God to act *b'tzelem elohim*—in the image of God—to support workers in achieving dignified and respectful treatment.

—ALANA SUSKIN

## Eating the Bitter Herb

As we eat the bitter herb,
may our hearts open
to the suffering of every living being.

אֲכִילַת מָרוֹר

יִפָּתַח לִבֵּנוּ,
תַּעֲמִיק הֲבָנָתֵנוּ
בַּאֲכִילַת מָרוֹר.

—MARCIA FALK

## Blessing over the Bitter Herb
## with Feminine God Language

בְּרוּכָה אַתְּ יָהּ אֱלֹהֵינוּ רוּחַ הָעוֹלָם
אֲשֶׁר קִדְּשַׁתְנוּ בְּמִצְוֹתֶיהָ וְצִוַּתְנוּ
עַל אֲכִילַת מָרוֹר.

*B'rucha at yah eloheinu ruach ha'olam asher kidshatnu b'mitzvoteha v'tzivatnu al achilat maror.*

You are Blessed, Our God, Spirit of the World, who makes us holy with *mitzvot* and commands us to eat bitter herbs.

—*THE JOURNEY CONTINUES: THE MA'YAN PASSOVER HAGGADAH*

# *Korech*

T
he haggadah tells us that the rabbinic sage Hillel combined the holiday's three central symbols—the paschal sacrifice, the matzah, and the *maror*—into one sandwich in order to fulfill the biblical commandment, "They shall eat it with unleavened bread and bitter herbs" (Numbers 9:11). Since the destruction of the Temple, there has been no paschal sacrifice, but the custom of making a sandwich out of matzah and *maror* at the seder has been preserved.

*Korech* brings the symbolic foods of the seder plate together in an evocative blend of flavors and textures. In many communities, this sandwich, widely known as the Hillel sandwich, includes not only matzah and *maror* but also *charoset,* a sweet mixture of fruit, wine, and nuts. The bitterness of the *maror* and the sweetness of the *charoset* temper each other, suggesting a deeper truth about life itself. We taste Hillel's sandwich and remember that even our greatest moments of happiness are mingled with sadness and loss. And yet, *korech* also reminds us that no bitterness is so great that we should let it eclipse our capacity to savor life's sweetness and beauty.

Some of the readings in this chapter reflect on the rich symbolism of the *charoset.* It is meant to recall the mortar that the Israelite slaves used while working in Egypt, but its sweetness also evokes the joy of our liberation. Of special significance for women's seders is the association in traditional sources between *charoset* and the women of the Exodus story. According to some commentaries, the apples in the *charoset* are reminiscent of the apple trees beneath which the Israelite women secretly bore children in order to protect their infants from Pharaoh's murderous decree.

For most Ashkenazi Jews, *charoset* is a mixture of apples, wine, nuts, and cinnamon. In many Sephardi communities, *charoset* is made from the fruits mentioned in the Song of Songs. There are hundreds of recipes for *charoset,* developed over centuries as Jews around the world have made this special Passover food from locally available ingredients. Many women's seders offer several varieties of *charoset* from different Jewish communities as a way of celebrating the diverse expressions of Jewish culture and tradition.

## Flavors of History

Although, like many cooks, I begin the seder meal with *gefilte* fish and chicken soup, I take a greater interest in the traditional foods of the Passover seder meal. Each of the foods in the Hillel sandwich—matzah, *maror,* and *charoset*—contains many layers of history and meaning. Becoming conscious of the history behind these foods makes our experience of tasting them even richer.

Matzah: Before the Jews' sojourn in Egypt, they ate unleavened bread. Indeed, before the Jews went to Egypt, they did not know about leavening. (Beer was first made in Egypt, and from beer, we have yeast. Yeast does not exist in the desert.) Their bread was unleavened, just as it is today in the few remaining Bedouin villages. Bedouin bread is made with stone-ground flour, water, and a bit of salt, flattened into a large round and then cooked on a cylinder placed over an open fire. Although it is slightly thicker, it looks deceptively like *shmurah* matzah and the floppy matzah that Yemenite Jews prepare at Passover. Bedouins believe that leavening is not pure and that one should serve only pure foods to friends, people who break bread with you. Is it possible that Jews ate unleavened bread because it referred to the purity of their lives before they went to Egypt and not because they were so hurried in fleeing the land of their slavery?

*Maror:* I do not believe that this bitter herb originally referred to the bitterness of slavery. In the springtime in Israel, bitter greens such as arugula and dandelion greens grow in the desert. In a place where so little grows at any time, these bitter greens were an excuse for a feast. They signaled the rebirth of spring. Later, they were linked with the bitterness of slavery. In Eastern Europe, where almost nothing grows in the spring, horseradish became a substitute for use during this ritual, as did romaine lettuce in the Sephardi countries.

*Charoset:* My seder includes at least five kinds of *charoset,* a fruit and nut dipping sauce that came to symbolize the mortar in the bricks laid by the Hebrew slaves during their captivity in Egypt. *Charoset* symbolizes, for me, the diaspora of the Jews. It is a wonderful example of how Jews change their foods according to the region where they reside. Originally this sauce, used at feasts during the first century, included dates, nuts, and raisins. For Jews who went to Babylonia, it was a date and honey mixture sprinkled with nuts, called *halek* today. As Jews wandered they changed their *charoset,* adapting the recipe to make use of the ingredients available where they lived.

As we eat the matzah, *maror,* and *charoset,* we taste the amazing history that these foods contain. The ingredients of *korech* bind us all to our legacy as Jews.

—JOAN NATHAN

## From Darkness to Light

From darkness to light, from slavery to freedom, from winter to spring, and now from bitterness to sweetness. But with the light, there is still darkness in the world. With our freedom, there are still those who are enslaved. It is still winter for some, and life remains bitter for many throughout our world.

Even in our own lives, we live within the tapestry of these contradictions. It is dark, and it is light; we are trapped, and we are liberated; we are cold, and we are warm; we experience pain and joy, just as we have eaten the *maror* with the *charoset,* taking the bitter with the sweet.

Through this act we acknowledge the fullness of life, shaded by the gradations of experience; never black and white but a reflection of the full range of possibilities.

—JOY LEVITT

## A Taste of Wisdom

As we sample the combination of bitter *maror* and sweet *charoset,* we taste an ancient wisdom. The *korech,* a metaphor for our simultaneous duty to mourn our sorrows and celebrate our joys, reflects one of the keys to Jewish survival. In Jewish tradition, suffering and joy exist side by side. Jews break a glass at a wedding, remembering loss even as we express appreciation for the gifts of life. In Israel, the sinking of the sun marks the end of Memorial Day—a day of ceremonies, remembrance, and grief—and in the same sunset, Independence Day, a holiday of fireworks and street dancing, is born. *Korech,* the mingling of life's bitterness and sweetness, can be seen as a symbol of the emotional capaciousness and agility that are the hallmarks of our history.

In the wake of September 11, 2001, a tragedy that altered each of our lives, the sweet-bitter wisdom of *korech* suddenly seems necessary to us not only as Jews but also as Americans. We can forget neither the sorrow of this moment nor the sweetness of life and our obligation to move forward.

At an arts retreat in the woods of New England, a Jewish woman explained to a group of fellow artists the tradition of laying stones at a grave or memorial. The artists were mostly New Yorkers, mostly non-Jews—all caught in the grief and bewilderment of those days following the attacks. Together, in an empty field with an open vista of the region's tallest peak, the group laid a sweeping, unbroken circle of stones.

Step into the circle. The grief is palpable; it is physical, shocking. Stand in that stunning, sun-choked field, with its view of the purple and black mountain, the pale blue sky. Remember the lost, the mourners, the fear that seized all of us who witnessed that day; remember, too, the beautiful vista laid before you. Taste them together, and gather strength to step outside the circle, into the uncertain, breathtaking future. *Korech*.

—RACHEL KADISH

## Bound in Community

The *charoset* symbolizes the mortar used to bind the bricks with which we, as slaves, were forced to build. Slavery is bitter; yet, we make the *charoset* sweet to the taste, remembering that when we bind ourselves to divinity and each other in community, companionship is sweet and everything becomes bearable.

—HEATHER MENDEL

# The Orange on the Seder Plate

T he objects on the seder plate tell the story of our liberation from Egypt in the most vivid and evocative terms. From a young age, children learn the essentials of the story through the foods they see and eat each year at the seder. Women's seders have played an important role in popularizing the tradition of placing a new food on the seder plate: an orange. Dr. Susannah Heschel first proposed including an orange on the seder plate in the early 1980s.[1] Originally, she intended the orange to symbolize our commitment to the inclusion of all who are marginalized within the Jewish community, particularly gays and lesbians. Over the past twenty years, as the orange has been incorporated into women's, family, and community seders, its meaning has been altered in significant ways. Today, the custom is often understood as a validation of women's central place and equal rights within Jewish life.

Some women's seders focus on the original intent of this new symbol, according a place of honor to gay and lesbian Jews at the seder table and in the life of the Jewish community. Others, either because they do not know the true origins of this custom or because they choose not to discuss its original intent, recognize the altered meaning of the orange, understanding it as an affirmation of the significant contributions of women to Jewish life and to the entire Jewish community. Now we can also examine the problematic history of this symbol and use it as a trigger for discussion about the relationship between sexism and homophobia in the Jewish community.

Whichever interpretation you choose to highlight, the conversation at your seder can be enriched by this powerful visual symbol. The orange takes its place alongside the other foods on the seder plate and adds a new chapter to the ancient story of liberation.

## A Woman's Idea

In the early 1980s, the Hillel Foundation invited me to speak on a panel at Oberlin College. While on campus, I came across a haggadah that had been written by some Oberlin students to express feminist concerns. One ritual they devised was placing a crust of bread on the seder plate as a sign of solidarity with Jewish lesbians, a statement of defiance against a rebbetzin's pronouncement that, "There's as much room for a lesbian in Judaism as there is for a crust of bread on the seder plate."

At the next Passover, I placed an orange on our family's seder plate. During the first part of the seder I asked everyone to take a segment of the orange, make the blessing over fruit, and eat it as a gesture of solidarity with Jewish lesbians, gay men, and others who are marginalized within the Jewish community (I mentioned widows in particular).

Bread on the seder plate brings an end to Pesach—it renders everything *chametz*, and its symbolism suggests that being lesbian is transgressive, violating Judaism. I felt that an orange was suggestive of something else: the fruitfulness for all Jews when lesbians and gay men are contributing and active members of Jewish life. In addition, each orange segment had a few seeds that had to be spit out—a gesture of spitting out, repudiating the homophobia that poisons too many Jews.

When lecturing, I often mentioned my custom as one of many new feminist rituals that had been developed in the past thirty years. Somehow, though, the typical patriarchal maneuver occurred: my idea of an orange and my intention of affirming lesbians and gay men were transformed. Now the story circulates that a *man* stood up after a lecture I delivered and said to me, in anger, that a woman belongs on the *bimah* as much as an orange on the seder plate. My ideas—a woman's words—are attributed to a man, and the affirmation of lesbians and gay men is simply erased.

Isn't this precisely what's happened over the centuries to women's ideas: a transfer to men's voices? And isn't this precisely the erasure of their existence that gay and lesbian Jews continue to endure, to this day?

—SUSANNAH HESCHEL

## *Hineini:* We Are Here

*Hineini.* Like the orange on the seder plate, we are now visible, but, unlike the orange, we are not newly here. For the past three decades, Jewish lesbian activists have been at the forefront of feminist transformations in every aspect of Jewish life. We have been central to moving the agenda of liberation forward. Homemade, cut-and-pasted, xeroxed haggadahs, a hallmark of lesbian-feminist seders, were among the first transformations of the telling, and now there are many dozens if not hundreds of such documents in use by Jewish lesbians around the world. These seders were joyous acts of liberation, for we had not yet been welcomed into Jewish life as lesbians, nor had we been welcomed into lesbian communities as visible Jews. With these lesbian-feminist Passover celebrations, we said boldly and clearly, *hineini,* "We are here."

These lesbian-feminist haggadahs provided liberation from the patriarchal Jewish practices that marked my childhood seders, which I now see as lost opportunities to make Jewish history meaningful to the next generation. As survivors of the Holocaust, my family had made its own journey from subjugation to freedom, but my father never shared his experience of having been enslaved in Dachau and Buchenwald in our telling. Nor did anyone ever mention that our family had lived under Nazi rule, or that grandparents, aunts and uncles, and friends had been left behind, never to be seen again. The wounds were raw—our stories as yet unspeakable. Thus, this portion of our history, which so powerfully mirrored the Passover story, remained hidden. By contrast, I did tell this story to my own children. Now that I also have grandchildren, I am even more deeply aware of the need to make our own histories and other liberation struggles part of the Passover story.

And that is what these homemade, lesbian-feminist haggadahs have enabled us to do. Each year at the seder, many of us recommit ourselves to the task of *tikkun olam,* the healing of the world. We name the contemporary plagues that are inflicted upon us. We bring the women of the story into sharper focus. In the process of retelling, the notion of *Dayeinu* is transformed. What we have accomplished is not enough. We must celebrate each step toward freedom as if it were enough—and then start out again on the next step, and the next.

In this spirit, the orange on the seder plate tonight not only acknowledges the contributions made by lesbians to Jewish life but also becomes a visible symbol of our recommitment to the full inclusion of lesbian, gay, bisexual, and transgendered people into Jewish communities.

—EVELYN TORTON BECK

## What's That Doing on the Seder Plate?

The orange on our seder plate makes several subtle spiritual and political statements. For one thing, it represents the creative piety of liberal Jews who honor tradition in a modern idiom. The orange also announces that women have arrived, finally, as coauthors of Jewish history. For many years, the orange on the seder plate was said to have grown from the remark of a rabbi who, when answering a question about the place of women in Judaism, said, "There is as much room for a woman on the *bimah* as there is for an orange on the seder plate."

We now know this simple explanation to be untrue, and the orange is now part of the ancient pedagogic strategy of Pesach. Just like the shankbone, the orange is there so that someone under the age of thirteen will ask, "What's that doing on the seder plate?"

The orange is there so that Mom or Dad can say, "I'm so glad you asked that question. The orange is a symbol of the struggle of people of who have been marginalized within the Jewish community; that includes gay and lesbian Jews, and indeed all Jewish women. The orange reminds us that the *bimah* is no longer an exclusively male bastion. The orange is a symbol of the juicy vitality of Judaism, which reseeds and reforms and reconstructs itself from generation to generation. And the orange is a mark of our confidence in the Jewish future, which means that someday, when you are a mom or a dad, maybe you too will bring something new to the seder plate."

The orange on the seder plate is both a playful and a reverent symbol of Judaism's ability to adapt and thrive. It also celebrates the abundant diversity of creation. After all, the God who made the heavens and the earth and humankind is clearly a great lover of variety and change—not to mention oranges.

—ANITA DIAMANT

## The Seeds of Rebirth

Divine Presence, bless us with creativity and invention that we may continue to honor you with new songs, stories, and blessings. As this orange contains the seeds of its own rebirth, may it represent a rebirth of the Jewish people as the voices of its women are heard.

—ELAINE MOISE AND REBECCA SCHWARTZ

# *Shulhan Orekh*

O ur story has been told. The ritual foods on the seder
plate have been discussed and explained. Questions have
been raised; new insights have been shared; blessings
have been offered. It is time to begin the festive meal.

It is common to begin the meal by eating a hard-boiled egg dipped
in salt water, while reclining. Explanations of the egg's significance vary
widely. According to one tradition, it is a symbol of mourning for the
destruction of the Temple. Another view associates the egg with the
Passover themes of birth and renewal.

At many women's seders, the meal is a time for participants to get
to know one another and to share their reactions to the first part of
the seder. Other communities choose a topic for conversation and
invite participants to discuss it during the meal.

Some of the readings included in this chapter explore topics related to the seder meal. Who has done all the work to prepare this festive
meal? Have we focused on the rituals of the seder while taking for
granted the labor of others who have made our feast of freedom possible? And what about the delicious food that has been thoughtfully
prepared and laid out before us? Can we allow ourselves the freedom to
enjoy the abundance and beauty of our seder meal, or do exaggerated

concerns about what we will see when we look in the mirror or stand on the scale impede our ability to celebrate?

## The Table Is Set

*Shulḥan Orekh.* "The table is set." The meal is served. We speak in a passive voice when we want to avoid the subject. Who set the table? Who is serving the meal? When I was growing up, the setter of the table and server of the meal was an African-American woman who did domestic work in my aunt's house. Even when I was a child, the painful irony of eating a meal to celebrate freedom served by someone whose ancestors were also slaves did not escape me. When I reached adulthood, I became the one who set the table and served the meal, and I often found that the work left me too tired to appreciate the rest of the seder. At this point in my life, the work is shared among friends, but someone is still taking on a huge amount of labor, often in the midst of an otherwise busy work week. What to do about this dilemma?

Whether women are serving or being served, we should pay more attention to this aspect of the Passover seder. Often we take the meal, and its preparation, for granted. We think about how to conduct the seder, what prayers to use, songs to sing, conversations to have. We assume that those parts of the seder are the most central to the theme of the holiday and will be the most memorable. Of course I love the music and the talk, but as a child I found my aunt's *gefilte* fish just as important. We surely couldn't imagine the seder without the meal. As Jews, we know the significance of food and of eating as an integral part of ritual. Anthropologist Ruth Gruber Fredman suggests that the beginning of the seder is meant to remind us of our past, our history, and so we tell the story. At the end of the seder we think about Elijah and about our hopes for the future. But the meal is what ties it together. It is about our present, our connections to family and friends, to being here today. Maybe we should find ways to make everyone as involved in the process of preparing and serving the food we eat as they are in the actual eating.

The tradition reminds us of this with the *motzi* before we eat and *birkat hamazon* after. When we say those prayers we should be careful to give thanks not only to the Source of Life but also to the people who work to set the table and serve the meal. Without us, there would be no seder.

—REBECCA T. ALPERT

## Shulhan Orekh

start without me
i'm ok really
i'll be right in

she never sat like i wanted her to
she would start to sing so pretty
an ancient melody
and a new melody from her ancient childhood
then i must check on the brisket
or the potatoes or the ceiling or the dishes or the kitchen
    floor

the festive meal was her palace
her beauty and radiance and sadness all laid out for us on her
    table
meat and vegetables and sweets and pretty dishes and table-
    cloths and
things she never had

her time to give us what God had given her:
a long table, a festive meal, and a taste of the world to come

—MAYIM BIALIK

## Low-Fat Manna

Jewish women's relationship with our bodies and food is as schizo-phrenic as the seder plate itself. It's the perfect roundness of a hard-boiled egg opposing the flat planes and sharp edges of the *afikomen*. It's the *charoset* sweetness of an indulgent meal, followed by the *maror*'s sharp rebuke of "Easy on the brisket, girl!"

If I may dare to generalize, many of my Jewish sisters—present company included—come built with extra padding. We've got more flank than shank. Some cushion to the tushin'. "Something to catch," as an Israeli boy once remarked, squeezing my upper arm flesh.

Alas, our well-roundedness is not so widely celebrated among our kin. While food continues to dominate Jewish culture as the pinnacle of comfort and connection, Jews have barreled headfirst into the dieting craze, pursuing svelteness with a zeal unmatched by other ethnic groups.

In a culture packed with food-lovin' holidays, there's an obvious conflict of interest.

But it's deeper than that. I recently learned from *Lilith* magazine that in a Brooklyn neighborhood populated by Syrian Jews and Chasidim, girls have a 50 percent higher rate of eating disorders than in the general population. Perhaps it's assimilation—the strain of living in a strict culture against the backdrop of Britney Spears and boot-cut jeans. For the Orthodox girls, the article cited mixed messages (or simple lack of education) about women's sexuality, and the pressure to marry young and become mothers right away.

As for secular Jews, I've got my own theories. Jewish women's confusion about what our bodies "should" look like may stem from a bigger identity crisis. Are we white or "people of color"? A race, a religion, or a culture? Perhaps we're all—or none—of the above. Either way, since we can't quite define our own niche, we have no beauty standards that really reflect our culture, and I believe this fuels Jewish women's body angst. (Or maybe it's just the fashion magazines. If so, whoever spread the rumor that Jews control the media obviously didn't look at the pictures.)

We were slaves in Egypt, and now that the manna is all-you-can-eat, we won't even take from the buffet.

Listen, I'm all for being healthy. Take the low-fat manna. But I'd like to know from each of you: Can you embrace your body as it's built—and learn to love your inner Julia Child—without sentencing yourself to an Exodus through a rice-cake, Stairmaster-strewn desert? Have another slice of brisket, and discuss.

—OPHIRA EDUT

# All Within

There is nothing more private than you, Egg. Inside your smooth temple, all of life teems, unborn universes of possibility, mutely waiting, pulsing. But outside, at your satin gates, Egg, you give away nothing, unbosom none of your secrets. Who would guess that worlds are queuing up inside you, restless to be born through generations, to be birthed and birthed again? Who would guess that worlds are queuing up inside of me, too, Egg, for I am like you, pregnant with what-might-be. On the outside you are flawless—clueless Eden before the fall—but inside, in that wild, un-Eden place, you realize your sensual aptitude for Creation.

Holding you in the cove of my hand, Egg, I hear you whisper, It is all within, it is all within. And I answer, Then let me in!

But what a fragile womb you are in my hand! How absently I have dropped you, how readily broken my dreams, passed over my own disciplines and desires. How I fail to bring waiting worlds to birth! You whisper, It is all within, it is all within. And I answer, So let me in!

Egg, we carry you within, as on a spoon across our hearts' lawn, cautiously, we ferry fevered plans, back and forth, back and forth, failing in execution. Look at me!, you shout, *Regardez moi! Tistakli!* My naked, shameless beauty. It is all within, it is all within!

Be strong, then, and enter who you are, enter your own body. There you will find a fruitful place. Don't go off somewhere else; don't wander forty years in a desert.

Think about it carefully. Consider this hand that cradles me, this palm in which I wait, winking: It is yours. Acknowledge me. Birth me. Birth your worlds.

—SUSAN SCHNUR

# Tzafun

Before we can conclude the meal, we must complete the search for the *afikomen*—the piece of matzah that was hidden earlier in the seder, the larger half of the middle matzah broken during *yachatz*. We now find the *afikomen* and divide it among the participants. Each of us tastes a part of the *afikomen*, bringing an end to the festive meal. Traditionally, this is the last food that we eat at the seder.

In most families, the children find and ransom the *afikomen*. Some of the readings in this section contemplate the significant role that the children are given in this ritual game of hide-and-seek. What might we learn from this negotiation between generations, in which the dynamics of power are playfully reversed? As our children return to the table, triumphant, *afikomen* in hand, *tzafun* invites us to consider the ways in which they might reveal hidden possibilities for wholeness and redemption.

Many communities also use *tzafun* as an opportunity to honor the heroic but secret acts of the women of the Exodus story. These women understood the power of hiding, and their clandestine acts remind us that there is a time to conceal and a time to reveal. *Tzafun,* the search for the *afikomen*, represents our own efforts to restore that which has been broken, to reveal that which has been hidden. At women's seders, *tzafun* provides an opportunity to reflect on the search for wholeness, integration, and openness in our own lives. What remains hidden within us, still waiting to be revealed? What are the costs of hiding; what is the price of invisibility? What broken parts of ourselves do we long to recover, uncover, make whole?

It is fitting that as we ask these questions we turn to our children and make sure that their voices—exuberant, unpredictable, and insistent—are heard.

## Restoring Wholeness

What is broken can be made whole
What is shattered can be restored.
Through our efforts, may the world be healed.

—*LICHVOD PESACH: A WOMEN'S COMMUNITY SEDER HAGGADAH*

## *Tzafun:* Hidden Treasure

The meal is almost complete. All that remains is to find and eat the *afikomen*. We sit in suspense, expectant, anxious. For in this final moment of the meal we savor a foretaste of redemption.

This is the moment of *tzafun,* when that which has been hidden will be revealed and restored to wholeness. For Jewish women there is special resonance in this moment. Women, ancient and modern, embody the *afikomen*. The Torah teaches that in Egypt, the act of concealment served as God's secret weapon, wielded time and again by the women who carried out the divine plan. The Hebrew midwives, Shifra and Puah, concealed the births of Hebrew male children so that the infants survived Pharaoh's death sentence. Moses' mother, Yocheved, hid her baby son—*titzpenayhu*—for three months until she could do so no longer, and then she concealed him in a basket and set him afloat on the Nile. Moses' sister, Miriam, hid herself in the reeds to watch over him. When Pharaoh's daughter, Batya, found the child, she brought him into her father's palace and raised him as her own son, concealing his Hebrew identity while he grew up.

So it is with the powerless. Unable to exercise power freely, they must resort to concealment; unable to speak up for themselves, they must express themselves in indirect gestures and silent acts. For much of our history, we Jews have found ourselves in such circumstances. How much more so for Jewish women.

Even now, at this celebration of our freedom, many Jewish women find themselves unwittingly in a place of *tzafun*. In the weeks leading up to Passover, many of us have cleaned and shopped, cooked and harried ourselves to get ready for this demanding holiday. We have turned our kitchens upside down to root out concealed *chametz*. We have turned our children upside down to empty their pockets of hidden crumbs. We have covered over our exhaustion as we covered our countertops, kept our panic under wraps as we unpacked our *pesachdik* (kosher for Passover) pots and pans, beat down our aggravation as we whipped up the dozens of eggs that went into our matzah balls, *kugels*, and sponge cakes. And how many of us even now are hidden in our kitchens, cleaning up after this extravagant meal?

How wise the Rabbis were to empower our children at this critical moment in the seder! For we realize that unless we negotiate with them to restore the hidden *afikomen* to the table, we cannot bring our ceremonies to an end. Thus, the least powerful among us now wield ultimate power. Until and unless they consent, we are powerless.

And so, our children teach us a powerful lesson at this moment of *tzafun:* that the secret of power lies in its very hiddenness. The resistance of Shifra and Puah. The self-discipline of Yocheved. The vigilance of Miriam. The audacity of Batya.

As we reassemble the broken middle matzah by bringing back into our ritual its hidden half, so let us resolve to make room in our lives for both wholeness and *tzafun*, for the power that comes from external action as well as that which comes from inner resolve. Our hearts and souls need them both to be truly free.

—ELLEN FRANKEL

## *Tzimtzum*

After the boisterous recounting of the Exodus is the quiet, secretive *tzafun*. Even as we recount the glory of our liberation from Egypt— God's outstretched arm, the parting of the Red Sea, Moses' song of victory—*tzafun* recalls the unspoken, concealed acts that brought redemption. Consider the acts of two mothers, one biological and one adoptive, who overcame their own powerful maternal impulses, who restricted their own needs to nurture, in order to make room for the presence of God in their son's life—and ultimately, in the life of their people.

The meaning of the Hebrew word *tzafun* is more layered than its common translation, "hiding." It also means keeping something— like a treasure—aside for a later time. In the Talmud it is written that while a fetus is formed in its mother's womb, the reward for the Torah he will learn in his life *tzafun lo,* is hidden away, set aside, for him.

Yocheved, Bat Pharaoh, and Miriam each set herself aside for Moses, for the divine redemption that he was to champion. Knowing that her baby's survival demanded that he be disassociated from her, Yocheved sent him off in a basket down the river. Moses' sister, Miriam, knowing that she too endangered her brother, "stationed herself at a distance" to watch for his safety in the basket (Exodus 2:4).

Bat Pharaoh, the daughter of Pharaoh, found the baby. The daughter of the ruler who oppressed the Hebrews not only felt compassion for this Hebrew baby (she knew he was Hebrew) but also played a crucial role in this story of Hebrew redemption. Bat Pharaoh *tzafun lo,* set aside her role as Pharaoh's daughter for Moses and for God. She limited her role as Moses' mother to make room for God's plan: for Yocheved to mother him, for Moses to know the family of his birth, and for Moses to return to, and lead, his people.

Yocheved and Bat Pharaoh made *tzimtzum,* the godly act of contracting oneself—constricting their emotions, their desires, and their actions to make room for each other, for Moses, and for God's will.

—SUSAN SILVERMAN

## Secrets and *Tzafun*

*Tzafun* is the act of finding what was hidden. *Yachatz,* the act of breaking and hiding the matzah, preceded the narration of our people's suffering and our journey through *mitzrayim,* the narrow passage, before our deliverance. Now we conclude the seder with the act of recovery; before we can transition from the story of our struggle to songs, praise, and rejoicing, we must find the *afikomen;* that which was concealed must be revealed and redeemed.

For many of us, the story of Passover is a reminder of our own stories of suffering. Tonight, let the *afikomen* remind us of the hidden parts of our personal stories. During *yachatz,* we each pretended not to see the act of hiding, not to know what was happening. So have we kept our own secrets or watched as others' secrets have been kept, as pain was hidden.

The seder can teach us about the nature of such hidden pain. At the beginning of our seder, before the story was told, the matzah was the bread of affliction. But through our telling, it has been transformed into the bread of redemption. So may our own personal stories of pain, abuse, and addiction be transformed as we bring them into the light. We break the matzah in silence, but tonight we must break the silence and tell our stories. As we move beyond our shame and share these truths, we allow others to reach out to us in support and begin our journey to healing.

We taste this matzah and savor this morsel as the final food of this festive meal. It is not a sweet dessert. There is no blessing to recite, no text to read. Once again we are silent. In this quiet, we take a moment to consider what is still hidden. At the seder, our collective story has been told and remembered. When each of us is also able to speak the truth about our lives and be heard, we may create a world where the children can grow whole and strong, and not need to repeat our personal journeys through *mitzrayim.*

—MARCIA COHN SPIEGEL

# Barekh

**B**arekh comes from the Hebrew word for blessing and refers to the recitation of *birkat hamazon*, the grace after meals, at the conclusion of the seder meal. *Birkat hamazon* reflects the profound rabbinic notion that one who eats without blessing is like one who steals from God. With *birkat hamazon*, we recognize our dependence on God for the most basic source of our sustenance, the food that we eat. The full *birkat hamazon* includes four blessings: we thank God for our food; we express gratitude for the Land God gave to our ancestors; we pray for the rebuilding of Jerusalem; and we ask for God's grace, mercy, and abundant blessings.

We recite *barekh* over the third cup of wine and say the blessing for the wine at its conclusion. Some women's seders include the full grace after meals; others use an abbreviated version, concluding with the blessing over the third cup. If you choose to recite the traditional grace after meals at your women's seder, you may wish to offer a version that uses feminized or gender-neutral God language.[1] Because the traditional grace after meals contains a series of short petitions that begin with the word *harachaman* ("May the Compassionate One..."), there is a custom of including additional *harachaman* petitions for special occasions. A new *harachaman* for women's seders is included here.

*Birkat hamazon* invites us to experience a sense of abundance, gratitude, and blessing in our own lives. This section includes contemporary readings, poems, and prayers that give expression to these themes.

*The following four blessings can be read either individually or together, as an alternative or supplementary grace after the meal.*

## Let Us Say Grace

Friends,
Let us say grace.
Or shall we ask for grace?

God,
Help us to be comforted by the faith that we are not alone,
And the understanding that there is meaning and purpose to
    our lives.
Help us to understand the desert journey.
Though we wander in an apparent wilderness,
The silence resounds with messages of comfort.
Guide us, O God of Miriam, show us the way.

So much of life is the steep climb up a mountain
That rumbles and shakes with Your presence, O God.
Teach us not to be afraid to climb enormous heights,
Though it takes our breath away
Because it leads to truth and helps us befriend life's mysteries.

Friends,
Shall we say grace?
Or shall we acknowledge that we live in grace
When we know that we are loved and chosen
For unique and wondrous things,
That we are called to greatness by our passion.

God, help me find my passion,
My mission.
Help me hear the melody of the silence.

And see the possibility in the vastness.
I know that the ground beneath my feet is holy
I know that it is,
Friends let us say grace.

—KARYN D. KEDAR

## We Ask for Your Blessing

There is nothing more profound than the breaking of bread.
God we ask Your blessing
For all who are hungry
And cannot come to eat.
Who do not know the feeling of a second helping,
Who know that the bread of affliction is real.

There is nothing richer than a sip of wine.
God we ask Your blessing
For all whose cups are empty
And who do not know the sweetness of redemption.
Whose cup of Elijah
Was never filled.

There is nothing more comforting than the company of others.
God we ask for Your blessing
For those who are alone and lonely,
Who are forever the stranger in a strange land,
Who do not know the way to
An open door.

There is nothing more enchanting than the telling of Your
    story.
God, we ask Your blessing for those
Who have forgotten their story
And wander without a people, without a past.
Or who are the heroes of a story that we have forgotten to tell
Whose lives and wisdom are excluded from the tale.

There is nothing more inspiring than the fight for freedom.
God, we ask Your blessing for
Those whose struggle goes unnoticed,

Who are too weak to find help,
Who search for a way to escape the thirst of the desert
And have not found Miriam to guide them to the wells.

—KARYN D. KEDAR

## Gratitude

The night is warm and flushed,
It is the wine.
Redemption lifts me to a higher place and
My cup runneth over.
It is an overflow of life
That stains the tablecloth.
Like this glass I drink,
I am emptied with diminished joy
And filled with abundant joy.
Nothing is perfect
And I am grateful.

I am grateful for the lingering taste
Of affliction which connects me
To a story of triumph and
Which makes me feel the suffering
Of the stranger.

I am grateful for the
Leftovers,
A sign of rich abundance.
A sign that the world is full of blessing,
More than I can grasp.
And I am grateful.

I am grateful for people around this table
We have retold, recited, sung, eaten, laughed, and argued.
We have listened and wondered,
And drifted off when we didn't understand
And we have spoken words of Torah.
The *Shekhinah* has blessed us with Her presence.

My cup runneth over
For I am not alone,
Not really, not if I join hands with others
In blessings of gratitude.

I am grateful for this moment.
For the children everywhere
Who are running around, refusing to settle down,
Defying authority
As we defied Pharaoh.
It is only with audacity that we cross the sea
And it is only after we cross the sea
That we can begin the journey
Which leads to understanding.

I am grateful for the courage that urges me to
Step into the unknown.

And mostly I am grateful to You, O God
The ultimate Mystery of Life
The Great Unknown.
You provide us with the sparks of meaning and
With moments like this.
Moments overflowing with abundance, community,
  belonging
And hope.

We are grateful.

—KARYN D. KEDAR

## *Bracha*

(In Hebrew, the word for "blessing" is the same as the word for "knee.")

*Bracha,*
A gentle bending
Bowing
Humbling of self
centeredness.

To ask of God a blessing
Is to place divinity at the core of your being. For this
Bending works best.

Dear God,
I long for Your blessing.
Help me turn aside my pain, fear,
Doubt
So that I may be filled with the
Light of Your goodness.

My God,
I reach out for Your staff
To guide and comfort me.
Lead me to stillness of soul,
So that my life may become
a blessing.

And I know
That there are those who bend because they are
Doubled over in pain.
Touch my fingers with kindness, dear One,
That I may wipe their tears with holiness.

Sweet God,
I bow my head in reverence,
Yearning to be free of
The silliness that makes me stumble,
The trembling that makes me falter and
The voices that take me off course.

*Bracha,*
A gentle bending
Bowing
Humbling of self
centeredness.
Oh, that I may be filled with the
Light of Your goodness.

—KARYN D. KEDAR

# *Harachaman* for *Birkat Hamazon* at a Women's Seder

הָרַחֲמָן הוּא יְבָרֵךְ אֶת כְּנֶסֶת הַנָּשִׁים הַזֹּאת.
הָרַחֲמַנָה הִיא תְּבָרֵךְ אֶת כְּנֶסֶת הַנָּשִׁים הַזֹּאת.

May the Merciful One bless this gathering of women.

הָרַחֲמָן הוּא יַשְׁקֵנוּ בְּמֵי בְּאֵר מִרְיָם הַנִּפְסֶקֶת.
הָרַחֲמַנָה הִיא תַּשְׁקֵנוּ בְּמֵי בְּאֵר מִרְיָם הַנִּפְסֶקֶת.

May the Merciful One replenish Miriam's well and sustain us with its waters.

—AYELET COHEN

## Blessing After the Meal

Let us acknowledge the source of life,
source of all nourishment.

May we protect the bountiful earth
that it may continue to sustain us,

and let us seek sustenance
for all who dwell in the world.

בִּרְכַּת הַמָּזוֹן

נוֹדֶה לְעֵין הַחַיִּים
הַזָּנָה אֶת הַכֹּל.

עַל הָאָרֶץ הַטּוֹבָה וְהָרְחָבָה
נִשְׁמֹר נָא, וְהִיא תְּקַיְּמֵנוּ,

וּנְבַקֵּשׁ מָזוֹן לְהַשְׂבִּיעַ בּוֹ
כָּל יוֹשְׁבֵי תֵּבֵל.

—MARCIA FALK

# Elijah's Cup

The redemptive possibilities intimated by *tzafun* are now brought into relief as we turn our attention to another ritual object on the seder table: *Kos Eliyahu*, Elijah's Cup. Jewish tradition teaches that the prophet Elijah will announce the coming of the Messiah. Expressing our longing for redemption, we symbolically welcome the prophet to our seder by including a cup of wine in his honor on our seder tables.

This part of the seder can be a powerful opportunity for participants to share the visions of redemption that inform our life's work and sustain us through difficult times. At women's seders in particular, we ask: What would it mean for our daughters and sons to speak, walk, love, learn, work, pray, dream, and wake up in a world free of sexism and misogyny? In some communities, it is customary to ask each person at the table to pour a bit of his or her own wine into Elijah's Cup, symbolizing that each of us has something precious to give and that unless we give it, redemption will not come.

After Elijah's Cup is filled, a seder participant opens the door. According to Jewish legend, Elijah visits the earth in every generation, disguised as a pauper. Depending upon how he is received, God will know whether humanity is ready to usher in the messianic age. Thus, we open our door on the night of the seder as a gesture of hospitality and compassion. We pray that the Messiah will not be delayed on our account.

The act of opening the door for Elijah is accompanied by reciting *shefoch chamatcha*, one of the most difficult and problematic passages in the entire haggadah. *Shefoch chamatcha* was added to the haggadah in response to intense anti-Semitic persecution during the Middle Ages. It is a plea for vengeance, addressed to God: "Pour out Your wrath upon the nations that do not know You, and upon the kingdoms that do not call upon Your Name."

This passage complicates the symbolism of the open door in ways that can have profound resonance at a women's seder. As we recite *shefoch chamatcha*, the open door becomes a symbol of our defiance: We are not afraid, we will not hide. We proclaim our indignation and our rage at the violence that has been perpetrated against us.

Yet, many women's seders approach this passage in an entirely different way. Uncomfortable with the desire for vengeance expressed in *shefoch chamatcha*, they opt to omit the passage entirely or to include readings that emphasize the dangers of retributive justice.

Because *shefoch chamatcha* is a cry of pain and fury at those who have persecuted and tried to destroy the Jewish people, many contemporary haggadahs devote this part of the seder to readings that commemorate the victims of the Nazi Holocaust. As we recall the murder of one-third of the Jewish people in our own time, the open door takes on new meaning. It evokes our profound admiration for those who opened their doors to Jews in need of refuge and, in so doing, risked their own lives. We open the door with gratitude that we can do so, and we remember those who, not long ago, were forced to live in hiding behind closed doors. We open the door, unwilling to submit to despair: May our prayers for redemption reach the heavens, and may they find there an open door.

# Welcoming Elijah

*For this ritual, Elijah's Cup should be empty. Participants will fill it with wine from their own cups, as described below. Everyone at the table should therefore have wine in her or his glass before the reading begins.*

As a child, I looked forward to this part of the seder all evening. Since my father let me open the door, giving me the opportunity, however brief, to leave the table, I thought of this ritual as fun. At the same time, it struck me as silly, since none of us really expected Elijah to show up. We filled a glass of wine, opened the door, and sang *"Eliyahu HaNavi"* simply because the haggadah instructed us to do so. Unlike other rituals performed during the seder, opening the door for Elijah seemed devoid of meaning.

And then, in the early 1990s, long after my father had died and I had assumed responsibility for leading the family seders, I came upon a prayer entitled "The Fifth Child," which imagined a child who didn't survive the Holocaust, unable to ask the question "Why?"[1] After recalling specific events linked to the Holocaust, each person was to pass the cup of Elijah in silence, filling the cup with some of his or her wine as an expression of hope that our efforts would one day bring about the Jewish people's redemption.

This prayer led me to reflect upon my own vision of redemption. Its hope is more universal, rooted less in the specificities of Jewish history than in the Jewish notion of *tikkun olam:* the human responsibility to repair, or perfect, the world.

According to Jewish tradition, the messianic age will be preceded by the appearance of Elijah the prophet. Thus, we place a wine glass on the table for him and open the door, hoping that this year he will join us and that an age of peace and justice, not only for us but for all people, will finally be at hand. And yet, we might ask, how long must we wait? How much more hatred, persecution, and bloodshed must the world endure before Elijah arrives?

According to rabbinic legend, Elijah is already here, though he has not yet revealed himself to us. Disguised as a leprous beggar, he sits by the gates of Jerusalem, slowly unbinding and binding his sores one at a time, ready to reveal himself once he is noticed. But people continue to walk by, turning their heads away, too busy or indifferent to help him. It is only when they stop to help—when we stop to help—that Elijah will reveal himself, for the messianic age will not be brought about by God alone. It also depends upon human effort.

*(The leader lifts up the cup of Elijah.)* The cup of Elijah is now empty. As we pass it to one another, let us each add some of our wine or juice, saying aloud or silently thinking of ways in which we plan to contribute to the world's redemption. In filling Elijah's Cup, we bind ourselves together as a community, pledging to do all that we can to bring peace and justice to the world and to all of humanity.

*After everyone has added wine or juice, the door is opened for Elijah, followed either by* Eliyahu HaNavi *or another song that expresses the group's own redemptive vision.*

—ELLEN M. UMANSKY

## Merger Poem

And then all that has divided us will merge
And then compassion will be wedded to power
And then softness will come to a world that is harsh and
    unkind
And then both men and women will be gentle
And then both women and men will be strong
And then no person will be subject to another's will
And then all will be rich and free and varied
And then the greed of some will give way to the needs of
    many
And then all will share equally in the Earth's abundance
And then all will care for the sick and the weak and the old
And then all will nourish the young
And then all will cherish life's creatures
And then all will live in harmony with each other and the
    Earth
And then everywhere will be called Eden once again.

—JUDY CHICAGO

## We Have Banished the Ghosts

In the 1940s, my Uncle Bernie used to lead the seder. He was the only family member who could read Hebrew, and he remembered a tune or two. The seder was held at my Aunt Libby's house at 941 Park Avenue. The table was covered with a lace cloth. The dishes were the finest Spode, and the crystal and the silver shone because the maids in the kitchen had worked hard.

My grandfather, who had died years before, had, without ever attending school after he arrived in America, made a considerable fortune in the shirt business. All his children considered everything that came from the Old World suspect, dingy, sodden with bad memories, and deserving of neglect. The women at the table, my aunts and older cousins, wore fine dresses and strings of pearls around their necks. The men were restless, listless, eager for the food. Through the very brief service, through the mechanical gestures of the adults, even as Mary, the maid from Poland, passed the chicken and the brisket on a silver platter embossed with silver fruit vines, I always waited for something magical to happen, for a moment to descend on us when perhaps the passage from Egypt would evoke a wonder that would infect the table with something beautiful, something grand, something beyond our ordinary days.

My father said that prayers were a waste of time. My aunts talked with one another about parties and dressmakers. No one said a word about the war that was being waged across the sea and what was happening to the Jews there. The family business was doing well. They talked about that.

I knew that my aunt held her husband in contempt for certain illegal jugglings of the annual report of the bank he had inherited from his father. Unfortunately, he had spent several years in jail. Those years did not improve his Hebrew. I knew my mother wept at night and wished herself in another marriage. I knew my brother wheezed and gasped for breath, and our nanny, who had been my cousins' nanny, worried that one day he might die of chest congestion. I knew my other aunt spent her days taking her chauffeur around town looking for bargains on essentials like lightbulbs and toothpaste.

I could tell from the English words I could read in the *Maxwell House Coffee Haggadah* that something marvelous had happened once and that important matters were at stake.

So when I was sent to the door to open it for Elijah, although I had done this before and been greeted only by the empty air in the outer hallway before the elevator, I had a shivering expectation, not so much of the real Elijah appearing before me, but of a solemn connection to the prophet who might bring word of a better world to come. I thought of all the other children who were opening the door at just that moment in their seders.

It was a bond, this turning of the door handle. I did it slowly, carefully turning the gold knob in my hand, listening to the click of the lock. I pulled back the green door, and there outside were two figures in sheets screaming "boo, boo" at me. It took me only a second to recognize the mother-in-law of one of my older cousins and her daughter. I could see their high-heeled shoes. I could hear their gold bracelets rattle. I could smell their perfume. "Boo, boo!" they shrieked, and disappointment washed over me. Nothing wonderful, nothing extraordinary was going to happen. It was a joke. The seder was a joke, and the joke was on me.

In later years, after I had found my way back into the Jewish tradition and we held seders in our own home, it made me sad that I did not know Hebrew and my husband had forgotten his. But one of my daughters had learned it well at the Park Avenue Synagogue, where she had joined a youth program. Now she leads our seder, and her soprano voice is as pure as anything I have ever heard, and each year something wonderful does happen. We become a part of the history of our people, and we sit in awe of our story, and we take our time to tell it all, and my daughter's Hebrew floats above us like a lifeline.

We have banished the ghosts at last.

—ANNE ROIPHE

## Opening the Door for Elijah

Elijah, we are told,
will precede the Messiah.
He will be a sign to us.
And so we welcome Elijah
at the end of Shabbat,
a taste of the ideal, the messianic.
We pray, we sing.
At the seder we even open the door.

At a *bris* we welcome a baby boy into the covenant. There we place a chair for Elijah, reminding us that each child born bears the potential...could make the difference...could be the Messiah.

But some would say that the Messiah will truly come when we welcome our daughters into the covenant with Elijah's chair present, bringing them into our people, recognizing their potential to make a difference.

We open the door. We welcome Elijah, girls and boys, women and men. Together we realize potential.

—NORTH SHORE CONGREGATION ISRAEL WOMEN'S SEDER

## Working Together toward Justice

On some days, the injustices in our world can seem too much to bear, and I am tempted to turn away from them. The bruises on a young woman's face, given by her boyfriend but not talked about because she is embarrassed. The antiabortion protesters outside the clinic, harassing a woman as she prepares to make one of the most difficult decisions of her life. A young girl, afraid to go to sleep at night, afraid of the visitor who comes to her bed. The elderly woman, uncared for, alone in her home with no one to turn to. I don't know these women. At least I don't think I do.

These are women I have learned about from news articles and reports. Every day I wish that my world did not include their harsh realities.

As we open the door for Elijah, we are not only inviting Elijah in but also refusing to shut ourselves off from the world around us. The task in front of us is to respond to these injustices and to fight the frightening demon of silence that surrounds them. This silence, this inability to tell one's story, plagues women all around me whose stories have remained hidden. This silence is the result of our own inability to stand up for the most vulnerable and defenseless among us, and it plagues the world we live in.

As Jews, belonging to a tradition that we both embrace and wrestle with every day, we must speak out against wrongs in our society wherever we find them. I think of the young Moses, a man of privilege, who one day realized that only if he verbally and physically protested the oppression of the Israelites in Egypt could he end the pain inflicted on his fellow human beings. He did not want to be a leader or a visionary. But he chose not to be silent, sacrificing his life of comfort and ease as an Egyptian prince for the sake of those he saw suffering around him.

We are all called, as Moses was, to fight against the oppression that surrounds us. Like Moses, we might fear and even dread this duty. On some days, it would be much easier to cover up our ears, to fold up the newspaper and put it in the trash. But when the day comes to an end, the world will remain no better than it was when we woke up, and we will be worse because of it.

When Moses saw the Egyptian slavemaster beating a Hebrew slave, it was certainly not the first time a slave had been beaten in Egypt. What was new was the way Moses allowed himself to *see* it. When we open our eyes to the cruelty around us, anger will follow. All is not right with the world, and we are not meant to make our peace with the way things are. Instead, we must all bear the weight of righting these wrongs together, knowing that while Moses was just one, we are many. Like Miriam and Yocheved placing baby Moses into the waters of the Nile, we must take action and work together toward justice.

—RACHEL ORKAND

## Who Where Is Elijah?

Down in the subway,
playing a fiddle,
blowing tenor sax
at Madison and State?
Foraging for scraps
behind Happy Foods?
Can you solve this
Passover riddle?

Was he the hiker
on Route 83
we speedily passed
when he thumbed a ride?
Or the beggar
refused at the door—
just being cautious,
weren't we?

Is Elijah a small
voice within,
keeping us on course,
like stars in orbit?
Or the silence—
deep, abiding—
twilight afternoons,
late in autumn?

Perhaps the infant
stranger to sorrow,
lying fast asleep
near Elijah's Chair,
offers the promise
of a better world
to come?

     Not today,
Then tomorrow.

—GERTRUDE RUBIN

# Reflections on *Shefoch Chamatcha:*
# Pour Out Your Wrath

## Proclaiming Anger

As we fill the fourth cup of wine and Elijah's goblet and open the door, the haggadah instructs us to read the following verses:

> Pour out Your wrath upon those who do not know You and upon the governments which do not call upon Your Name. For they have devoured Jacob and laid waste his dwelling place (Psalms 79:6–7). Pour out Your fury upon them; let the fierceness of Your anger overtake them (Psalms 69:25). Pursue them in indignation and destroy them from under Your heavens (Lamentations 3:66).

These are not verses that I remember reciting at past seders. In the seders I remember, we opened the door and sang "Elijah the Prophet." And yet, as I read these disturbing verses, I am struck by their power. They are a visceral reminder that part of the experience of oppression is the anger it produces in those of us who have been oppressed.

Revenge is not pretty; it is even embarrassing. And yet, these passages acknowledge that anger and the desire for revenge are a part of our legacy. They seem to suggest that before the Messiah can come, we must be able to express our rage at what has been done to us.

As I reread these passages from the haggadah, I am keenly aware of the necessity as well as the difficulty of expressing anger. As feminist poet Audre Lorde reminds us, anger is loaded with information and energy. It is not something to shy away from or to be afraid of. This is why the author of these verses devotes so much of his text to expressing his rage. Although these violent passages are difficult to read and recite aloud, I believe they need to be spoken.

Audre Lorde argues for the eventual translation of anger into "action in service of our vision and our future" but first demands that we claim our anger. There can be no final time, no messianic era unless we first acknowledge these brutal desires. If they cannot be expressed, we may never know a better future. And, for those of us less inclined to imagine this ritual as a step toward a distant messianic future, the expression of such emotions may simply enable us to live more fully in the present.

Although these brutal biblical passages express a real desire for revenge, it is important to remember that they are revenge *fantasies*—creative, imaginative interventions. They are to be recited, not acted out. For those of us who have been brutalized, whose lives have been threatened, who have known oppression in our bodies, these fantasies can be truly liberating only if we find the courage to fully express our indignation, our pain, and our fury.

—LAURA LEVITT

## Women and Anger

Women, however, have long been discouraged from the awareness and forthright expression of anger. Sugar and spice are the ingredients from which we are made. We are the nurturers, the soothers, the peace-makers, and the steadiers of rocked boats. It is our job to please, pro-tect, and placate the world. We may hold relationships in place as if our lives depended on it.

Women who openly express anger at men are especially suspect. Even when society is sympathetic to our goals of equality, we all know that "those angry women" turn everybody off.... The direct expression of anger, especially at men, makes us unladylike, unfeminine, un-maternal, sexually unattractive, or, more recently, "strident".... Cer-tainly, you do not wish to become one of *them*....

Why are angry women so threatening to others? If we are guilty, depressed, or self-doubting, we stay in place. We do not take action except against our own selves, and we are unlikely to be agents of per-sonal and social change. In contrast, angry women may change and challenge the lives of us all.... And change is an anxiety-arousing and difficult business for everyone, including those of us who are actively pushing for it.

Thus, we too learn to fear our own anger, not only because it brings about the disapproval of others but also because it signals the necessity for change.

—HARRIET LERNER

## We Remember Idit

*When we read the* shefoch chamatcha *passage of the haggadah, we ask that God deliver wrath on the nations that have tried to destroy us. Lot's wife, Idit, who turned back to see the town of Sodom as it was being destroyed, witnessed the outpouring of such divine anger. In the reading below, Sandy Sasso brings Idit and her wisdom to this part of the seder ritual.*

*Place a container of salt next to Elijah's Cup in remembrance of Idit.*[2] *As you open the door to invite both Elijah and Idit to your family table, lift the container of salt and add these words to* shefoch chamatcha:

We remember Idit—once known only as Lot's wife—
who wept at the destruction of her enemies.
This is the salt of her tears.

"Our eyes run with tears,
Our pupils flow with water" (Jeremiah 9:17).

We remember Idit—once known only for her act of disobedience—
who turned out of compassion for life destroyed.
This is the salt of her tears.

Welcome, Idit, to our seder.
Teach us deeds of lovingkindness.

*Hodu la'adonay ki tov, ki l'olam hasdo.*
Give thanks to the Eternal who is good, whose lovingkindness endures forever.

*Yomar na yisrael, ki l'olam hasdo.*
Let all Israel say, "God's lovingkindness endures forever."

*Yomru na yirey adonoy, ki l'olam hasdo.*
Let all in awe of God declare, "God's lovingkindness endures
    forever."

—SANDY EISENBERG SASSO

# Readings on the Holocaust

## *Bashert*[3]

*These words are dedicated to those who died*

These words are dedicated to those who died
because they had no love and felt alone in the world
because they were afraid to be alone and tried to stick it out
because they could not ask
because they were shunned
because they were sick and their bodies could not resist the
    disease
because they played it safe
because they had no connections
because they had no faith
because they felt they did not belong and wanted to die

These words are dedicated to those who died
because they were loners and liked it
because they acquired friends and drew others to them
because they took risks
because they were stubborn and refused to give up
because they asked for too much

These words are dedicated to those who died
because a card was lost and a number was skipped
because a bed was denied
because a place was filled and no other place was left

These words are dedicated to those who died
because someone did not follow through
because someone was overworked and forgot

because someone left everything to God
because someone was late
because someone did not arrive at all
because someone told them to wait and they just couldn't
any longer

These words are dedicated to those who died
because death is a punishment
because death is a reward
because death is the final rest
because death is eternal rage

These words are dedicated to those who died

*Bashert*

*These words are dedicated to those who survived*

These words are dedicated to those who survived
because their second grade teacher gave them books
because they did not draw attention to themselves and got
lost in the shuffle
because they knew someone who knew someone else who
could help them and bumped into them on a corner on a
Thursday afternoon
because they played it safe
because they were lucky

These words are dedicated to those who survived
because they knew how to cut corners
because they drew attention to themselves and always got
picked
because they took risks
because they had no principles and were hard

These words are dedicated to those who survived
because they refused to give up and defied statistics
because they had faith and trusted in God
because they expected the worst and were always prepared
because they were angry
because they could ask

because they mooched off others and saved their strength
because they endured humiliation
because they turned the other cheek
because they looked the other way

These words are dedicated to those who survived
because life is a wilderness and they were savage
because life is an awakening and they were alert
because life is a flowering and they blossomed
because life is a struggle and they struggled
because life is a gift and they were free to accept it

These words are dedicated to those who survived

*Bashert*

—IRENA KLEPFISZ

## A Seder Night to Remember

We inmates who strictly observed Passover, got three mazzoth a day, this meant still more starvation than usual. On this eve of the first Seder, we assembled in our room, occupied by five persons. As chairs were not available, people were sitting on the floor, perhaps twenty to thirty men and women. The seder plate consisted of a carrot, a little bit of not eatable green, a bone, and salt water; tears you could have enough there. The rabbi, my late husband, celebrated the seder, reading the haggadah, and a *chasen* [cantor] from Prague with a wonderful voice (the Czech Jews were especially gifted in art and music) chanted the well-known songs. It belonged to the satanic tricks of the Nazis, that on Jewish holidays they invented special cruel punishments. So all of a sudden, the lights went out and we were surrounded by complete darkness. But the rabbi went on saying the haggadah by heart, as good as he could, and the *chasen* went on singing the beautiful songs, [in] Hebrew and Yiddish...till the sun rose at the horizon. Never *"L'shanah ha-ba'ah b'Yerushalayim"* [Hebrew for "next year in Jerusalem"] has been said with more fervor, never the dream of independence and freedom for our people thought of in more hope. Living in bondage and slavery and danger of death like our forefathers in Egypt, these Jews held...up their spirit, their faith in the help of the Almighty. I do not know how few of them survived and lived to see the redemption and the rebirth of our people. But our children and grand-children and their children must know this story, that they may be proud of the heroism of their ancestors and be proud to be a Jew.

*This account of a Passover seder in Theresienstadt was written by Klara Caro, an active member of the Jewish feminist movement in Germany before the Nazis came to power. She was also the wife of Rabbi Isidor Caro of Cologne. The Nazis deported the Caros to the Theresienstadt concentration camp in Czechoslovakia in 1942. Established in late 1941, Theresienstadt was intended for the elderly, war veterans, and functionaries of the Jewish communities. The Nazis touted it as a "model Jewish settlement," and most German Jews considered it to be a "preferred" camp. However, although the German-Jewish survival rate was higher there than in other camps, Jews still died en masse from disease, exposure, and malnutrition. Most of the rest were sent on to extermination camps.*

*Caro organized some of the few cultural activities allowed in Theresienstadt. She wrote about these works to teach us about the events of her time, to memorialize the victims, and to show hope in the midst of hell. Well versed in Jewish learning, she understood the meaning of Passover—to tell how, as the haggadah states, "in every generation some have risen against us to annihilate us" but also to tell of the miracle of our escape from slavery in Egypt. Her story illustrates what Yosef Hayim Yerushalmi meant when he wrote about Passover: "Here the memory of the nation is annually renewed and replenished, and the collective hope sustained."*

—KLARA CARO, WITH COMMENTARY BY MARION KAPLAN

# *Hallel*

T he Hebrew name for Passover, *Pesach*, has been translated
interpretively as *peh sach*, or open mouth. The Passover
seder requires that we open our mouths to ask and to
answer, to recount and retell, to give voice to the story of
our people. We are asked now, once again, to open our mouths. But
this time, we open our mouths in song!

Before we conclude the seder, we recite a collection of psalms
known as *hallel*, or Songs of Praise. Although *hallel* is sung on many
festivals and special occasions throughout the year, the seder is the only
time when we sing *hallel* at night. And though we customarily stand
to recite *hallel*, at the seder we recline as we sing.

The recitation of *hallel* at the seder traditionally begins after *maggid*, with Psalms 113 and 114. It continues after Elijah's Cup with
Psalms 115 through 118 and 136, as well as two ancient prayers, *yehal-
leluchah* and *nishmat*. While Psalms 113 and 114, recited earlier in the
seder, focus on our liberation from bondage in Egypt, Psalms 115
through 118 express our deep yearning for a future redemption. We
praise God as a loving, saving redeemer who brings us out of all the
narrow places in which we suffer.

We pour the fourth cup of wine before reciting *hallel* and drink the wine after concluding the singing. If participants at your seder know the *hallel* melodies, you may want to sing all or part of the traditional *hallel*. Or you may wish to read the beautiful poetry of the psalms aloud. This chapter includes several commentaries on *hallel* for the seder, bringing the wisdom of contemporary Jewish women to the ancient melodies of our people.

## The *Shekhinah* Who Dwells Among Us

The psalms we sing in *hallel* are ascribed to David—the musician, the poet, the king. In fact, many of the psalms begin with *l'David mizmor* (to David a psalm) or *mizmor l'David* (a psalm of David).

The Talmud teaches that when a psalm *(shira)* begins with the words *L'David mizmor,* it signifies that the *Shekhinah* rested upon David and inspired him to utter this *shira*.[1] The *Shekhinah* is the mystical term for the most close-dwelling God and carries the feminine attributes of the Divine. What a beautiful image this is—being inspired by a feeling of closeness to an intimate God and then being moved to sing.

The text also explains that when the psalm begins with the words *mizmor l'David,* David first began to sing the *shira* and only then did the *Shekhinah* rest upon him. This text speaks to the remarkable power of music: Uttering a *shira* brings the Divine Presence to a place where She did not dwell before! I remember this experience at my first women's seder. We gathered together from many places, unsure of what the seder experience would offer, and then we began to sing. The sound of women's voices raised in song elevated the experience and made me feel a sense of closeness to the community of women and to God.

During the seder, we sing many songs—songs of enslavement, songs of redemption, and songs of gratitude. When we utter these psalms of praise in *hallel,* may we each reflect the *Shekhinah* who dwells among us. And if we are not sure that the *Shekhinah* dwells among us, it is all the more important that we sing and bring Her here.

—ANGELA WARNICK BUCHDAHL

# We Will Sing a New Song Before You

Why is this *hallel* different from all other *hallels?* It is the only time during the year that we sing *hallel* at night instead of during the day. We praise God in the evening because the miracle of Passover took place under a midnight sky; the Israelites hastily shed their shackles in the depths of an Egyptian night.

In all other *hallels* we praise God for the miracles performed for our ancestors, while on this night we praise God for the miracles performed for us. We preface our singing of *hallel* by proclaiming that we will praise God for the miracle that God has performed, both for our ancestors and for us. Attempting to see ourselves tonight as though we personally have been freed from slavery in Egypt, we allow ourselves to be transported from despair to joy, from mourning to celebration, from disheartenment to hope; and thus we move from slavery to freedom.

*V'nomar lefanav shira chadasha*—we will sing a new song before You. This new song is *hallel* at night. It is *hallel* at the moment of our transformation; it is a song that reflects the moment of discovery. If something we have read or heard, thought or spoken tonight has influenced us in any way, then these words of praise for God, which speak not only about the miracle of the Exodus from Egypt but also about our hopes for future redemption, will have new meaning as well.

*Ana Hashem hoshiah nah! Ana Hashem hatzlichah nah!* "Please God, save us now! Please God, bring us success now!" As we ask for God's salvation tonight, our request may be refocused or slightly altered from that of yesterday. We speak tonight about our ancestors' journey to freedom as well as our own journeys in search of personal and communal freedom. In sharing our stories, we weave together a new narrative of what it means to be a slave and what it means to be a free person. As our personal and communal narratives are transformed, so must our relationship with God be altered. Tonight we have composed a new song of praise to God, with new rhythms and melodies, with new questions and desires, with new hopes and new faith.

—ALIZA DZIK

## In Praise of the Holy One

*Hallel* is chanted during the prayer service on major and minor festival days, giving us some fifty opportunities during our yearly cycle to call out in joy to God. Of those fifty opportunities within the formal service, this is our one *hallel* of family and friends, of intimacy.

Our seder meal is framed by the psalms of *hallel*. Psalms 113 and 114 are sung before the meal and Psalms 115 through 118 after it. We delight in our meal of freedom surrounded by the sounds of hope in and awe of God.

Concentrate on the differences between praising God on an empty stomach and on a full stomach. How much easier it seems to call forth with the quick *hamotzi* when one is hungry and anxious to eat! And how much easier to forget the important *mitzvah* of praising the Holy One of Being when we are comfortable and sated.

The Talmud records, "There was only as much as an olive of the Passover-offering [to eat], yet the *hallel* split the roofs!"[2] During many of our festival services, we hear in the often-melancholy sounds of *hallel* our Jewish history, our determination to call out God's praises in the midst of adversity and oppression.

But tonight there must be no questioning or uncertainty in our song. We must find ways to split the roofs of our homes as we sing out in praise. We are redeemed; we are crossing the sea on dry land; we are free to serve God in full glory. Tonight we sing genuinely, knowing and feeling that truth.

It is said that in our ancient Temple ritual, men were the musicians and singers. Women, on the other hand, were the leaders and teachers of the songs of the people, the weavers of melody and drummers for the world around these centers of religious life. Tonight, let us bring our voices and rhythms to the praise of the Holy One of Blessing at our seder tables.

—LOREL ZAR-KESSLER

## Song of Praise

Holy Mother, *Shekhinah* Soul, *Rachamema*
Compassion fills your womb of love *T'hallel hah!*
Holy Mother, *Shekhinah* Soul, *Mikor Hayim*
Fountain of life flows from you, *u'shavten mayim.*
Holy Mother, *Shekhinah* Soul, *Shechinat-el*
On wings of light we soar to You, *natchil l'hitpalel.*
Holy Mother, *Shekhinah* Soul, *Eheyeh Asher Eheyeh*
You were, You are, You'll always be, *Gam anachnu Nihiyeh.*
Holy Mother, *Shekhinah* Soul, *Melechet Shamayim*
You rule skies and earth with a gentle hand, *borchi et Yerusha-
   layim.*
Holy Mother, *Shekhinah* Soul, *Rachmana Yah*
You heal the wounds of a heavy heart, *Ayl na r'fanah la.*
Holy Mother, *Shekhinah* Soul, *b'air l'chai ro-i*
I drink deep of your love, *Ki at emadi.*

—GEELA RAYZEL RAPHAEL

# *Nirtzah*

As our seder comes to a close, we bless and drink the fourth cup of wine. "I will take you to be My people and I will be your God" is the promise of the fourth and final cup. *Nirtzah* reminds us that the Exodus is not the end of our story; it is the beginning. As Jews, as women, as human beings deeply aware that the world is not yet as it should be, we must continue to look toward a vision of the Promised Land.

*L'shanah ha-ba'ah b'Yerushalayim!* Next year in Jerusalem! We conclude our seder with this declaration, which demands that we ask where we will be a year from now. Where do we hope to be? When we leave the seder table, how will we set ourselves in the right direction? What steps will we take—in our own lives, in our families, in our communities, in our workplaces—toward fulfilling our highest visions of righteousness, wholeness, and peace? What kind of changes do we wish to make in the world, and what have we learned at our seder about how to enact them?

*L'shanah ha-ba'ah b'Yerushalayim!* We affirm that our destiny is bound up with the well-being of Jerusalem and all her inhabitants. What claim will Jerusalem make on us in the coming year? How can we help end the hatred and bloodshed in the City of Peace?

Because *nirtzah* is the last section of the seder, many women's seders also include a reading that serves as a conclusion to the event. Reflections that address the themes of the holiday or the entire seder ritual allow participants to reflect on the rituals and conversations of the evening and can provide a meaningful way to end the event. Alternatively, *nirtzah* can be time to look forward, to explicitly acknowledge and address the challenge of maintaining the feelings of inspiration, community, and empowerment created at the seder during the rest of the year.

*L'shanah ha-ba'ah b'Yerushalayim!* Next year in Jerusalem! We cry out with renewed hope, determination, and courage for the challenges that lie ahead. Our seder is over, but our journey has just begun.

## Jerusalem

Jerusalem a child reborn every day
A tear-away teen enlightened and rebellious
A woman, raped, loathed but forever loved
Jerusalem, widowed mother, solitary sufferer.
Mystic dust is the balm that soothes
Your torn and exposed body
Sheltering and unshielding all its pains, hopes and despairs.

Shalem of King David. Herodian. Roman. Byzantine.
Biblical and pre-Biblical
Your soil cannot bear any more broken bodies
You were not born to be a burial city, embalmed museum,
stately ruins reserved for tourists' eyes

How difficult to tread on your sacred soil, too painful,
my body too heavy for your sensitive ground,
history of all humankind

I enter the gateways whose very name makes one dream
I climb to the summit of your walls, your steps and hidden
     nooks
On every side the scars, the open wounds, the excavations

Perhaps on a day that can't be distant now
The courage of your grey-winged doves
Will transform the deadly bullets that yet assail you
into milk and honey?

Oh spirit of Jerusalem
The outcasts who hunger and thirst for justice
Pray for you, Jerusalem
Humanity needs you
In you alone can we celebrate
The great unending universal festival

Wall of lamentations
Gethsemane
Mount of the Olives
Sea of Galilee
Haifa, Beer-Sheba
Jerusalem, Israel

Transcendent songs unite us all as one
We meet again and, again, farewell was and is impossible.
This we have known since that dawn woven of yellow
    confidence
on the edge of the desert
witnessed in the distance by bedouins and their favorites
hidden wells and stars within range of our grasping hands

—SARA RIWKA ERLICH, TRANSLATED BY AURISTELA XAVIER,
SARA RIWKA BR'RAZ ERLICH, AND J. M. DEISLER

## Yearning for Jerusalem

Jerusalem has always had historical, religious, political, and intensely emotional dimensions. Even as a religious concept, the City of Peace comprises a duality that has permeated Jewish texts, literature, poetry, and liturgy for centuries, for millennia. There is Jerusalem-the-real and Jerusalem-the-ideal.

Now, at the conclusion of the Passover seder, we express our fervent wish to be privileged to repeat the experience "next year in Jerusalem." A plain reading of that age-old prayer interprets it as a literal yearning to be situated in that city when the next Passover is celebrated. A deeper apprehension of what the petition entails recognizes it as a more mystical yearning for the supernal, sublime concept of Jerusalem-on-High, a spiritual state of peace and fulfillment, of safe harbor, of homecoming to God's house, of closeness to the Divine.

Many of us who reside in or visit Jerusalem-the-real, while transported by the physical beauty of the modern City of Gold, also experience the tension of a bitterly contested city. We are surrounded by constant divisiveness—between Arabs and Jews, between Orthodox and secular Jews. The pride and love we feel for the actual Jerusalem is tinged with anxiety and fear for the future. The torrent of emotions evokes within us yearnings for Jerusalem-the-ideal, as we declare that we feel closer to God there, that we are imbued by a mystical association with the center of the universe and a more immediate connection to the heavenly spheres.

Our generation has witnessed the creation of yet a third version of the city: the Jerusalem-of-fear. In recent years, the political situation has run to a murderous extreme. That city's residents and visitors live in fear of being butchered or dismembered by implacable, pitiless, indiscriminate, homicidal bombers. "Next year in Jerusalem" also expresses our solidarity with Jews forced to live with fear and with sorrow in a distorted version of the biblical Zion.

Restoring tranquility to the City of Peace should be our first resolve. Bringing the reality of Jerusalem ever closer to the ideal version has been a goal of Jews throughout history, regardless of political or religious ideology. May that vision inform our own time and our responses to the true Jerusalem.

—CAROL DIAMENT

## For Anne at Passover, Part III

Given the vagaries of the calendar, Good Friday sometimes coincides with the first night of Passover, as was the case the year I was working on "For Anne at Passover." Despite my early years as a student at the convent of the Sisters of St. Joseph, a teaching order next door to my childhood home, I think I was a college student before I understood that the Last Supper depicted Jesus and his disciples ranged around the seder table on a Friday that was to become Good Friday.

The poem is dedicated to the poet Anne Sexton, to whom, at that time, Judaism was a curiosity faintly tinged with disrepute. It was remarkable luck that we were able to break through the stereotypes and forge a deep personal and professional friendship.

Part III, included below, takes up the story of Passover, focusing on the rituals of the seder service while contrasting them with the Christian belief of Jesus' burial in and subsequent resurrection from the cave. The sacrament of the Eucharist and the symbolism of the matzah, which I call "our fetishes," are set alongside the ritual entombment of the placenta by the people of the Bakongo region in Africa, a custom that ensures that the soul of the newborn is safely hidden from evil spirits.

The roots of Jewish holidays are centuries deep, and the seder service carries a heavy load of emotional baggage. The poem, and I as its composer, deplore the parochialism that still locks away recognition of our common heritage and religious practice between Jews and Christians and among Jews, Christians, and Muslims.

> Tonight, the damask cloth laid, the loving cup
> brimmed with sweet wine, I think of those my kin
> who sat that Friday, inviting Elijah in
> and swore he never came, nor comes again.
> I think of Judas, the prophecy fetched up
> to truth at our mutual season: yours to take
> your pierced and honored Son out of His cave
> and sing *resurgam,* drink His winy life;
>    there at the rail for pity's sake
>    redeem yourself, all men, as if
> there were still time in this hard-budding time;
>
> and mine to mind another book: remind
> my blood relations we are marked in the blood
> of an earlier lamb, and call God good,
> Who thumped our Moses so to send us out

and turned aside and hardened Pharaoh's heart
    ten times, Antagonist! to put
    us on that dusty pathway through
Your hot sea. So we come to praise You.

Yearly, the youngest child, asking why
this night is different from all other nights,
is told, his soft mouth crammed with bittersweet,
the bondage years in Egypt, and in some way
learns to perpetuate them from that day.
I remember my father's mother boiled
chickens with their feet on, and we ate,
blasphemous modern children, from her plate
both meat and milk and stayed up loved and late,
no letter law applying to a child.
I have sealed her in me, her fierce love
    of kindred all she had to give,
    and my drowned Polish ancestry,
washed out of Europe, rises up in me.

We pray tonight, dip herbs, and pour out wine,
forever what we are. I hear the rain
swelling the hard buds, all our fetishes
the simple sum of promises or wishes:
a radioactive rain in Pakistan
and Haifa, Yucca Flats, the Vatican,
    on all my kind: Manhattan rich
    or Yemen poor, who break hard bread
tonight and bless their unforgotten dead.

What do we do, who eat to celebrate
with Eucharist and matzoh man's old fate?
I take a funny comfort, reading how
Bakongo folk, hard on the pulsing spew
of the afterbirth, would kiss that cord
and fix it in the belly of their god
    so that its navel bud protrudes
    where we are, mewling, swathed to hold
our secret in. We die, that knob unsealed.

Now God forgive us where we live
The ways we love are relative.
Yours, Anne, the sacramental arts
which divide Him in three parts;
mine, the vengeful King of pride
despite Whose arm His chosen died;
theirs, the unction and the fuss
who bless the lost umbilicus.

Guests of our glands, slaves to our origins,
we pray and eat tonight in greening weather.
Time swells the buds. A sharper rain begins;
we are all babes who suck at love together.

—MAXINE KUMIN

## Pesaj in Chile

Tonight,
Unlike any
Other night,
Spring returns
To its dominions of jasmine.
Tonight,
Unlike any
Other night,
We lean over the places
Where the memory
Of another time
Also recline.
Our learning springs forth in songs.

The younger ones
Ask:
Why is tonight
Unlike any other night?
The elders repeat:
Because we were also slaves
In the land of Egypt
And the jasmine moistens the lips

And the song is fragrance.
Our learning springs forth in songs.

My son reads the haggadah.
We answer him.
Braided voices,
Restless gardens,
Like words
And it is this history a gesture in the womb
Of our beginning.
Our learning springs forth in songs.

Your daughter opens the door,
For the arrival of the foreigners
The women with empty baskets.
My daughter opens the window to dream
Of the times of wheat and honey,
Or an open sky like the *Aleph,*
A sky of imaginary boundaries.

The sky is different tonight,
It is not like the other nights,
Winged, covered by prayers,
Soft like a song over
The shadows of God.
We name the stars and we repeat the name of those camps
Where we also died:
Bergen-Belsen, Dachau, Treblinka
Auschwitz

Tonight, like every other night
We dream of love
Of the time when women gathered olives
And sang amidst the thresholds of sand.

The old man of the round table,
The Jewish King Arthur
Whispers, moans or prays.
Sanctifies the wine and its lights,
The land and its festive torches.
We sing

Leaning
Over the haggadah of Sarajevo or Alexandria
And the wind of God covers
Our cheeks
Moistened by salt,
Thankful and fulfilled.
This night so different from all the other nights:
This night where I love you, foreigner,
My body receives you
As if you were also a lost people.

—MARJORIE AGOSIN

## Redemption Seemed as Close as the Kitchen Sink

We have reached the end of the seder. We have traveled through sacred time, making the journey from slavery to freedom. We have pushed the limits of our imaginations, embracing the idea that we, too, were slaves in Egypt, and we, too, will celebrate next year's seder in a Jerusalem filled with peace. We have savored the taste of a dry, humble cracker—at once the bread of poverty and the symbol of our redemption. Tonight, we have shared our table with prophets and let the voices of our ancestors mingle with our own songs of praise. And now, that intensity begins to fade away. We look around through tired eyes— there is wine spilled on the table, matzah crumbs cover the floor. It is time to do the dishes.

We are poised, right now, somewhere between Jerusalem and our kitchen sinks. The demands of the ordinary pull us away from the seder's extraordinary delights, and we are faced with the task of keeping the songs of freedom ringing in our ears. There is no easy way to do this; no simple formula can guide every one of us. But each of us needs to reflect: What does it mean to say that God brought our ancestors out of Egypt? What does it mean to say that we, too, were slaves in that place? What are the consequences of these words? What kinds of responsibilities do they place on us? How do we walk away from this table and still keep the teachings of this evening close to our hearts? Tonight, let's turn away from platitudes and easy answers. Let's acknowledge how hard it is to keep the seder with us, how difficult it is to stay in touch with wonder, gratitude, and the call to justice.

Soon we will clear away the glasses and sweep up the crumbs. But sometime in the coming year, we may notice the smallest crumb of matzah stuck between the cracks in the floor. And if that happens, perhaps we will hold that crumb in our hands and be brought back to this moment, when redemption seemed as close as the kitchen sink.

—DEBORAH GLANZBERG-KRAININ

## By the Merit of Our Righteous Mothers

By the merit of our righteous mothers, our foreparents were redeemed from Egypt (BT *Sotah* 11b).

Deep in the darkness of Egyptian slavery, our foremothers caught glimpses of light. The pyramids of hardship did not persuade them; they dreamed themselves openings and moved swiftly. How could they weep at night, when a nation was waiting to be born?

These ingenious women devised elaborate plans to reawaken desire in their work-worn husbands. They fed them, bathed them, and drenched them with sweet-smelling oils. And their magic worked wonders. Our mothers' wombs grew to be as full as pomegranates. The midrash relates that each woman could have birthed the whole nation—six hundred thousand in each womb!

Shifra and Puah, the mighty pair of midwives, defied Pharaoh's strict orders to ensure that life would continue for a new generation. But our mothers' foresight and skill extended outside the birthing room. With Miriam the prophetess as their able guide, they greeted God's splitting of the sea with an eruption of their own beautiful music. "From where did they have instruments in the middle of the desert?" asks the midrash. They were believers in God's miracles, these women; they were prepared for redemption.

As we greet redemption at Passover each year, we too are the engines of our people. Preparing our houses and families for the holiday is a true labor of love, fueled by fear of God and faith in the future. We too are able to see new possibilities where there appears to be darkness. We gather strength from Shifra and Puah, Miriam and Yocheved, joining our forces together to effect change. Let us allow Miriam's song of praise to inspire us and guide our steps.

—TAMMY JACOBOWITZ

## Next Year

They arrived at the Seder,
unannounced and tried to squeeze
their thin bodies in a chair.
They had more than four questions
to ask. Four cups of wine
could not slake their thirst.
They were ghosts from Brazil,
Iran, Russia, Poland; lost shtetls.
Jews of the blackened chimneys.

They knew secret places
to hide the *afikomen*. They sang
and danced wildly to invisible
violins. Later, exhausted,
they reclined like noblemen
at a grand feast.

When it was time to leave,
they used threadbare sleeves
to wipe the matzah crumbs
from their grape-stained lips.

They vanished into the night.
The host, sensing something
amiss, ran outside. Gazing up,
he found them clustered, like stars.
He whispered hoarsely, "Come back,
next year! Next year!"

—GERTRUDE RUBIN

## The Seder Is Complete

The seder is complete, the ritual fulfilled.
Our daughters' questions awakened our hearts;
our sisters' music invited us to dance;
our mothers' stories welcomed us home.
Nourished by words ancient and new,
We tasted a future of justice and care.
Tonight, a new history begins:
in the cities of Judah and wherever our people gather,
the voices of daughters join the voices of sons
in songs of freedom and celebration.

*L'shanah ha-ba'ah b'Yerushalayim.*

—SUE LEVI ELWELL

## The Dusk of Our Ritual

We have reached the dusk of our ritual. Our table is rich both with tradition and with promise. As those who will bear the next generation we look to tomorrow's Passover as we close this one, waiting for its promise to bloom.

—*YALE WOMEN'S HAGGADAH*

# Afterword: A Guide to Planning a Women's Seder

The planning process for a women's seder can be as meaningful as the event itself. Many women find that taking part in the creation of this ritual strengthens their connection to Jewish tradition, helps them form close bonds with other Jewish women, and introduces them to a variety of issues central to Jewish feminism and contemporary Judaism. This guide to planning a women's seder will help your planning process reach its full potential as a powerful, community-building experience.

Compiled with the help of more than fifty women's seder organizers, this guide is a collection of the opinions and advice of the experts—the women who have been through the planning process themselves. The information presented here is taken from survey responses by organizers in diverse communities throughout North America. We have included a wide array of their suggestions and advice so that you may incorporate the ideas most relevant to you.

## Create a Planning Committee

Gather a group of women to work with you, and think about how, together, you will create the seder. Larger seders will often need a formal planning committee with several members, and many of the suggestions below are most applicable to such groups. However, smaller seders as well as those opting for a more informal planning group will also find helpful ideas here.

**Create a planning committee that represents the communities you hope will join you at the seder.** If you want to attract attendants from the entire Jewish community, be sure to include women from different movements and backgrounds on your committee. If it is important to you to have an intergenerational seder, include women of many ages. For example, Dorothy Flippen recalls that the Wilmington, Delaware, seder planning committee included "an Orthodox feminist, the former president of Delaware NOW, an intellectual property attorney, the former editor of the local Jewish biweekly, a synagogue choral director, and a professional calligrapher.... It was an all-lay group with members from all four of the congregations in northern Delaware."

**Invite organizations to cosponsor your seder.** Cosponsors provide organizational support for your event and can help draw a diverse group of participants. Congregational sisterhoods and other women's groups; Jewish Community Centers; Federations; Hadassah, ORT, and NCJW chapters; and campus Hillels and women's centers often work together to plan a women's seder. Ask cosponsors to donate money, volunteer, or both, and encourage them to publicize the seder to their members.

**Involve Jewish professionals or others knowledgeable about the seder.** Many communities find the involvement of a female rabbi or cantor to be invaluable to the planning process. Alternatively, there may be a woman in your community who is particularly knowledgeable about Jewish traditions and can serve on your planning committee. A male rabbi in your community may also be interested in lending support.

**Select a seder leader, and include her on the committee.** Many women's seders are led by female cantors or rabbis; others are led by lay members of the community. It is important that the seder leader be involved in the planning process so that she will understand your community's plans and goals for the event.

**Personally recruit women to be a part of your planning committee, considering the talents of individual women in your com-**

**munity.** Rabbi Lisa Greene of North Shore Congregation Israel in Glencoe, Illinois, advises: "Capitalize on the strengths of your community members by inviting writers in your community to write and musicians to help with the songs for the seder. Tap women's interests and talents and play on your community's strengths. Many women with important skills and input to offer will become a part of the seder planning process *if* you approach them; invite their participation."

## Begin the Planning Process

Once you have gathered a group of women who would like to be a part of your planning committee, begin to structure and schedule the planning process.

**"You can never start too early,"** Margo Lazar of the Jewish Federation of Metropolitan Detroit points out. The most common suggestion offered by women's seder organizers is to begin planning far in advance of the seder. If you are holding your first seder, writing a haggadah, or hoping to hold a very large seder, you may want to begin as early as six months to a year before the event. Most large seders leave between three and eight months for planning, while smaller seders tend to allow about six weeks.

**Educate the committee about women's seders.** At a meeting early in your planning process, you may want to review some sample women's haggadahs and articles on women's seders from *The Women's Passover Companion: Women's Reflections on the Festival of Freedom* (Jewish Lights Publishing) or other resources.

**Form a study group.** Many communities find that including a formal educational component in the planning process greatly enriches the experience of organizers as well as the seder itself. Particularly if you are writing your own haggadah, consider forming a group to study the haggadah, the Book of Exodus, related midrash, and the textual and ritual innovations of other women's seders. Or, if this is too significant a time commitment, simply hold one or two study sessions for your committee. You can use *The Women's Passover Companion, The Women's Seder Sourcebook,* or the materials listed in their bibliographies to find materials for your study group.

**Delegate responsibilities by creating committees.** These committees can be responsible for specific aspects of the seder, such as publicity, rituals, decorations, haggadah, and food.

**Designate cochairs.** Having two or three women cochair the event and assigning cochairs for individual committees can make the planning process more manageable and enjoyable.

**Alternatively, create an informal, nonhierarchical planning committee** and allow women to volunteer for various responsibilities as they come up. This approach tends to work best for smaller seders and can make the planning process more collaborative.

**Keep minutes from each of your meetings.** Francine Osinoff, Eve Landau, and Jane Nusbaum of Women of Reform Judaism at the Westchester Reform Temple in New York suggest recording not only your decisions but also the reasons for them. Women who miss meetings can stay up to date by reading these minutes, and referring back to them in future years can be very useful.

**Accommodate busy schedules by doing some planning by phone and e-mail.** In New Orleans, the women gather for the first meeting about four months before the seder and then take care of the rest of the planning by e-mail. This can be ideal if it is difficult for your committee to meet in person.

## Issues to Consider Early in the Planning Process

### What Are the Goals of Our Seder?

Begin to answer important questions about the vision and goals of your seder. As the planning committee in Westchester, New York, remarked, this stage is critical: "The discussion at our first meeting—what we liked and didn't like about other seders and what we wanted to achieve—influenced all of our decisions, i.e., what kind of haggadah to choose, what kind of tables to use, how many people we could accommodate and still make people feel involved, how to ensure maximum participation, how to reclaim our role in Jewish history without being strident, how to introduce new rituals, etc." Here are some questions to consider in developing a vision for your seder:

- Who is the seder for? Are we aiming to draw women from the entire community, or do we want this event to bring together women in our specific organization or group of friends?

- What do we want women to take away from the seder? A sense of sisterhood and personal connection to other women in the community? Greater knowledge about Jewish women's history or the Jewish tradition? New rituals and readings to incorporate into their family seder?

- What are our priorities this year? For example, do we want to focus our energy on writing a community haggadah, hosting an elaborate event, or reaching out to a broad spectrum of women in the community?

It is also important to know when you need to stop discussing decisions and start implementing them. Lisa Adelman, of the Jewish Federation of Metropolitan Detroit, had her committee identify a "point of implementation." At this date (a few months before the seder) the women stopped brainstorming and began moving forward.

### When Will We Hold the Event?

**Before Passover.** Holding the seder two or more weeks before Passover enables participants to incorporate rituals and readings from the women's seder into their family seders and ensures that it will not conflict with the time-consuming work of preparing their own homes for the holiday.

**During Passover.** For many women, holding the event during the week of Passover validates its significance and better reflects its important role in their observance of the holiday. In addition, if you are on a college campus, holding the seder during Passover offers students a wonderful way to celebrate the holiday together. (However, remember that many students return home for the first few days of the holiday as well as for the weekends preceding and following it.) Also, if you hold your seder during Passover, you should remember that the first, second, and last days of Passover are *hagim* (holy days when the laws of the Sabbath apply), and you will need to be sensitive to participants who observe halakhah.

**On your organization's meeting night.** As Edith Tuber of NCJW Brooklyn B and P Branch noted, if your seder is intended for a group that meets regularly, holding your seder on this regular meeting night will ensure that members have the evening free.

**Sundays are often the most flexible day of the week.** Communities often hold their seders on Sunday, as many women have too many time constraints on weekdays.

### Where Will We Hold the Event?

As you decide where to hold the seder, consider the following questions: Is it conveniently located? Does it offer microphones or other sound equipment? Will women be able to see the seder leader from all parts of the room? Is there adequate space for dancing? Are the kitchen, bathroom, parking, and wheelchair facilities sufficient? What kind of atmosphere does it provide? Will you be allowed to decorate the room for the event?

There are several possibilities for where you can hold the seder:

**In a home.** Holding a small seder at the home of one of the women on your committee is economical and can make your seder feel more intimate.

**In your temple.** This can be a very convenient location, but you may find it more difficult to attract participants who belong to other congregations.

**In a Jewish communal space.** Many organizers find that holding the event in a JCC or Federation space helps attract a diverse group of women.

**In a reception hall.** Very large seders are often held in hotel ballrooms. This can be beautiful but is often an expensive option.

**At your Hillel, women's center, or other campus space.** Be sure to consider the ways in which the space you select may affect how comfortable various students feel attending the event.

**Change your location from year to year.** The Wilmington, Delaware, seder has been held in individual homes, the JCC, the social hall of a senior apartment complex, and the Delaware Nature Center. These different venues keep the seder vibrant and encourage new participants to attend each year. More observant Jews came to the Orthodox woman's home, unaffiliated Jews came to the JCC, senior citizens came to the apartment complex, and younger women and non-Jewish women came to the nature center.

## How Will We Create an Appropriate Space for This Ritual?
Wherever you choose to hold your women's seder, there are several ways to create a festive and warm environment for the event:

**Include decorations and ritual objects made by members of your community.** Hold a pre-seder event where women can make their own ritual objects, such as Miriam's Cups or matzah covers. Invite local artists to create Miriam's Cups that can be displayed and used at the seder.

**Ask local children to help personalize your decorations.** The planning committee in Clearwater, Florida, asked preschool and elementary school classes to make table centerpieces. In Detroit, Michigan, nursery and elementary school classes created wall decorations. The women in Worcester, Massachusetts, asked local religious schools to decorate wine glasses to be used as Miriam's Cups. This not only enhances the seder but also teaches children from a young age about women's seders and the Miriam's Cup ritual.

**Have members of your committee bring in their own ritual objects,** such as seder plates, Miriam's Cups, Elijah's Cups, and *kiddush* cups for the seder. The women of Glencoe, Illinois, found that this made the seder feel more intimate and personal.

**Fill the space with images of Jewish women from history.** Contact the Jewish Women's Archive (http://www.jwa.org) about their "Women of Valor" posters, and hang these around the room.

**Arrange the space carefully.** Do your best to set up the room so that the women can see and hear one another as well as the seder leaders and song leaders.

### What Food Will Be Served at the Seder?

Serving food at the seder is difficult but rewarding. While some communities feel that a meal is a central part of the event, others conclude that it is too expensive, time-consuming, and distracting from the ritual. There are several ways to handle food at the seder:

**Serve a catered meal.** Although this is expensive, many organizers find that the meal is important to participants and therefore hire a catering service. Consider whether your participants will need a kosher meal, and ask around in your community to ensure that you get a reliable caterer.

**Serve a meal prepared by volunteers.** It can be fun to prepare the food as a group. In Worcester, Massachusetts, the planning committee meets in a committee member's home the night before the seder, eats dinner together, and then prepares the foods to be served at the seder.

**Have a potluck meal.** This can help keep the cost of your seder low and allows every woman to contribute to the event.

**Serve only the ritual foods.** Hire a caterer, or have organizers prepare only the foods directly involved in the seder: wine, spring water, *karpas*, salt water, matzah, *maror*, oranges, *charoset*, roasted eggs, and roasted shankbones (or beets).

**Provide light refreshments.** The Kansas City seder serves dessert as well as the seder plate foods. Some communities provide light foods such as *gefilte* fish, hors d'oeuvres, and dessert with coffee. Other organizers serve a signature dish. For example, the women of Latham, New York, make a *charoset* with oranges in celebration of their special seder.

Some other things to keep in mind about food at the seder:

**Remember that the meal can take up a lot of time.** Account for serving and eating the meal in your estimation of how long the seder will last.

**Be clear about what food will be served.** If you are not providing dinner and your seder is being held during dinner hours, inform attendants that a meal will not be a part of the event.

**Be aware of participants' *kashrut* observance.** This will affect your decisions about what food to serve, which caterer to use, and where the food can be prepared.

**Use egg matzah.** There is a halakhic restriction on eating matzah for the thirty days before Passover begins. To avoid violating it, the Yale Women's Seder uses egg matzah.

**Consider using a buffet.** Many communities prefer this solution, as no one is responsible for serving the food at the seder.

**Serve "Passover-style" food.** If your seder is held before Pesach, it is not necessary to avoid serving *chametz*. However, you probably don't want to have challah at your seder! Providing a meal that is kosher for Passover or Passover-style will make the seder feel more authentic.

**Incorporate Passover recipes from all Jewish cultures.** Many communities include a variety of styles of *charoset* at their seders. Consider preparing different versions of the other ritual foods as well, including *karpas* and *maror*. You may find that the women in your community have very different traditions for many of these foods.

**Make a plan for dealing with leftovers.** Arrange in advance to drop off leftover food at a local charity that feeds the needy, or inquire about donating it to the temple or facility where the event is being held. To avoid being wasteful, the Worcester, Massachusetts, seder leaders note how much food is left over after the seder so that they can adjust their purchases accordingly the following year.

### *How Will We Incorporate Music into the Seder?*

Many organizers feel that music is a central part of the ritual and suggest it be a priority as you plan the seder.

**Have live music at your seder.** This can be extremely energizing and will encourage the women at your seder to join together in song and dance.

**Incorporate a variety of contemporary Jewish women's music into the seder.** You can refer to the Bibliography and Resources section of this book for information about many musicians who have written music appropriate for women's seders.

**Reserve a good song leader early in your planning process.** The leader should be familiar with the songs you would like to include and able to contribute her own ideas for music to the seder. It is also important for her to be skilled at leading and energizing participants. If you aren't sure how to find a song leader, you might check for musicians through a local college. Union of American Hebrew Congregations regional offices also keep lists of available song leaders in the United States as well as several international locations: http://keshernet.com.

**Use high-quality sound equipment.** This may be available at your facility, or you may have to rent or borrow it. Song leader Peri Smilow suggests that you make sure your song leader has a microphone if you have even a medium-sized women's seder.

**Consider including a choir of women.** Congregational groups often feature women from the temple choir; other seders simply bring together a group interested in singing to perform during the seder.

**Bring, or ask participants to bring, percussive instruments,** such as drums, maracas, and tambourines, advises Peri Smilow. You can purchase "eggs" (small percussive instruments) at any music store for a few dollars each. Alternatively, drums, guitars, and table-banging add enthusiasm and spirit to any chant. Cantor Lorel Zar-Kessler of Lexington, Massachusetts, also suggests reading or singing Psalm 150 to help you introduce the importance of these instruments at your seder.

**Provide lyric sheets for all the music that will be sung at the seder** so that everyone can join in the singing. Choose music that will be easy to learn and sing.

### *How Large Should the Seder Be?*

Many women's seder organizers have found it helpful to address the question of size early so they can then create a budget and make appropriate choices about food, location, and the ritual itself. For example, readings and activities that work in small groups often don't work as well with large groups, and vice versa. When thinking about the desired size of your seder, you may want to consider the following:

**A large seder can be very powerful** both visually, as the women gather together, and audibly, as they sing and pray in unison. The energy generated by hundreds of women at these seders is inspiring.

**A small seder provides intimacy.** Everyone can participate in the ritual, and many organizers feel that such participation is crucial. Attendants also often have more of an opportunity to form connections with one another.

## *What Is the Desired Length of the Seder?*

**Decide in advance on the length of your seder.** Most seders are planned to last no longer than three hours, including the meal. Some communities find that a shorter event is more practical for their community.

**Plan how you will end the seder.** Some communities complete the entire seder, including rituals that usually follow the meal, before the meal. Some simply omit these later portions of the ritual and end the seder with the meal or with song and dance. Other communities follow the traditional order and resume the ritual after the meal. Decide in advance what you will do, so that the seder comes to an energetic and formal conclusion.

**Stick to your desired length at the event.** Keep a detailed schedule of the seder, marking readings that are the highest and lowest priority. The women of Westchester, New York, found this particularly helpful: If they began to run behind schedule, they immediately knew which sections of the seder to cut.

**Include the time that the seder will end on invitations and publicity** so that participants can plan their schedules accordingly.

## *How Will We Fund the Seder?*

Hosting a women's seder can be costly. Many women's seder leaders find it a challenge to balance the desire for a beautiful meal, haggadah, and atmosphere with their desire to keep the ticket price of the seder reasonable. Here are several strategies for funding the event while keeping costs down:

**Create a budget.** Principal items include food and drink, room rental, payment for a song leader and seder leader, copying or purchasing the haggadah, invitations, publicity, and objects for the rituals (such as candles).

**Set a ticket price that will cover the cost of the event.** This is one simple way to pay for your seder. Ticket prices generally range from

$5 to $50. Be sure to set aside funds to assist women who cannot afford the ticket price. The Ma'yan women's seder reservation form invites women to become a "seder sister." By paying twice the ticket price, seder sisters make it possible for a woman who would not otherwise be able to afford the ticket to attend. You may want to recognize women who have made this type of contribution in your haggadah.

**Seek outside funding** to ensure that the event is affordable for all. The simplest way to do this is to enlist the financial support of organizational cosponsors. Local chapters of women's organizations, women's divisions of local Jewish Community Centers, Jewish Federations, or synagogues may be willing to cosponsor your seder and underwrite a part of the cost. You may want to ask these organizations for monetary contributions, or you can request that they cover specific costs for your seder, such as purchasing advertisements or sponsoring women who cannot afford to attend. Some communities have successfully secured corporate and individual donations, but if you plan to fundraise this way, you will need to begin six months to a year in advance.

**Ask for in-kind donations.** Local businesses such as grocery stores, florists, or copy shops may be willing to donate items or services. In Clearwater, Florida, the community donated the net proceeds from the seder to provide Passover meals for the needy. Grocery stores were more enthusiastic about donating to the seder because it was also a charity event.

**If your seder generates a profit, put the proceeds to a good use.** Put extra funds towards a *tzedakah* project such as a local charity or a project related to Jewish women. The women in Orlando, Florida, used profits to fund future women's seders in their community.

### What Haggadah Will We Use?

The process of putting together a women's haggadah can be an incredible learning experience for all involved. Creating a unique haggadah also allows organizers to personalize the seder for their community.

However, particularly in your first year of planning, many women's seder organizers insist that writing a haggadah can feel like reinventing the wheel. Because it is such a time-consuming endeavor, many communities use an already published work, supplement an existing haggadah, or compile one from a variety of existing sources.

**Read through several women's and traditional haggadahs.** Arielle Derby of the Smith College Hillel in Northampton, Massachusetts, suggests: "Do your homework! Read every women's or other non-traditional haggadah you can find to see what works for you. Really think about what aspects of Passover make the ritual meaningful to you and your community." This will help you get a sense of what you do and do not like and prepare you to make decisions about your own haggadah.

**Use *The Women's Seder Sourcebook*** to find readings and rituals for your haggadah, learn about each part of the seder, or gather ideas about writing original material.

**If you plan to write your own haggadah, create a haggadah committee.** In some committees, each woman takes responsibility for writing material for particular sections of the seder. Alternatively, you may want to form smaller study groups or pairs within the seder planning committee. Each group can find or write several readings for your haggadah based on their research and discussions.

**If you plan to use a previously written haggadah, it is also helpful to have a committee** to choose a haggadah that represents the interests and needs of your community.

**Make the haggadah committee as diverse as the population you hope will attend your seder.** Particularly because they will be dealing with liturgy, try to include women of different movements in this group.

**Hold study sessions with your rabbi.** The women of Glencoe, Illinois, studied traditional sources with their rabbi to inform their decisions and the material they wrote for the haggadah.

**If you plan to use a previously written haggadah, consider supplementing it** with writings from women in your community. Marilyn Doore from Congregation Beth Sholom in Anchorage, Alaska, advises: "We added some of our own readings because they were more relevant to our members—poetry and prose, stories from our own lives."

**Use new material to vary your haggadah from year to year.** You can easily and inexpensively alter the haggadah by including a different insert sheet each year. Change the theme of the seder and add a handful of readings on that theme, vary the four questions or the women honored with the four cups, or add different participatory rituals or activities to the seder. But pay attention to what participants mention as favorite moments so that you can include them each year.

**Allow participants to take their haggadahs home** so they can incorporate new readings and rituals into their family seders.

## Publicity for Your Seder

Because publicity is so important to the success of large community-wide women's seders, be sure to begin early.

Included here are several suggestions for undertaking the most effective publicity effort possible.

### Use Personalized Invitations and Publicity Whenever Possible

**Send "save the date" cards** to women in your community far in advance of the seder. Ask your cosponsors or other local Jewish organizations if you can add these cards to one of their mailings or use their mailing lists.

**Encourage women who are involved to talk up the event.** Many organizers said that word of mouth was their most effective method of publicizing the seder.

**Call women who have attended your seder in past years.** Myrna Kasser of the United Synagogue of Hoboken in New Jersey has found reminding past participants particularly effective because these women are the most enthusiastic about the seder: "If someone comes once, it's hard to stay away!"

**Send personal invitations.** This kind of personal touch is very effective and lets women know that their presence is important to the seder. In Worcester, Massachusetts, organizers take lots of pictures at their seder. The next year, they match invitations with any photographs taken of the recipient and enclose a personal note as well.

**Use table hostesses.** Table hostesses volunteer to "host" a particular table at the seder. They are responsible for inviting several individual women to join them at their table. As Beverly Jacobson of the Women's Division of Jewish Federation of Kansas remarked, this attracts participants and makes women feel personally invited to the seder.

**A week or two before the event, send a postcard reminder to participants.** On this postcard you can also note things participants should bring, such as Miriam's Cups or tambourines.

**Host a pre-seder event that will spark enthusiasm** for your women's seder. Rabbi Laurie Katz Braun of the Westchester women's seder holds a workshop in which women make their own Miriam's Cup a few weeks before the seder. Women who attend can bring the Miriam's Cup they created to use at the seder. Alternatively, Stacie Funk and Evie Raphael of the Women of Temple Judea Sisterhood in California hold a *charoset* party the night before the seder. Each woman who attends provides her own recipe for *charoset,* and everyone helps make each dish.

### Publicize Widely in Your Local Community

**Mention the event on your website.** The women in Orlando, Florida, also ask sponsoring organizations to do the same, and they have found this to be an invaluable publicity tool.

**Post flyers around the community:** at the JCC, Jewish Federation, synagogues, and—to reach an unaffiliated population—community centers, stores, and public areas.

**Get media coverage before the seder.** Articles written about your seder in advance of the event publicize it at no cost. Several weeks before the seder, send a press release to local Jewish and secular newspapers as well as to local radio and television stations. The women of Clearwater, Florida, suggest that you make sure the articles or other publicity notices run at least one week before your reservation deadline.

### Capitalize on Existing Publicity Channels in Your Community

**Ask local JCCs, Jewish Federations, and synagogues to mention the event** in their bulletins and e-mail lists as well as on their websites.

**Ask sponsoring organizations to take responsibility for publicizing the event to their membership.**

**Ask local rabbis to announce the seder from the *bimah*** for several weeks preceding the event.

### Include Pertinent Information on Your Publicity Materials

**Advertise who will be leading the seder.** If your leader is a local rabbi or cantor, or another prominent member of the community, include this in your publicity.

**Bring a featured speaker to your seder.** Advertise this speaker in order to give women another reason to attend.

**Be clear that no woman will be turned away for financial reasons.** Advertise a "recommended ticket price" or make the seder "pay what you can."

### Reach Out to Special Populations

**Young women.** Post flyers at college Hillels, Jewish day schools, and Hebrew schools; include young women in the planning process; and offer a student discount on the ticket price. It can also be effective to hold a pre-seder event for young women. The Detroit seder held a brunch for teenagers a few weeks before the seder. They went to a pottery store, where they painted matzah plates, seder plates, and Miriam's Cups.

**Women in need.** Ask an organization such as Jewish Family Services to invite clients to the seder, as Randi Kraus did in Clearwater, Florida: "This year we asked Gulfcoast Jewish Family Services to invite some of their women clients as our guests. These are women who are clients because of financial needs, family problems, or medical problems and could use a connection to the Jewish community. Without identifying these women to the other guests, we made sure that they were sitting with people we knew would make them feel welcome." Be sure there is an easy and confidential way for women who cannot afford the cost of the seder to speak to someone about attending.

**Women not yet connected to the Jewish community.** Advertise in secular media, and post flyers in shopping centers, libraries, parks, and other public places. In Houston, Texas, Beverly Sufian was "amazed as to how many unaffiliated women come to the women's seder—these are people who are seldom seen at other Jewish events. It shows that people seek out events such as these where there is a feeling of community and continuity."

**Men.** Most women's seders choose not to invite men, and those that do find that few choose to attend. However, if you want men to be a part of your seder, clearly communicate on all your publicity that they are welcome to join you. The Smith College seder chose to call the event a feminist seder, rather than a women's seder, to suggest that it was open to all feminists—male and female.

**Children.** While some communities find it meaningful to include children old enough to sit through and understand the events at the seder, many insist that this is a time for women to join together and experience the seder free of their parental duties. Whatever you decide, clearly explain the policy on the invitation. If you feel that excluding children will be a major obstacle for many women, consider offering child care at the facility or coordinating your event with a Passover event for children at your congregation or community center.

**Women from the community surrounding your campus.** If you are holding a campus seder, you may want to use this as a time to connect with women from the wider community. Invite these women, or cosponsor the seder with a local Jewish women's group or community organization. Or invite teenage girls from the local synagogue or religious school.

## Creating a Meaningful Experience for Participants

Almost all of the women's seder organizers who responded to our survey commented that one of the biggest challenges they faced was creating an intimate, participatory event. And when we asked organizers what they and other attendants found to be the most memorable part of the seder, many spoke about a participatory moment such as a ritual or time for discussion.

While some communities make an effort to keep the seder small, many women's seders grow in size each year. Particularly for these groups, it is crucial to ensure that everyone feels that she has participated in a ritual and not merely observed a performance. As Dorothy Flippen of Wilmington, Delaware, advises, "The participation of those in attendance is most important. They have to have input at the seder to experience it." Women's seder organizers use several different strategies to make the seder a personal, participatory experience:

**Capitalize on and celebrate the unique assets of your community in all aspects of the seder.** Many seder organizers echo the comments of Lisa Adelman of the Jewish Federation of Metropolitan Detroit: "If it's going to be special, it should be a program with a thumbprint of the community hosting it."

**Consider opening the seder with a brief learning session on a text related to the holiday.** The Plano, Texas, women's seder found that beginning with a short study session on the Song of Songs, led by the seder leader, set an appropriate tone for the evening and actively involved the women from the start.

**Perform rituals at individual tables.** Although it is generally more time efficient to have the seder leader perform rituals for the group, women will feel more engaged if they themselves perform rituals such as candlelighting, the breaking of the middle matzah, and handwashing. Be sure to account generously for the time it will take to perform these rituals.

**Bring women together in song and dance.** Include music throughout the seder to set a celebratory tone. Cantor Lorel Zar-Kessler advises that "even the simplest *hallelu/Hodu LaShem* melody offers opportunities for a stand-up–sit-down game that will enliven your table and your guests."

**Make sure that as many women as possible participate in the readings.** There are several ways to do this. The Minneapolis women's seder highlights one reading in each haggadah. Every woman then has a highlighted passage to read aloud at the seder. At the NCJW Brooklyn seder, the seder leader says the blessings in Hebrew, and participants repeat them in English. The Westchester seder names each table for a biblical woman, and the rabbi calls on tables to read parts of the haggadah. At the Ma'yan seder, odd-numbered and even-numbered tables read the haggadah responsively. Large seders often provide the leader or someone else with a microphone who can read along with the tables so that they can be heard clearly.

**In your invitations, encourage women to begin thinking about the seder before the event itself.** The Yale Women's Seder asks participants to include with their RSVP a question that they will be bringing with them to the seder. You can compile a list of these questions and read them aloud at the seder, choose a few to discuss, or select four to serve as your seder's "Four Questions." Alternatively, Cantor Lorel Zar-Kessler suggests that each participant be asked to bring a favorite song of hope, praise, or delight with her. During *hallel,* ask everyone to share a song with the group. Your seder can create a unique, informal *hallel* of rejoicing and thanksgiving.

**Plan opportunities for discussion.** Women will feel more engaged if they meet and talk with other participants. Set aside a time for discussion at individual tables early in the seder or over dinner.

**Assign individual roles.** Approach individual women about leading one of the blessings or readings or performing one of the rituals.

**Assign parts to small groups of family members or friends.** For many women, one of the most memorable aspects of the seder is sharing the experience with a mother, sister, cousin, or close friend. Beverly Sufian notes that it is particularly meaningful to watch three generations of a family perform a ritual, such as candlelighting, together.

**Honor women who have made a special contribution to your community with special parts.** Make the event a celebration not only of women from Jewish history but also of the women in your community.

**Ask four women to prepare speeches for the Four Cups.** Beverly Jacobson of the Women's Division of the Jewish Federation of Kansas suggests that you choose four women, preferably ranging in age, to present four short (two- to four-minute) monologues, one to follow each cup of wine. Ask each woman to speak on the same topic, such as "A Passover Memory" or "My Jewish Heroines."

**Dedicate each of the Four Cups to a local woman** who has contributed to your community. You can ask seder participants to help with these dedications by speaking about the important roles these four women have played.

**Enable each participant to speak about an important woman in her life** during the Four Cups. Ask participants to share stories about a family member, teacher, mentor, or friend, and dedicate one of the cups of wine to her. In a medium-sized or large seder, this can be done at individual tables; at a smaller seder, you may want to devote time for women to share with the entire group.

**Encourage women to participate in asking the Four Questions.**
This section of the seder is among the most familiar for many women.
The NCJW Brooklyn seder invites all who are the youngest children
in their families to stand and sing the Four Questions together in
Hebrew. Alternatively, the Hadassah Nurses Council in Irvine, California, asks women from each of the countries represented at their
seder to recite the Four Questions in their native language.

**Assign table leaders in advance of the seder.** They can welcome
guests and facilitate conversation and activities at the table. If rituals are
performed at the tables, the leader can start the pouring of wine and
water, and ask someone to perform rituals such as breaking the middle matzah and lighting the candles.

**Set up the room so that the women can see each other.** Many organizers have found that this is very important to participants' experience.
The Westchester women's seder set up one large U-shaped table to seat
all one hundred twenty participants. The women's seder of Congregation Rodef Sholom in San Rafael, California, sets up the tables in a
large circle.

**Balance your seder with light moments as well as serious ones.**
Your seder will have many serious and moving moments, but this tone
and intensity are hard to sustain for two or three hours. Seder organizers advise that humor is important and can help make women feel
a part of the event. The women of Providence, Rhode Island, suggest
that your seder leader should help everyone in the room find the joy
in each moment of the seder.

## Other Details for the Event

**Expect last-minute reservations.** Be prepared to receive many
reservations during the week before the seder. Set aside extra space
for walk-ins. If you are holding a small seder and need to know how
many women will attend, consider calling women to ask about their
plans.

**Provide relevant organizational information at the seder,** particularly about those groups sponsoring the seder, as this event often draws new members into sisterhoods or other groups. Recognizing that the seder is also an opportunity to reach hundreds of women in the community, many seders feature a table with information about events, health and social services, domestic violence hotlines, and other community resources for women.

**"The pace of the seder needs to move, and the leader must be flexible and sense how the women are feeling,"** the women of Worcester, Massachusetts, have found. If women are enjoying a particular dance or discussion, it is not necessary to rush the seder along. However, if they seem hungry or bored, a seder leader should be flexible enough to skip or substitute readings.

**Have a clean-up plan.** Some seders have set-up and clean-up committees. Smaller seders can simply ask everyone to help. If everyone helps clear the tables and clean the room, it will make the job much easier.

**Incorporate a *tzedakah* project.** Give a portion of the proceeds to a *tzedakah* project and have a venue at the seder for women to donate further, such as *tzedakah* boxes on each table. Or ask participants to bring canned food or clothes with them to the seder to be donated to a local food bank or other nonprofit organization.

**Create a Passover recipe book for participants.** Before the seder, ask guests to send you a favorite Passover recipe. Combine these recipes into a packet to give to each participant.

**Consider finding a partner community in Israel.** This unique project was undertaken in Detroit, Michigan: "The women in our partnership region in Israel planned their first women's seder this year. We shared information with each other and really weaved each other's seders into our own." The women in Israel featured reflections from the women in Michigan, and vice versa.

**Ask seder participants to fill out evaluations.** This will be invaluable in planning future women's seders.

**Take lots of pictures.** They can be useful in advertising for future seders. And surely, you and your community will want to have a record of this memorable event!

# Notes

## Preface

1. Hellman, Lillian. *An Unfinished Woman: A Memoir* (New York: Little, Brown and Company, 1969).

## Introduction

1. From "Miriam's Song: A Womanly Strain in the Song at the Sea" in *Beshalach: The Chassidic Masters*, a project of the Chabad Lubavitch World Headquarters, produced by the Lubavitch New Service. Accessed at http://www.chabadonline.com.

## Candlelighting

1. *Tkhines* are an important resource for learning about the religious lives of our foremothers. While many *tkhines* were written by women, and many others by men for women, the majority of these texts, including the *tkhine* translated here, are anonymous. Nonetheless, Yiddish-speaking women loved these prayers, whoever wrote them. Women's conceptions of God and of themselves as Jewish women, their hopes for the redemption of the people of Israel, and their prayers for the health and prosperity of the family were all shaped by and expressed through these devotions.

2. As in many *tkhines*, this text has a place for the woman herself to address God, in her own name and as the daughter of her mother. Furthermore, this prayer recognizes the tremendous effort and expense involved in preparing for Passover. If we remember the widespread poverty of Jews in Eastern Europe, we realize how difficult it was to meet the expenses of the special foods for the holiday, and the burden of both preparation and household budget management usually fell to women. Note as well the way in which the text relates many aspects of Passover preparations to wider themes: Eating matzah, for example, is connected to the hope to be saved from hunger throughout the year.

287

### The Four Cups

1. It is only since the 1970s, and not even entirely so today, that the bat mitzvah parallels the bar mitzvah in what it looks like. At Judith Kaplan's bat mitzvah in 1922, her father received the *aliyah,* and he read from the Torah. She sat in the front row during this part of the service. By the 1950s, some Reconstructionist congregations held bat mitzvah ceremonies during which females were called to the Torah. In 1950, the Society for the Advancement of Judaism finally voted to start calling women to the Torah independently, that is, on occasions other than a bat mitzvah.

### *Karpas*

1. For a more complete telling of Idit's story to complement this reading, refer to Sandy Eisenberg Sasso's chapter "The Open Door: The Tale of Idit and the Passover Paradox" in *The Women's Passover Companion,* the companion volume to this book.

### Miriam's Cup

1. For more information on the history and evolution of the Miriam's Cup ritual, refer to Vanessa Ochs' "Setting a Cup for Miriam" in *The Women's Passover Companion,* the companion volume to this book.
2. The ritual was adapted from a reading by Matia Rania Angelou and Janet Berkenfield.
3. *Moment* Magazine, August, 1997, 26–27.
4. Eliahu KiTov, *The Book of Our Heritage,* 62.
5. 4Q364: 6, 2.
6. *Ma'aseh Rokeach* 59.
7. *Kol Bo* 41.
8. *Tkhine* for Shabbat before Rosh Chodesh Iyar.
9. *Maor V'Shemesh, B'shalakh.*

### *Ha Lachma Anya*

1. Midrash Psalms 118:17.

### *Avadim Hayinu*

1. In the haggadah, the phrase appears in Hebrew, whereas in the Hillel story, the phrase appears in Aramaic. But the literal meaning of both is "Go and learn."

### The Four Children

1. BT *Sotah* 11b.

### Go Forth and Learn

1. BT *Sotah* 11b.
2. *Midrash V'eleh Toldot Aharon u'Moshe, Otzar Midrashim.*
3. Ginsberg, Louis. *Legends of the Jews, Vol. II* (Philadelphia: Jewish Publication Society, 1968), 271.
4. Ibid., 270.
5. *Yalkut Shimoni, Parshat Lech Lecha*, 64.
6. *Exodus Rabbah* 1:13 and 1:15.
7. BT *Megillah* 13a.
8. *Exodus Rabbah* 1:23.
9. BT *Megillah* 14a.
10. *Song of Songs Rabbah* 2:15.
11. BT *Megillah* 15b.
12. BT *Sotah* 11b.
13. "Then Sarah treated her harshly, and she ran away from her."
14. "The Egyptians dealt harshly with us and oppressed us; they imposed heavy labor upon us."

### The Ten Plagues

1. Unpublished data from the Vital Statistics System, Centers for Disease Control and Prevention, National Center for Health Statistics, 2000. Accessed at http://www.bradycampain.org/facts/issuebriefs/kidsandguns.asp.

### B'chol Dor Vador

1. Center for Reproductive Law and Policy, "The Bush Global Gag Rule: Endangering Women's Health, Free Speech and Democracy." April, 2001. Accessed at http://www.crlp.org.
2. From "Buffalo Soldier," written by Bob Marley and N. G. Williams.

### Maror

1. UNAIDS Report on the Global HIV/AIDS Epidemic 2002, 8.

### The Orange on the Seder Plate

1. For a more in-depth explanation of the complex history of the orange on the seder plate, please refer to Susannah Heschel's "The Orange on the Seder Plate" in *The Women's Passover Companion*, the companion volume to this book.

### Barekh

1. *The Journey Continues: The Ma'yan Passover Haggadah*, edited by Tamara Cohen, features a grace after meals with feminized God language.

### Elijah's Cup

1. This prayer was written by members of a liturgical task force developed by the National Jewish Center for Learning and Leadership, then under the direction of Rabbi Irving (Yitz) Greenberg.
2. For a more complete telling of Idit's story to complement this reading, refer to Sandy Eisenberg Sasso's chapter "The Open Door: The Tale of Idit and the Passover Paradox" in *The Women's Passover Companion*, the companion volume to this book.
3. *Bashert* (Yiddish): inevitable, (pre)destined.

### *Hallel*

1. BT *Pesachim* 117a.
2. BT *Pesachim* 85b.

# Glossary

**Adonai** A commonly used Hebrew name for God, often translated as "Lord." "Adonai" is a pronounceable substitute for the tetragrammaton, the four-letter Name of God, written YHVH.

*afikomen* Lit. "dessert" (Greek). Half of the middle matzah at the seder, which is set aside to be eaten at the conclusion of the meal. It is customary for young children to hide the *afikomen* in the hope that the leader of the seder will reward them with a gift if they return it.

*agunah* Lit. "chained woman" (Hebrew). A woman whose marriage has ended and who has not been given a *get* (divorce) from her husband. Traditionally, only a man can initiate a Jewish divorce. Plural: *agunot.*

**Aramean** A person of the tribe of Aram, referred to in Deuteronomy 26:5; a verse recited at the seder: "My father was a wandering Aramean and with just a few people he went down to Egypt and sojourned there. And he became a great nation, mighty and numerous." The Aramean is traditionally taken to refer to the patriarch Jacob, who lived in Aram for a while.

*Arov* Locusts; the fourth plague with which God struck Egypt (Exodus 8:16–28).

**Ashkenaz** The Hebrew word for Germany; term used to refer to Jews whose families come from eastern France, Germany, and Eastern Europe. Plural: Ashkenazim.

*Avadim hayinu* Lit. "We were slaves" (Hebrew). The opening words of the *maggid* section of the haggadah, which chronicles the history of the Jewish people's enslavement and redemption.

*Ayl na r'fanah la* Lit. "God please heal her" (Hebrew) (Numbers 12:13). Moses' prayer to God to heal his sister Miriam, who was afflicted with leprosy.

*Barad* Hail; the seventh plague with which God struck Egypt (Exodus 9:13–35).

*barekh* Lit. "bless" (Hebrew). The twelfth of the fourteen parts of the seder, consisting of the Grace After Meals.

*bashert* From *sher*, the Yiddish word meaning "to cut," as in "the one cut out for you." 1. One's future mate. According to the Talmud (*Sotah* 2a), a heavenly voice calls out a destined soul mate for each person forty days before birth. 2. Pre-destined.

*bat* Daughter of (Hebrew).

bat mitzvah Lit. "daughter of the commandment" (Hebrew). 1. A girl who has reached the age of twelve or thirteen and is consequently considered an adult according to Jewish law and obligated to observe all the commandments. 2. The ceremony marking this milestone.

*bimah* Lit. "pulpit" (Hebrew). The raised platform in a synagogue from which the rabbi or leader conducts the prayer service.

*B'nai Yisrael* Lit. "the sons of Israel" (Hebrew). Biblical term for the Jewish people.

*bracha* Blessing (Hebrew). Plural: *brachot*.

*bubbe* Grandmother (Yiddish).

*chalutz* Pioneer (Hebrew). Plural: *chalutzot*.

*chametz* Lit. "leaven" (Hebrew). A grain product that has risen for eighteen minutes or more and is consequently prohibited on Passover.

*charoset* A mixture of apples, dates, nuts, wine, and spices placed on the seder plate and eaten on Passover as a symbol of the mortar that the Israelites used to make bricks in Egypt. Recipes vary in Jewish communities around the world.

*chasen* Cantor (Hebrew).

Chasid An adherent of Chassidism, a movement of Orthodox Judaism initiated in White Russia by the Baal Shem Tov (1698–1760).

*Chesed* Lovingkindness (Hebrew).

*Choshech* Darkness; The ninth plague with which God struck Egypt (Exodus 10:21–29).

*chuppah* Lit. "canopy" or "covering" (Hebrew). The *chuppah* is a canopy held up by four poles under which a Jewish wedding ceremony is conducted. The term can also be used to refer to the wedding ceremony itself.

*conversos* Lit. "converts" (Spanish). Jews who converted to Christianity to save their lives or livelihoods during the Spanish Inquisition, beginning in the fourteenth century.

*Dam* Blood; the first plague with which God struck Egypt (Exodus 7:14–25).

*daven* To pray (Yiddish).

*Dayeinu* Lit. "It is enough" (Hebrew). Title of a Passover song chronicling God's beneficent actions on behalf of the Israelites, beginning with the Exodus from Egypt and culminating in the still-awaited rebuilding of the Temple in Jerusalem.

*Dever* Cattle disease; the fifth plague with which God struck Egypt (Exodus 9:1–7).

*Eheyeh Asher Eheyeh* Lit. "I will be what I will be" (Hebrew). Name with which God identifies Himself to Moses at the burning bush in Exodus 3:14.

*Eliahu HaNavi* Elijah the prophet; a prophet of the northern kingdom of Israel in the ninth century B.C.E., who ascended to heaven in a whirlwind with a chariot of fire (II Kings 2:11). According to tradition, Elijah comes to each Jewish household on the night of the Passover seder to offer his protection to the household, and thus a fifth cup of Elijah is placed on the seder table. Since Elijah is the forerunner of the Messiah, this cup represents God's future redemption of the Jewish people.

*emunah* Belief (Hebrew).

*genug* Enough (Yiddish).

*Ha lachma anya* Lit. "This is the bread of affliction" (Aramaic). Opening line of a paragraph recited at the beginning of the *maggid* section of the haggadah, in which the seder participants invite those who are hungry or needy to partake of the food on the table.

**haggadah** Lit. "saga" or "tale." The haggadah is the text of the Passover seder and tells the story of the Exodus from Egypt. It is a collection of passages from the Bible, Mishnah, and rabbinic midrash as well as prayers, hymns, and blessings. It was likely compiled during the time of the Second Temple, but the earliest surviving complete haggadah is from tenth-century Babylonia.

**halakhah** Lit. "way" or "path" (Hebrew). Jewish law, established by rabbinic authority.

*hallel* Lit. "praise" (Hebrew). A group of Psalms praising God, remembering the Exodus, and expressing hope in God's salvation. *Hallel* is recited on festivals and new moon days, and it is included in the haggadah as the thirteenth step of the seder.

*haredi* Lit. "one who trembles" (Hebrew). Term used to describe ultra-Orthodox Jews who typically minimize their contact with the secular world.

*hineini* Lit. "Here I am" (Hebrew). This word is Moses' response when God calls out to him at the burning bush (Exodus 3:2–3).

**Iyar** The second month of the Jewish calendar, occurring in April/May.

**kabbalah** Lit. "receiving" (Hebrew). Jewish mysticism, which flourished in southern France and Spain in the thirteenth century.

**kaddish** Lit. "holy" (Aramaic). Prayer extolling the greatness of God, recited by the cantor to mark the end of a section of liturgy, and by mourners following the death of a relative.

*kadesh* Lit. "sanctify" (Hebrew). First of the fourteen parts of the seder, consisting of the *kiddush*.

*kadosh* Holy (Hebrew).

*karpas* Leafy green vegetable, usually parsley or celery, placed on the seder plate and eaten at the seder to symbolize the freshness of spring. In the third of the fourteen parts of the seder, the *karpas* is dipped in salt water and eaten.

**kibbutz** Lit. "community" (Hebrew). A kibbutz is an egalitarian community, usually agricultural, where there is no private wealth, everyone shares responsibility for the welfare of all, and decisions are made by majority vote. The first kibbutz was founded in 1909; approximately 120,500 people live in 269 kibbutzim across Israel today. Plural: kibbutzim.

*kiddush* Lit. "sanctification" (Hebrew). Prayer of sanctification recited over a cup of wine on the Sabbath and festivals. The recitation of the *kiddush* is the first of the fourteen steps of the seder.

*Kinim* Lice; the third plague with which God struck Egypt (Exodus 8:12–15).

*korech* Lit. "bind" or "combine" (Hebrew). Sandwich of matzah, *charoset*, and *maror* eaten as the ninth step of the seder. This practice was initiated by Hillel in the first century B.C.E.

*Kos Miryam* Miriam's Cup (Hebrew). A recent Passover custom of placing an additional goblet filled with water next to Elijah's Cup on the seder table to honor the talmudic story of Miriam's well, which provided water as the Israelites traveled through the desert, just as Miriam nurtured the people throughout their journey.

*Kotel* Lit. "wall" (Hebrew). The western section of the outer wall of the Temple Mount, the only remaining structure of the Second Temple in Jerusalem, which was destroyed by the Romans in 70 C.E. The Kotel has become a site of pilgrimage and is considered the holiest place in the world for Jews.

*kugel* A dish resembling a pudding or casserole often eaten on the Sabbath and holidays. Most commonly a sweet noodle pudding, a *kugel* may also be made with matzah, shredded potato, or farfel.

*lechem oni* Lit. "bread of affliction" (Hebrew). Term used in the Bible (Deuteronomy 16:3) and the haggadah to refer to the matzah eaten on

Passover, which is a symbol of freedom, enslavement, and the humility of a person not puffed up with egotism.

*Lo dayeinu* Lit. "It is not enough" (Hebrew). An allusion to the popular Passover song *Dayeinu.*

*L'shanah ha-ba'ah b'Yerushalayim* Lit. "Next year in Jerusalem" (Hebrew). The closing words of the seder, with which the participants express the hope that next year will bring the messianic redemption and the return of the Jewish people to Jerusalem.

*machzor* Lit. "cycle" (Hebrew). Festival prayer book; most commonly used to designate the Rosh Hashanah and Yom Kippur prayer book.

*maggid* Lit. "One who tells" (Hebrew). The fifth and longest of the fourteen parts of the seder, consisting of the retelling of the Exodus narrative. The *maggid* includes the *mah nishtanah,* the four children, the Ten Plagues, *Dayeinu,* and the second cup of wine.

*Mah nishtanah* Lit. "What changes" or "How is [it] different" (Hebrew). Opening two words of a famous passage in the haggadah which consists of the Four Questions recited by the youngest person at the seder. The child asks the reason for some of the holiday's more unusual rituals, and the rest of the haggadah is devoted to answering these questions.

*Mahatanim* Relative by marriage (Yiddish).

*Makat bechorot* Lit. "Striking of the firstborns" (Hebrew). The tenth plague with which God struck Egypt, in which God killed all the first-born Egyptians at midnight on the eve of the Exodus (Exodus 12:29).

*Makot* Lit. "Plagues" (Hebrew). The ten plagues with which God struck Egypt (Exodus 8–12).

manna Lit. "portion" (Hebrew). The food miraculously given to the Israelites on their journey in the wilderness.

*maror* Bitter herbs (Hebrew). The bitter horseradish eaten during the seder to remind Jews of the bitter enslavement of the Israelites in Egypt. The eating of the *maror* constitutes the eighth of the fourteen steps of the seder.

*marrano* Lit. "swine" (old Spanish). Derogatory term for Jewish converts to Christianity who retained a secret adherence to Judaism during the Spanish Inquisition in the fourteenth to eighteenth centuries. The *marranos* would sometimes descend into their cellars to conduct Jewish rituals such as the Passover seder.

matzah Unleavened bread (Hebrew). Flat bread made of flour and water, eaten on Passover in memory of the unleavened bread prepared by the Israelites during their hasty flight from Egypt, when they did not have time to wait for their bread to rise.

*maycha'la d'asuta* Lit. "bread of healing" (Aramaic). Term used in the *Zohar* to describe the matzah on the second night of Passover.

*maych'la d'mhaymenuta* Lit. "bread of faith" (Aramaic). Term used in the *Zohar* to describe matzah on the first night of Passover.

*mayim* Water (Hebrew).

*mechitzah* Lit. "partition" (Hebrew). The wall or curtain separating men and women in Orthodox religious prayer services.

**midrash** From the Hebrew *darash*, "to inquire." 1. The commentary and expository literature developed in classical Judaism to interpret the Bible differently from its literal meaning. 2. The method of interpreting the Bible this way.

*mikveh* Lit. "gathering" (Hebrew). A ritual bath formed from a pool of "living water" collected from rain or from a spring, used for spiritual purification. The *mikveh* is used primarily in conversion rituals and after a woman's menstrual cycles.

*minyan* Lit. "number" (Hebrew). A quorum of ten Jews over the age of thirteen, required for communal prayer services.

*mishkan* Tabernacle (Hebrew). The portable sanctuary that accompanied the Jews during their forty years of wandering in the desert; it was eventually replaced by the Temple in Jerusalem.

**Mishnah** Lit. "teaching" (Hebrew). The rabbinic interpretation of biblical law edited and compiled by Judah Ha-Nasi in the early third century C.E. The Mishnah is divided into six sections, or orders, concerned with all aspects of Jewish law.

*Mit'chila* Lit. "from the beginning" (Hebrew). Opening word of a section in the *maggid* section of the haggadah recalling our ancestors' worship of idols and Abraham's faith in one God.

*mitzrayim* Biblical name for Egypt, the kingdom that, under the rule of the Pharaohs, enslaved the Israelites until God led them to freedom.

*mitzvah* Lit. "commandment." *Mitzvah* refers to the 613 commandments given to Jews in the Torah. Commonly used to denote any Jewish religious obligation or good deed. Plural: *mitzvot*.

**Mizrahi** Lit. "oriental" (Hebrew). Generally refers to Jews of Asian or African origin.

*motzi* matzah Lit. "removes unleavened bread" (Hebrew). The seventh step of the seder, involving the recitation of two blessings and the eating of the matzah. These blessings are the regular *motzi* blessing and one specifically mentioning the commandment to eat matzah on Passover.

*Neshume-le* Lit. "little soul" (Yiddish). Diminutive form of *neshama*, the Yiddish word for soul. A term of endearment.

*ner tamid* Lit. "eternal light" (Hebrew). The lamp kept perpetually lit over the ark in the synagogue as a symbol of God's eternal presence.

*nirtzah* Lit. "accepted" (Hebrew). The final section of the seder, following the *hallel* and culminating in the prayer "Next year in Jerusalem."

**Nisan** Seventh month of the Jewish civil calendar and first month of the Jewish religious year. Passover begins on the fourteenth day of Nisan.

*parsha* Lit. "section" (Hebrew). One of the fifty-four sections of the Torah read in synagogue liturgy on an annual cycle.

**Pesach** Passover (Hebrew). One of the three pilgrimage or harvest festivals enumerated in the Bible; a celebration of the Israelites' liberation from Egyptian bondage. The name of the holiday originates in the last of the ten plagues, when God "passed over" the houses of the Israelites and spared their firstborns. The term "Pesach" also refers to the paschal sacrifice commanded by God on the eve of the Exodus.

*pesachdik* From the Hebrew *pesach*. Kosher for Passover.

**Pharaoh** Name of the kings of Egypt in biblical times; particularly used to refer to the Egyptian ruler during the enslavement and Exodus of the Israelites.

**Purim** From the Persian for "casting of lots". Festival on the fourteenth of Adar celebrating the deliverance of the Jews of Persia, as recounted in the Book of Esther.

*Rebbe* Rabbi (Yiddish). The title of the spiritual leader of the Chasidim.

*rochtzah* Lit. "washing" (Hebrew). The sixth step of the seder, involving the ritual washing of the hands and the recitation of a blessing sanctifying this act.

**Rosh Chodesh** Lit. "head of the month" (Hebrew). The new moon festival celebrated at the beginning of each lunar month in the Jewish calendar, when the *hallel* psalms and a *musaf* (additional) service are added to the regular liturgy. In recent years, Jewish feminists have reclaimed the holiday and observed it as a day of special significance for Jewish women.

**Rosh Hashanah** Lit. "head of the year" (Hebrew). The Jewish New Year, Rosh Hashanah occurs on the first and second days of the month of Tishrei, the seventh month of the Jewish year. One of the holiest days of the Jewish year, Rosh Hashanah is referred to in the Bible as Yom Ha-Zikkaron (the day of remembrance) or Yom Teruah (the day of the sounding of the shofar).

**seder** Lit. "order" (Hebrew). The festive ritual meal eaten in the home on the first night of Passover (on the first two nights in the diaspora). The seder is divided into fourteen steps and includes the retelling of the story of the Exodus from a haggadah text.

**Sephardi** Lit. "Spaniards" (Hebrew). Term used to designate Jews of Spanish and Portuguese descent whose ancestors spread throughout Africa, the Ottoman Empire, part of South America, Italy, and Holland following the expulsion of 1492. Plural: Sephardim.

**Shabbat** Sabbath (Hebrew). The Jewish Sabbath, lasting from sundown Friday night to sundown Saturday night. According to the Bible (Genesis 2:1–4), God rested from creation on the seventh day, so Jews are commanded to rest on this day.

*shaleym* Complete (Hebrew).

**shalom** Peace (Hebrew). Also, a term of greeting and farewell.

*shalom bayit* Lit. "peace of the house" (Hebrew). Domestic tranquility; peace between husband and wife, held to be a very important ideal in Judaism.

*Shechin* Boils; the sixth plague with which God struck Egypt (Exodus 9:8–12).

*Shechinat-el* Lit. "indwelling of God" (Hebrew). The divine presence.

*shefoch chamatcha* Lit. "pour out your wrath" (Hebrew). Passage in the haggadah in which Jews ask God to pour out anger on those nations who do not worship God. This section, which consists of three verses from Psalms (79:6–7, 69:25) and one from Lamentations (3:66), is recited as the door is opened for Elijah.

*shehecheyanu* Lit. "who has sustained us" (Hebrew). Blessing recited for any special, long-awaited occasion, such as the celebration of a holiday or bar mitzvah ceremony. The blessing is included in the *kiddush* recited at the seder.

*Shekhinah* Lit. "indwelling" (Hebrew). The divine presence; in kabbalah, the *Shekhinah* was associated with the feminine aspect of God.

*shira* Lit. "song" or "poem" (Hebrew). The feminine form of the Hebrew word for "song" or "poem." Used in the Bible to refer to a long poem of praise extolling God.

*shmurah* **matzah** Lit. "guarded matzah" (Hebrew). Special matzah that has been watched by rabbis from the time the wheat is cut until the flour is mixed with pure water and cooked for less than eighteen minutes, to ensure that it is kosher for Passover.

**shofar** Lit. "horn" (Hebrew). A ritual instrument dating back to biblical times, the shofar is blown on Rosh Hashanah and Yom Kippur.

*shtetl* Lit. "little town" (Yiddish). Small Eastern European village of Jews; the main demographic center of Ashkenazim in the eighteenth and nineteenth centuries.

**Shulhan Arukh** A sixteenth-century compilation of Jewish ritual laws by Rabbi Joseph Caro, considered authoritative by most traditionally observant Jews.

*Shulhan Orekh* Lit. "set table" (Hebrew). The tenth step of the Passover seder, consisting of the festive meal.

*tallit* Lit. "cloak" (Hebrew). Four-cornered shawl with knotted fringes worn during Jewish morning prayers. According to the Bible (Numbers 15:38–39), the fringes are intended to serve as a reminder of God's commandments.

**Tanach** A Hebrew acronym for the three parts of the Bible: Torah (Five Books of Moses), Nevi'im (Prophets), and Ketuvim (Writings).

*tikkun olam* Lit. "fixing the world" (Hebrew). The Jewish obligation to repair the world through acts of social justice.

*tzafun* The eleventh step of the seder, consisting of the eating of the *afikomen*. After this step, no more food may be eaten at the seder.

*tzar* 1. Enemy 2. Narrow (Hebrew).

*tzedek* Justice (Hebrew).

*Tzefardeya* Frog (Hebrew). The second plague with which God struck Egypt (Exodus 7:26–8:11).

*ur'chatz* The second step of the seder, consisting of the ritual washing of the hands by the leader of the seder, with the blessing omitted.

*yachatz* The fourth step of the seder, in which the middle matzah is broken and half is set aside to serve as the *afikomen*.

**yeshiva** Lit. "sitting" (Hebrew). A Jewish rabbinic academy of higher learning, in which learning is undertaken for its own sake as a religious duty.

**Yom Tov** Lit. "good day" (Hebrew). A Jewish festival.

*zayde* Grandfather (Yiddish).

*zeroah* Lit. "limb" (Hebrew). 1. The roasted lamb shankbone placed on the seder plate to commemorate the paschal sacrifice offered by the Israelites on the eve of the Exodus. 2. The term used in the Bible to describe the outstretched arm with which God delivered the Israelites from Egypt.

*Zohar* Lit. "splendor" (Hebrew). Chief literary work of the kabbalists, written as an Aramaic midrash on the Bible. The *Zohar* is traditionally attributed to the followers of Simon Bar Yochai in the second century, though modern scholars accept that most of the book was written by Moses de Leon, a twelfth-century Spanish rabbi.

# Bibliography and Resources

## Published Women's Haggadahs

Broner, E. M., and Naomi Nimrod. "The Women's Haggadah" in *The Telling: A Group of Extraordinary Jewish Women Journey to Spirituality through Community and Ceremony* by E. M. Broner. San Francisco: HarperCollins, 1993.

Cohen, Tamara, ed. *The Journey Continues, The Ma'yan Passover Haggadah*. New York: Ma'yan: The Jewish Women's Project, 2000.

Elwell, Sue Levi, ed. *And We Were All There: A Feminist Passover Haggadah*. Los Angeles: American Jewish Congress Feminist Center, 1994.

Moise, Elaine, and Rebecca Schwartz. *The Dancing With Miriam Haggadah: A Jewish Women's Celebration of Passover*. Mountain View, Calif.: Rikudei Miriam Press, 1997.

Shelley, Martha. *Haggadah: A Celebration of Freedom*. San Francisco: Aunt Lute Books, 1997.

Stein, Judith. *A New Haggadah: A Jewish Lesbian Seder*. Cambridge, Mass.: Bobbeh Meisehs Press, 1997.

Zones, Jane, ed. *San Diego Women's Haggadah*. San Diego, Calif.: Woman's Institute for Continuing Jewish Education, 1986.

Zuckoff, Cantor Aviva. "A Jewish Women's Haggadah" in *Womanspirit Rising: A Feminist Reader in Religion* edited by Carol Christ and Judith Plaskow. San Francisco: HarperSanFrancisco, 1992.

## Sources on Passover and Holding a Seder

Bokser, Baruch. *The Origins of the Seder*. Berkeley: University of California Press, 1984.

Dishon, David, and Noam Zion. *The Leader's Guide to the Family Participation Haggadah: A Different Night*. Jerusalem: Shalom Hartman Institute, 1997.

Elias, Rabbi Joseph. *The Artscroll Haggadah*. Brooklyn, New York: Artscroll Mesorah Publications, Ltd., 1999.

Fredman, Ruth Gruber. *The Passover Seder: Afikomen in Exile*. Philadelphia: University of Pennsylvania Press, 1981.

Steingroot, Ira. *Keeping Passover: Everything You Need to Know to Bring the Ancient Tradition to Life and Create Your Own Passover Celebration*. San Francisco: HarperSanFrancisco, 1995.

Wolfson, Ron. *Passover, 2nd ed.: The Family Guide to Spiritual Celebration*. The Art of Jewish Living Series. Woodstock, Vt.: Jewish Lights Publishing, 2003.

———. *Passover Seder Workbook*. Woodstock, Vt.: Jewish Lights Publishing, 1988.

Yerushalmi, Yosef Hayim. *Haggadah and History*. Philadelphia: Jewish Publication Society, 1975.

## Additional Related Jewish Feminist Resources

Adelman, Penina V. *Miriam's Well: Rituals for Jewish Women Around the Year*. New York: Biblio Press, 1990.

Adler, Rachel. *Engendering Judaism: An Inclusive Theology and Ethics*. Boston: Beacon Press, 1999.

Agosin, Marjorie, and Roberta Gordenstein. *Miriam's Daughters: Jewish Latin American Women Poets*. Santa Fe: Sherman Asher Publishing, 2001.

Alpert, Rebecca. *Like Bread on the Seder Plate*. New York: Columbia University Press, 1998.

Ashton, Dianne, and Ellen M. Umansky, eds. *Four Centuries of Jewish Women's Spirituality: A Sourcebook*. Boston: Beacon Press, 1992.

Baskin, Judith, ed. *Jewish Women in Historical Perspective*. Detroit: Wayne State University Press, 1991.

Beck, Evelyn Torton, ed. *Nice Jewish Girls: A Lesbian Anthology*. Revised edition. Boston: Beacon Press, 1999.

Broner, E. M. *The Telling: The Story of a Group of Jewish Women Who Journey to Spirituality through Community and Ceremony*. San Francisco: HarperSanFrancisco, 1993.

Chesler, Phyllis, and Rivka Haut. *Women of the Wall: Claiming Sacred Ground at Judaism's Holy Site*. Woodstock, Vt.: Jewish Lights Publishing, 2003.

Cohen, Debra Nussbaum. *Celebrating Your New Jewish Daughter: Creating Jewish Ways to Welcome Baby Girls into the Covenant*. Woodstock, Vt.: Jewish Lights Publishing, 2001.

Diament, Carol, Ph.D., ed. *Moonbeams: A Hadassah Rosh Hodesh Guide*. Woodstock, Vt.: Jewish Lights Publishing, 2000.

Falk, Marcia. *The Book of Blessings: New Jewish Prayers for Daily Life, the Sabbath, and the New Moon Festival.* Boston: Beacon Press, 1999.

Falk, Marcia. *The Song of Songs: A New Translation.* San Francisco: HarperSanFrancisco, 1993.

Frankel, Ellen. *The Five Books of Miriam: A Woman's Commentary on the Torah.* San Francisco: HarperSanFrancisco, 1998.

Goldstein, Elyse. *Revisions: Seeing Torah through a Feminist Lens.* Woodstock, Vt.: Jewish Lights Publishing, 2001.

———. *The Women's Torah Commentary: New Insights from Women Rabbis on the 54 Weekly Torah Portions.* Woodstock, Vt.: Jewish Lights Publishing, 2000.

Gottlieb, Lynn. *She Who Dwells Within: A Feminist Vision of a Renewed Judaism.* San Francisco: HarperSanFrancisco, 1995.

Greenberg, Blu. *On Women and Judaism.* Philadelphia: Jewish Publication Society, 1981.

Harlow, Jules. *Pray Tell: A Hadassah Guide to Jewish Prayer.* Woodstock, Vt.: Jewish Lights Publishing, 2003.

Hendler, Lee Meyerhoff. *The Year Mom Got Religion: One Woman's Midlife Journey into Judaism.* Woodstock, Vt.: Jewish Lights Publishing, 1999.

Heschel, Susannah. *On Being a Jewish Feminist.* New York: Schocken, 1983.

Hyman, Paula. *Jewish Women in America.* New York: Routledge, 1997.

Kaye/Kantrowitz, Melanie, and Irena Klepfisz, eds. *The Tribe of Dina: A Jewish Women's Anthology.* Boston: Beacon Press, 1989.

Ochs, Vanessa L. *Words on Fire.* New York: Harcourt Brace Jovanovich, 1990.

Orenstein, Debra. *Lifecycles Volume 1: Jewish Women on Life Passages and Personal Milestones.* Woodstock, Vt.: Jewish Lights Publishing, 1994.

Orenstein, Debra, and Jane Rachel Litman. *Lifecycles Volume 2: Jewish Women on Biblical Themes in Contemporary Life.* Woodstock, Vt.: Jewish Lights Publishing, 1997.

Ostriker, Alicia Suskin. *The Nakedness of the Fathers: Biblical Visions and Revisions.* New Brunswick, N.J.: Rutgers University Press, 1997.

Plaskow, Judith. *Standing Again at Sinai: Judaism from a Feminist Perspective.* San Francisco: Harper & Row, 1990.

Pogrebin, Letty Cottin. *Deborah, Golda, and Me: Being Female and Jewish in America.* New York: Crown Publishing Group, 1991.

Ruttenberg, Danya, ed. *Yentl's Revenge: The Next Wave of Jewish Feminism.* Seattle: Seal Press Feminist Publishing, 2001.

Spiegel, Marcia Cohn, and Deborah Lipton Kremsdorf, eds. *Women Speak to God: The Prayers and Poems of Jewish Women.* San Diego: Woman's Institute for Continuing Jewish Education, 1987.

Weissler, Chava. *Voices of the Matriarchs: Listening to the Prayers of Early Modern Jewish Women*. Boston: Beacon Press, 1998.

Zornberg, Avivah Gottlieb. *The Particulars of Rapture: Reflections on Exodus*. New York: Doubleday, 2001.

Zuckoff, Aviva Cantor. *Jewish Women/Jewish Men: The Legacy of Patriarchy in Jewish Life*. San Francisco: HarperCollins, 1995.

## Passover Music for the Seder

**Debbie Friedman's** *The Journey Continues* features twenty-four Hebrew and English songs that parallel the Ma'yan Passover Haggadah of the same name. The album includes the new songs "The Time Is Now," *"B'chol Dor Vador,"* and *"Birkat Hamazon";* seder appropriate renditions of "Miriam's Song," *"L'chi Lach," "Shir Hama-alot," "Hodu, Hal'luyah,"* and more; and traditional Pesach songs *"Ha Lachma," "Mah Nishtana," "Avadim Hayinu," "Ma L'cha Hayam," "L'shana Ha-ba-a";* and others. All songs are available in cassette, compact disc, and songbook from SoundsWrite Productions, P.O. Box 601084, San Diego, CA 92160-1084 or http://www.soundswrite.com; by phone at 800-976-8639; or by e-mail at soundswrite@aol.com.

**Linda Hirschorn's** Passover and women's seder music includes "Women Gathering Round," about the courage of women around the world gaining strength from each other; "Blessed Is the Flame," appropriate for candle-lighting; *"El na R'fah nah Lah*—Please Heal Her," a healing song for *yachatz; "Zog Maran,"* to be sung before reciting the Ten Plagues; "Miriam's Snake Dance at the Riverside"; *"Rue Platz,"* a tribute to the women who worked for the labor movement and the women who died in the triangle shirtwaist factory; "I Have a Million Nightingales," with words based on a poem by Palestinian poet Mahmoud Darwish; "Circle Chant," a song of freedom for the ages, appropriate for a women's seder closing. All songs are available through Oyster, Box 3929, Berkeley, CA 94730. In addition, Linda Hirschorn has composed a version of Marcia Falk's *Kiddush* set to music, available from Half Note Productions, Box 3929, Berkeley, CA 94703. Available on Vocolot's 2002 album *"B'chol Dor Vador,"* which praises the accomplishments of women throughout the generations, are *"Los Biblicos,"* a Ladino song about spring appropriate for *karpas; "Pitchu Li"* or the Yiddish version, *"Effen Oyf;"* songs of praise for *hallel; "Yesh Lanu Koach Yesh Lanu Ruach";* and "Sarah and Hagar," which tells the story of these biblical women from a contemporary viewpoint. More information is available at http://www.vocolot.com.

**Geela Rayzel Raphael's** Passover songs include "Shifra and Puah," which tells the story of the midwives' courage and faith; "Batya—Daughter of God," which recounts Pharaoh's daughter's rescue of Moses and her bond with Miriam and Yocheved; and "By The Shores," a joyful song about the women's celebratory dance of freedom with Miriam at the Reed Sea. All songs are available through Geela Rayzel Raphael by contacting the a capella trio MIRAJ at 610-771-0831, or at mirajtrio@aol.com.

**Peri Smilow's** Passover music includes *The Freedom Music Project: The Music of Passover and the Civil Rights Movement,* an entire album of music sung by an electrifying choir of young black and Jewish singers celebrating the freedom music of their traditions. Songs include "Wade in the Water," *"Avadim Hayinu,"* "Keep Your Eyes on the Prize," *"Ha Lachma Anya,"* "One Small Step," "Where Was God," and an innovative rendition of *"Chad Gadya."* Other Passover songs such as *"Kos Miryam"* are included on *Ashrey.* You can learn more about Peri's music at www.PeriSmilow.com. All music is available through SoundsWrite Productions, P.O. Box 601084, San Diego, CA 92160-1084 or http://www.soundswrite.com; by phone at 800-976-8639; or by e-mail at soundswrite@aol.com.

**Margot Stein's** songs include *"Avadim Hayinu,"* a gently humorous look at women's Passover preparations; "Wilderness," a funky pop exploration of the wilderness generation; "Desert Dances," Tziporah's song, longing for a second chance with her beloved, Moses; *Limnot Yameynu* (Psalm 90), which celebrates counting our days as an opportunity to count our blessings; and "Miriam So Brave and Strong" to the tune of *"Eliyahu HaNavi,"* based on the Hebrew text written by Rabbi Leila Gal Berner. All songs are available by contacting the a cappella trio MIRAJ at 610-771-0831 or mirajtrio@aol.com. Some songs also available from SoundsWrite Productions, P.O. Box 601084, San Diego, CA 92160-1084 or http://www.soundswrite.com; by phone at 800-976-8639; or by e-mail at soundswrite@aol.com.

**Judith Wachs'** recordings of Sephardic women's *romanceros,* folk songs, and other songs appropriate for Passover can be found on Voice of the Turtle albums. *"Kuando Moshe Rabeynu"* is on *Balkan Vistas: Songs of the Spanish Jews of Bulgaria and Yugolsavia-Ti-103* (Volume III, "Paths of Exile" Quincentenary Series). *"Mosé salió de Misrayim"* and *"Mosé, Mosé, Mosé"* are recorded on *Bridges of Song: Songs of the Spanish Jews of Morocco-Ti-189* (Volume II, "Paths of Exile" Quincentenary Series). *"Kuando d'Aifto fueron salidos," "Ah Moshe," "Par'ó era estreyero," "Ken supiese i entendiense," "Ke komiash duenya," "Tenia yo,"* and *"Yaakov le disho a Yosef"* can be found on *A Different Night: A Passover Anthology-KHT-018.* All recordings are available from http://www.voiceoftheturtle.com.

## Other Resources for a Women's Seder

**Ma'yan: The Jewish Women's Project of the JCC of the Upper West Side** offers a wealth of information about women's seders on their website, http://www.mayan.org. In addition to *The Journey Continues: The Ma'yan Passover Haggadah,* the organization produces a guide to planning a women's seder that they mail by request.

**Ritualwell,** a website at http://www.ritualwell.org, features a number of readings, ritual suggestions, and background information for women's and family seders.

***Lilith: The Independent Jewish Women's Magazine*** has a Passover packet of articles that they mail by request. In addition, the magazine features creative writing and articles on a variety of issues relating to Jewish feminism. More information is available at their website, http://www.lilithmag.com, or by contacting *Lilith* directly at lilithmag@aol.com.

***Bridges: A Journal for Jewish Feminists and Their Friends*** is a resource for articles, personal essays, and poetry by and about contemporary Jewish women. More information is available at http://www.bridgesjournal.org.

# About the Contributors

**Rabbi Stephanie Aaron** is rabbi of Congregation Chaverim, a Reform synagogue in Tucson, Arizona.

**Penina Adelman** is a writer and social worker. She authored *Miriam's Well* and *The Bible from Alef to Tav,* which was a finalist for the National Jewish Book Award. Currently, she is writing about Jewish girls coming of age and is a visiting scholar at the Brandeis Women's Studies Research Center.

**Dr. Rachel Adler** is assistant professor of modern Jewish thought at Hebrew Union College in Los Angeles and assistant professor of religion at the University of Southern California. Her book *Engendering Judaism: An Inclusive Theology and Ethics* won the 1999 National Jewish Book Award for Jewish Thought.

**Dr. Marjorie Agosin** is a poet, human rights activist, and professor of Latin American literature at Wellesley College. She is an award-winning poet and has been recognized internationally for her work on behalf of women and human rights. Her most recent publications are *The Angel of Memory* (poetry), *Amigas: Letters of Friendship and Exile,* and *The Invisible Dreamer: Memory, Judaism and Human Rights.*

**Jenny Aisenberg** is currently a women's studies major at Smith College, where she has been the cohead of the kosher kitchen. She was born and raised in Providence, Rhode Island, and has spent a semester studying at the University of California at Santa Cruz.

**Rabbi Renni S. Altman** is the associate rabbi at Temple Beth-El in Great Neck, New York, where she has served since July 1994. Her varied responsibilities there have included overseeing a very successful Rosh Chodesh group and women's seder. Renni was ordained at the New York Campus of Hebrew Union College–Jewish Institute of Religion in May 1988.

**Dr. Rebecca T. Alpert** is codirector of the women's studies program and associate professor of religion and women's studies at Temple University. She is the coauthor (with Jacob Staub) of *Exploring Judaism: A Reconstructionist Approach,* author of *Like Bread on the Seder Plate: Jewish Lesbians and the Transformation of Tradition,* and editor of *Voices of the Religious Left: A Contemporary Sourcebook.*

**Matia Rania Angelou** is a poet, ritual artist, spiritual teacher, and healer. She is a member of the musical trio Ashira and performs with the drumming group Olamot and The Tribe of Dinah, a collective of women artists, dancers, and musicians. In 1990, Matia founded Nishmat HaNashim/WomenSoul to provide opportunities to deepen spirituality through Jewish study, meditation, healing, and the creative arts.

**Rabbi Sharon Cohen Anisfeld** is director of education and programming at Harvard Hillel. While associate rabbi at Joseph Slifka Center for Jewish Life at Yale from 1993 to 2001, she was an advisor to Jewish Women at Yale. She has been a faculty member of the Bronfman Youth Fellowships in Israel since 1993. She is coeditor of *The Women's Passover Companion* and *The Women's Seder Sourcebook* (both Jewish Lights Publishing). Sharon lives in Boston with her husband and two children.

**Dr. Katya Gibel Azoulay** holds a Ph.D. in cultural anthropology from Duke University and a B.A. and an M.A. in African studies from Hebrew University of Jerusalem. Katya is associate professor of anthropology and chair of the Africana studies concentration at Grinnell College. She is author of *Black, Jewish and Interracial: It's Not the Color of Your Skin but the Race of Your Kin, and Other Myths of Identity.*

**Zoe Baird** is president of the Markle Foundation, a private philanthropic organization that works to realize the potential of emerging communications tools to improve people's lives. She was associate counsel to President Jimmy Carter and attorney in the Office of Legal Counsel of the U.S. Department of Justice. Zoe served on the President's Foreign Intelligence Advisory Board. She founded and chairs Lawyers for Children America, which is concerned with the impact of violence on children.

**Rachel Barenblat** is cofounder of Inkberry, a literary organization in the Berkshires in Massachusetts. Her second chapbook of poems, "What Stays," was recently published by the Bennington Writing Seminars Alumni Chapbook Series. She holds an M.F.A. from Bennington College.

**Dr. Evelyn Torton Beck** is a lesbian feminist activist, writer, and teacher, working on issues related to "difference," Jewish women's studies, lesbian studies, and feminist transformations of knowledge. She is professor of women's studies at the University of Maryland and the editor of *Nice Jewish Girls: A Lesbian Anthology.*

**Miriam Benson** is the executive director of the Connecticut Valley Region of United Synagogue of Conservative Judaism. She serves as legal liaison between the International Committee for Women of the Wall and the attorneys in Israel. Miriam is married to Rabbi Jon-Jay Tilsen of Congregation Beth El-Keser Israel in New Haven, Connecticut, and has three children.

**Barbara H. Bergen** is associate director and general counsel of MAZON: A Jewish Response to Hunger. After a long career as general counsel of a savings bank, Barbara changed her professional focus to civil rights and social justice. Before joining MAZON, she served as Associate Western States Counsel and Central Pacific Regional Director of the Anti-Defamation League.

**Ruth Berger Goldston** is a psychologist in Princeton, New Jersey. She is a long-time *havurahnik* and former chair of the National Havurah Committee.

**Janet Berkenfield**'s ties to Judaism are through her writing: poetry; meditations; and translations of Jewish prayer, many of which appear in Havurat Shalom's prayer book, *Birkat Shalom.* She grew up in El Paso, Texas, and now resides in Boston.

**Susan Berrin** is the editor of *Sh'ma: A Journal of Jewish Responsibility.* She teaches and lectures on Jewish issues, specifically in the areas of Jewish women and spirituality, midlife and aging issues, and values-oriented parenting. She is editor of *A Heart of Wisdom: Making the Jewish Journey from Mid-Life through the Elder Years* (Jewish Lights Publishing) and *Celebrating the New Moon: A Rosh Chodesh Anthology.*

**Mayim Bialik** is a second-generation American of Eastern European descent who enjoys Ramban, random acts of *tzedakah,* and the ocean. Mayim starred in "Blossom," one of the first prime-time network television shows to depict a strong, independent, and dynamic young woman. She is very active in Jewish life at University of California at Los Angeles, where she is a graduate student in neuroscience.

**Judith Bolton-Fasman** lives with her husband and two children in Newton, Massachusetts. Her reviews and essays have appeared in the *New York Times,* the *Boston Globe,* the *Washington Post,* and other venues. She is the founding editor of JBooks.com, an online book review of Jewish literature.

**Senator Barbara Boxer** became a United States senator in January 1993, after ten years of service in the House of Representatives, and was elected to a second, six-year term in 1998. The Senate's leading advocate of a woman's right to choose, Senator Boxer authored the Family Planning and Choice

Protection Act and helped lead the floor fight for passage of the Freedom of Access to Clinic Entrances Act.

**Dr. Esther Broner** organized the first women's seder in 1976 and published *The Telling: The Story of a Group of Jewish Women Who Journey to Spirituality through Community and Ceremony,* a memoir of the historic event. She is also the author of *A Weave of Women* and *Bringing Home the Light: A Jewish Woman's Handbook of Rituals.*

**Rabbi/Cantor Angela Warnick Buchdahl** is a graduate of Yale University and has been involved with the Yale Women's Seders since their inception in 1994. Angela is the first Asian American to be invested as a cantor or ordained as a rabbi from Hebrew Union College. She serves Westchester Reform Temple in Scarsdale, New York, and lives in that community with her husband, Jacob, and son, Gabriel.

**Rabbi Nina Beth Cardin** is the director of Jewish Life at the JCC of Greater Baltimore. Her two most recent books are *The Tapestry of Jewish Time: A Spiritual Guide to Holidays and Lifecycle Events* and *Tears of Sorrow, Seeds of Hope: A Jewish Spiritual Companion for Infertility and Pregnancy Loss* (Jewish Lights Publishing).

**Ayelet Cohen** is a Cooperberg-Rittmaster Rabbinical Intern and is coordinator of children's programs at Congregation Beth Simchat Torah. She is in her final year of rabbinical school at the Jewish Theological Seminary. She holds a B.A. in comparative literature and Judaic studies from Brown University, where she was a founder of B'GLAL, one of the first university groups for Jewish LGBT students and allies.

**Tamara Cohen** was the program director at Ma'yan: The Jewish Women's Project of the JCC in Manhattan for seven years. She edited *The Journey Continues: The Ma'yan Passover Haggadah* and led numerous Ma'yan seders. She continues to consult with Ma'yan, write poetry, and serve as the spiritual leader of the Greater Washington Coalition for Jewish Life. She lives in Gainesville, Florida, with her partner.

**Naida Cohn** is presently on the board of trustees of Temple Beth Shalom in Austin, Texas. She has served on the national and executive boards of Women of Reform Judaism. Naida's writings in *The Women's Seder Sourcebook* were originally composed for the women's seder of the National Council of Jewish Women, Austin Section.

**Rachel R. Cymrot** served as the Jewish Campus Service Corps Fellow at Yale University after graduating from Bates College in 2000. Originally from Newton, Massachusetts, she now lives in New York City, working as a health educator at Mt. Sinai's Adolescent Health Center and studying social work and public health at Columbia University.

**Rebecca L. Davis** graduated from Yale University in 1998. For two years in New York City she worked at a nonprofit agency for low-income people with HIV/AIDS, freelanced, and served as synagogue and youth group song leader. She is currently pursuing her Ph.D. at Yale, focusing on modern Jewish history and American religious history.

**Arielle Derby** recently graduated from Smith College, where she organized the campus women's seder. Her reflection in *The Women's Seder Sourcebook* was originally included in *Across the Sea: A Haggadah,* created for the Smith College Hillel women's seder. She lives in Brooklyn with her favorite Hillel cochair and her cat, Princess.

**Anita Diamant** is a Boston-based writer and lecturer. She is the author of the international best-seller *The Red Tent.* Her other books include *Good Harbor, The New Jewish Baby Book* (Jewish Lights Publishing), *The New Jewish Wedding,* and several other guides to Jewish life.

**Dr. Carol Diament** is director of the National Department of Jewish Education at Hadassah. She is the first woman to have completed a doctorate in Jewish studies at Yeshiva University. Carol received the Shazar Prize for excellence in Jewish education in the diaspora as well as the Simon Rockower award for excellence in journalism. She is the editor of *Moonbeams: A Hadassah Rosh Hodesh Guide* (Jewish Lights Publishing), *Jewish Women Living the Challenge,* and *Zionism: The Sequel.*

**Aliza Dzik** is currently a book jacket designer at Penguin Putnam in New York. She studied literature at Yale University, with an emphasis on French and Hebrew literature. Upon graduation, she went to Israel on a Fulbright scholarship to study Israeli women's and Israeli Arab literature.

**Ophira Edut** has been an independent magazine publisher, writer, and website developer since 1992. She is the editor of *Body Outlaws: Young Women Write about Body Image and Identity,* a contributing editor to *Ms.,* and the founding publisher of *HUES* (Hear Us Emerging Sisters), an award-winning national magazine for young women of all cultures and sizes. A Detroit native and Israeli American, Ophira now lives in New York and spends her time speaking publicly, developing her Ophira.com website, writing, and consulting on online projects.

**Rabbi Sue Levi Elwell, Ph.D.,** edited *The Open Door,* the new Reform haggadah. The founding director of the Los Angeles Jewish Feminist Center and the first rabbinic director of Ma'yan: The Jewish Women's Project of the JCC of the Upper West Side, she directs the Pennsylvania Council of the Union of American Hebrew Congregations.

**Eve Ensler** is an award-winning playwright, activist, and screenwriter. The world tour of her Obie Award–winning play, *The Vagina Monologues,* initiated V-Day, a global movement to stop violence against women. Eve has written plays about nuclear disarmament, homeless women, and death, and is working on a documentary about women in prison.

**Susan Estrich** was the first woman president of the *Harvard Law Review* and the first woman to run a presidential campaign. A professor at Harvard Law School for ten years, she is currently the Robert Kingsley Professor of Law and Political Science at the University of Southern California. She is a nationally syndicated columnist and the author of five books, including *Real Rape* and *Sex and Power.*

**Sara Riwka Br'raz Erlich** was born in Recife, northeast Brazil, the daughter of Jews who emigrated from Poland. She is a psychiatrist and training analyst. She has published books and scientific and literary papers, and her work is included in anthologies in Brazil and abroad.

**Dr. Marcia Falk** is a poet, translator, and Judaic scholar. She is the author of the highly acclaimed *The Book of Blessings: New Jewish Prayers for Daily Life, the Sabbath, and the New Moon Festival; The Song of Songs: A New Translation and Interpretation,* and *With Teeth in the Earth: Selected Poems of Malka Heifetz Tussman.*

**Tali Farimah Farhadian** is a student at Yale Law School. She graduated in 1997 from Yale College, where she helped create the original *Yale Women's Haggadah.*

**Sherry Farzan's** parents went to Israel, where she was born, after escaping from Iran during the revolution of 1979. Her family then moved to Great Neck, New York, where Sherry was raised. She pursued her academic interest in biology at Yale University and developed and shared her passion for Israel as leader of Yale Friends of Israel. Sherry graduated from Yale in 2001 and is currently in her second year of medical school at Harvard University.

**Merle Feld** is an award-winning playwright and poet. She is the author, most recently, of *A Spiritual Life: A Jewish Feminist Journey.*

**Rabbi Marla J. Feldman** is assistant director of the Jewish Community Council of Metropolitan Detroit and director of the Michigan Board of Rabbis. She is a Reform rabbi, a lawyer, a teacher, and a community activist. Her articles and "modern midrash" have been published in numerous periodicals.

**Rabbi Susan P. Fendrick** is the editor of SocialAction.com and rabbi-in-residence at Jewish Family & Life!, a nonprofit Jewish media group in Newton, Massachusetts. A former Hillel rabbi, she recently served as vice-chair of the National Havurah Committee, and for several years she was on the faculty of the Institute for Contemporary Midrash as a trainer in bibliodrama.

**Rabbi Tirzah Firestone** is a Jungian therapist and the founding rabbi of the Jewish Renewal Congregation of Boulder, Colorado. Her first book, *With Roots In Heaven: One Woman's Passionate Journey into the Heart of Her Faith,* was hailed as "spiritual autobiography at its best" and a "must read" for spiritual seekers. Tirzah lectures widely on the lost Jewish women's mystical tradition. Her book *The Receiving,* about Jewish women saints and sages, will be available in 2003.

**Dr. Ellen Frankel** is currently the CEO and editor in chief of the Jewish Publication Society. She received her Ph.D. in comparative literature from Princeton University. Dr. Frankel has published numerous books on Jewish topics, including *The Classic Tales: 4,000 Years of Jewish Lore* and *The Five Books of Miriam: A Woman's Commentary on the Torah.* She is also a contributor to volumes 3–8 of *My People's Prayer Book: Traditional Prayers, Modern Commentaries,* edited by Lawrence A. Hoffman (Jewish Lights Publishing). Ellen travels widely as a storyteller and lecturer.

**Dr. Nancy Gad-Harf** is director of the East Central Region (Michigan and Ohio) of the American Technion Society. She also sits on a wide range of Jewish organization boards. She received a Ph.D. in politics from Brandeis University and an M.S.W. from Washington University.

**Nan Fink Gefen** is codirector of Chochmat HaLev, a center for Jewish meditation in the San Francisco Bay Area, and the author of *Discovering Jewish Meditation: Instruction and Guidance for Learning an Ancient Spiritual Practice* (Jewish Lights Publishing).

**Justice Ruth Bader Ginsburg** is an associate justice of the United States Supreme Court. She has taught at numerous universities, including the University of Amsterdam, Harvard Law School, and New York University Law School. Justice Ginsburg was instrumental in launching the Women's Rights Project of the American Civil Liberties Union. Throughout the 1970s she litigated a series of cases solidifying a constitutional principle against gender-based discrimination.

**Rabbi Deborah Glanzberg-Krainin** is a doctoral student at Temple University, where her work focuses on Jewish feminism and issues of memory and loss. She lives in West Chester, Pennsylvania, with her partner, David, and their three children.

**Beth Gomberg-Hirsch** is a speech pathologist by vocation, a eulogist by avocation, and the mother of two daughters.

**Rabbi Lynn Gottlieb** was one of the first ten women in the world to be ordained as a rabbi. She is a storyteller, performer, and author of *She Who Dwells Within: A Feminist Vision of a Renewed Judaism.*

**Naomi Graetz** teaches at Ben Gurion University of the Negev in Beersheba, Israel, and is the author of *S/He Created Them: Feminist Retellings of Biblical Stories* and *Silence Is Deadly: Judaism Confronts Wifebeating.*

**Dr. Cheryl Greenberg** is professor of history at Trinity College in Hartford, Connecticut, where she teaches African-American and twentieth-century United States history. She has written and edited books and articles on various topics in African-American history and is currently writing a history of black-Jewish relations in the twentieth century.

**Rabbi Lisa S. Greene,** ordained by Hebrew Union College–Jewish Institute of Religion in 1995, is associate rabbi of North Shore Congregation Israel in Glencoe, Illinois. After leading several women's seders and writing and editing haggadahs, she worked with women of many ages to create a haggadah for her congregation's 2001 women's seder.

**Ruth Halperin-Kaddari** is a senior lecturer at Bar-Ilan University Faculty of Law in Israel and is the head of the Ruth and Emanuel Rackman Center for the Promotion of the Status of Women. She teaches and publishes in the areas of family law, feminist critique of law and of Jewish law, and bioethics. She wrote and presented the formal reports of the State of Israel to the UN Committee on Elimination of Discrimination Against Women (CEDAW) and is currently completing a book on women in Israel.

**Toby Hecht** has taught Jewish education for preschool, middle school, and high school students for several years and now serves as codirector of Chai, the Jewish Society at Yale University. Originally from Seattle, Washington, she lives in New Haven, Connecticut, with her husband and three children.

**Dr. Susannah Heschel** is the Eli Black Associate Professor of Jewish Studies at Dartmouth College. She is the author of numerous studies of modern Jewish thought, including *Abraham Geiger and the Jewish Jesus,* which won the National Jewish Book Award, and a classic collection of essays, *On Being a Jewish Feminist.*

**Ronnie M. Horn** is the author of *The Children's Seder* and one of the principal authors and editors of the Ma'yan haggadah. She is the director of communications for Capital Gifts and Special Initiatives of UJA–Federation of New York. A Barnard graduate, she holds an M.A. in literature from New

York University and an M.A. in religious education from Hebrew Union College–Jewish Institute of Religion. She has worked for the Reform movement, Hadassah, and national UJA; has two grown sons; and, with her husband, Arthur, has made thirty-six seders.

**Tammy Jacobowitz** is a doctoral candidate in rabbinic literature at the University of Pennsylvania. She is a Wexner graduate fellow. Tammy received her B.A. in English literature from the University of Pennsylvania and completed the Talmud/Tanach program at the Drisha Institute. She has taught adult education in a wide variety of communities. Her writings in *The Women's Seder Sourcebook* were originally featured at "A Place at the Table: An Orthodox Feminist Exploration of the Seder," an exhibit hosted by the Jewish Orthodox Feminist Alliance.

**Rachel Kadish** is the author of the novel *From a Sealed Room*. She is currently a fiction fellow of the National Endowment for the Arts and is at work on another novel as well as on a nonfiction book about Holocaust reparation claims.

**Hilary Kaplan** is an ecofeminist and writer. Her work in the Jewish community covers racial and ethnic diversity, economic justice, environmental ethics, gender issues, and community-building for young adults. She holds a degree in comparative literature from Yale University and lives in San Francisco.

**Dr. Marion Kaplan** is the author of *Between Dignity and Despair: Jewish Life in Nazi Germany* and professor of modern Jewish history at New York University.

**Rabbi Karyn D. Kedar** is the author of *God Whispers: Stories of the Soul, Lesson of the Heart* and *The Dance of the Dolphin: Finding Prayer, Perspective and Meaning in the Stories of Our Lives* (both Jewish Lights Publishing). She is a frequent speaker and scholar-in-residence on matters of the spirit. She and her husband, Ezra, are the parents of three children.

**Rabbi Naamah Kelman** is coordinator of Beit Midrash/A Liberal Yeshiva at Hebrew Union College. She was the first female rabbi to be ordained in Israel.

**Loolwa Khazzoom** is founder and director of the Jewish Multicultural Curriculum Project, through which she developed a cutting-edge fourth- through sixth-grade curriculum about Jews from Africa, the Middle East, Central and East Asia, Central and South America, and southern Europe. Loolwa is the author of *Consequence: Beyond Resisting Rape* and the editor of the forthcoming *Behind the Veil of Silence: North African and Middle Eastern Jewish Women Speak Out.*

**Melissa Klein** is a student at the Reconstructionist Rabbinical College in Philadelphia. From 1993 to 1995, she studied at the Pardes Institute in Jerusalem, where she gained a love of Mishnah. She has led several women's seders, including a seder at the battered women's shelter in Jerusalem. Melissa grew up in Los Alamos, New Mexico, and enjoys rabbinic work with all ages, ranging from the elderly to young children.

**Naomi Klein** is an award-winning journalist and author of the international best-selling book *No Logo: Taking Aim at the Brand Bullies,* which has been translated into eighteen languages. The *New York Times* called *No Logo* "a movement bible." Naomi's articles have appeared in numerous publications, including *The Nation, The New Statesman,* and the *New York Times.* She writes an internationally syndicated column for the *Globe and Mail.*

**Irena Klepfisz** is an activist in the lesbian and Jewish communities, with much of her work focused on publishing and distributing women's writing and on peace in the Middle East. A committed secularist, she promotes and translates the poetry of Yiddish women writers. She teaches courses on Jewish women at Barnard College and is the author of *A Few Words in the Mother Tongue* (poetry) and *Dreams of an Insomniac* (feminist Jewish essays).

**Maxine Kumin** has published several books of poetry, including *Up Country: Poems of New England,* for which she received the Pulitzer Prize. She is also the author of a memoir, *Inside the Halo and Beyond: The Anatomy of a Recovery;* four novels; a collection of short stories; more than twenty children's books; and four books of essays.

**Ilana Kurshan** graduated from Harvard University with a degree in history of science and has studied English literature at Cambridge University. She lives and works in New York City.

**Rabbi Noa Rachel Kushner** is the rabbi for Hillel at Stanford University. She and her husband, Michael, have a daughter, Zella.

**Cantor Marilyn J. (Sternberg) Ladin** apprenticed with her father, also a cantor, from the age of eight and served her first professional pulpit at the age of seventeen. Since 1970, Marilyn has been providing cantorial and spiritual leadership for congregations in Mt. Pleasant, Michigan; Chicago; Seattle; and Houston. Also a psychotherapist, she is well known for her work with women in transition, intergenerational/family reconciliation, and loss and grief issues, providing spiritual counseling and workshops.

**Dr. Harriet Lerner** is a nationally acclaimed expert on the psychology of women. Her books have been published in more than fifty foreign editions, with book sales of more than three million copies. She is the author of the popular trilogy *The Dance of Anger* (1985), *The Dance of Intimacy* (1989), and *The Dance of Deception* (1993). Harriet is a senior staff psychologist and psychotherapist at the Menninger Clinic. She travels nationally to lecture, consult, and present workshops.

**Kiera Levine** graduated from Yale University in 1996 with a B.A. in philosophy. As an undergraduate she studied with Rabbi Sharon Cohen Anisfeld. She has worked in nonprofit medicine and human rights and is preparing to enter medical school. Her poem "A Sip of Kadosh" was originally included in the *Yale Women's Haggadah.*

**Dr. Sara Buchdahl Levine** is a pediatrics resident at the Children's Hospital at Montefiore. She graduated from the Albert Einstein College of Medicine of Yeshiva University. Sara is also a board member of Physicians for Reproductive Choice and Health. She received an M.P.H. from Columbia University and a B.A. from Yale.

**Rabbi Joy Levitt** is the associate executive director for programming at the Jewish Community Center in Manhattan. For the past twenty years she has served as a congregational rabbi on Long Island and in New Jersey. She is the coeditor of the new haggadah, *A Night of Questions,* and the coauthor of *The Guide to Everything Jewish in New York.* She has two daughters and is married to Rabbi Michael Strassfeld.

**Dr. Laura Levitt** is the director of Jewish studies at Temple University, where she teaches in the religion department and in the women's studies program. She is the author of *Jews and Feminism: The Ambivalent Search for Home* and the coeditor, with Miriam Peskowitz, of *Judaism Since Gender.* She is currently at work on a book about American Jews and family photography, *Ordinary Jews,* and is also coediting, with Laurence Silberstein and Shelley Hornstein, *Transforming Memory.*

**Lisa Lidor** lives in Thornhill, Ontario, and is currently a student at the University of Toronto. Her poetry won first prize in the Ontario Provincial Holocaust Writing Contest in 2001 and was published in *Parchment: Canada's Journal of Jewish Creative Writing.* Lisa is extremely honored to be included in this collection.

**Hadassah Lieberman** has made a significant contribution to improving public health, education, and international understanding through both her professional and her volunteer work. As a member of the American Committee for Shaare Zedek Medical Center, she is working on the development of an advisory network for women's health.

**Evelyn Gershon MacPhee** belonged to the MoVFTY youth group during her teenage years. After traveling in Europe, she worked as an administrator for the University of Kansas. She recently retired early to New Mexico with her husband. She enjoys *t'ai chi*, reading, computers, and e-mailing and talking to friends.

**Heather Mendel** was born in South Africa. She is a mother, feminist artist, author, activist (a 2002 NOW Local Hero), storyteller, and mystic. A student of diverse spiritual pathways, she combines her love of lettering and spirituality through her calligraphic "word-paintings." She performs programs of midrash and melody. She is married to a rabbi and currently resides in California.

**Ruth W. Messinger** is the president of American Jewish World Service (AJWS). She recently completed twenty years of public service in New York City, where she demonstrated a commitment to work with grassroots groups changing people's lives. Ruth is continuing her lifelong pursuit of social justice at AJWS, expanding its programming and visibility.

**Deena Metzger's** latest novel is *The Other Hand,* in which a woman astronomer confronts the Holocaust. In another novel, *What Dinah Thought,* the love between a Jewish-American filmmaker and a Palestinian archeologist echoes the love between the biblical Dinah and Shechem. Her other books include *Writing for Your Life, Tree: Essays and Pieces,* and *A Sabbath Among the Ruins.*

**Sarah Anne Minkin** graduated in 1999 from Yale University, where she was an active member of Jewish Women at Yale. She spent a few years in Haifa, Israel, working in feminist, social justice, and peace-building organizations. Now in the United States, Sarah Anne works in the field of economic empowerment and is active with Women in Black, the international women's peace movement, and other groups working for a just settlement to the Middle East conflict.

**Celine Mizrahi** is a student at New York University Law School. After graduating from Yale University in 2000, she worked for the Women's Housing and Economic Development Corporation, which is dedicated to the economic advancement of low-income women, men, and children.

**Tara Mohr** graduated from Yale University in 2000 with a B.A. in English literature. The coeditor of *The Women's Passover Companion* and *The Women's Seder Sourcebook* (both Jewish Lights Publishing), Tara works on Jewish outreach and organizational change programs as a Koret Synagogue Initiative consultant in the San Francisco Bay Area. Currently, she is also writing a study of Shakespeare's comedies.

**Elaine Moise** has been involved in Jewish women's rituals since the late 1970s, when she wrote her first Rosh Chodesh service. She is a founder and currently the president of a Reconstructionist synagogue in Palo Alto, California. Elaine is coauthor, with Rebecca Schwartz, of *The Dancing with Miriam Haggadah: A Jewish Women's Celebration of Passover.* She writes songs and develops liturgy, both for women and for congregational use.

**Jo-Ann Mort** is coauthor, with Gary Brenner, of *Our Hearts Invented a Place: Can Kibbutzim Survive the New Israel?* and editor of *Not Your Father's Union Movement: Inside the AFL-CIO.* She has written about Israel, Jewish issues, and social justice issues for *The Jerusalem Report,* the *LA Weekly,* the *Los Angeles Times* opinion section, *Dissent* magazine (where she is an editor), and elsewhere. She was formerly a columnist for *The Forward* newspaper.

**Dr. Faye Moskowitz,** chair of the English department at George Washington University, is author of *A Leak in the Heart; Whoever Finds This: I Love You; And the Bridge is Love;* and *This Time We'll Look at the Falls* (forthcoming). She is the editor of *Her Face in the Mirror: Jewish Women on Mothers and Daughters.*

**Dr. Pamela S. Nadell** is professor of history and director of the Jewish studies program at American University. Her book *Women Who Would Be Rabbis: A History of Women's Ordination, 1889–1985* was a finalist for the National Jewish Book Award. Her most recent book, coedited with Jonathan D. Sarna, is *Women and American Judaism: Historical Perspectives.*

**Joan Nathan** is author of several cookbooks, including the award-winning *Jewish Cooking in America.* She contributes articles to the *New York Times, Food Arts, Gourmet,* and the *B'nai B'rith International Jewish Monthly.* She lives in Washington, D.C., with her husband and their three children.

**Naomi Nimrod** is a founder of the Israeli feminist movement and the co-author of *The Women's Haggadah,* the first published women's haggadah.

**Rachel Orkand** received a B.A. in sociology from Rice University in 2000. She worked as a legislative assistant for the Religious Action Center of Reform Judaism.

**Dr. Alicia Suskin Ostriker** is a poet, essayist, and writer of midrash. Her books include *The Nakedness of the Fathers: Biblical Visions and Revisions,* the prize-winning *The Crack in Everything,* and *The Volcano Sequence.* Her work appears in numerous journals of Jewish writing and anthologies of Jewish poetry. She is professor of English at Rutgers University.

**Dr. Judith Plaskow** is professor of religious studies at Manhattan College and author of *Standing Again at Sinai: Judaism from a Feminist Perspective.*

**Marge Piercy** is author of the memoir *Sleeping with Cats,* as well as *The Art of Blessing the Day: Poems with a Jewish Theme* and *Three Women,* among other books. Those with a particularly Jewish theme include *Gone to Soldiers* and *He, She and It*.

**Elana Ponet** has been director of the Hillel Children's School at Yale University for the past nine years. She lives in New Haven, Connecticut, with her husband, Jim Ponet, the Howard M. Holtzmann Jewish Chaplain at Yale. They have four children.

**Rabbi Geela Rayzel Raphael** was ordained at the Reconstructionist Rabbinical College and has studied at Indiana University, Brandeis, Pardes, and the Hebrew University of Jerusalem. She is the rabbinic director of the Jericho Project, an Interfaith Family Support Network of the Jewish Family and Children's Service of Greater Philadelphia. Rayzel is a songwriter and liturgist and sings with MIRAJ, an a cappella trio, and Shabbat Unplugged. "Bible Babes A-beltin'" is Rayzel's most recent recording.

**Dr. Rachel Naomi Remen** is clinical professor of family and community medicine at University of California at San Francisco School of Medicine and director and founder of the Institute for the Study of Health and Illness at Commonweal. She is the author of *Kitchen Table Wisdom* and *My Grandfather's Blessings*.

**Daphna Renan** received her B.A. from Yale University in 2000. She recently completed postgraduate studies in international and comparative legal studies at the University of London and is currently a student at Yale Law School. Her poem "Pharaoh's Daughter" was originally included in the *Yale Women's Haggadah*.

**Anne Roiphe** is the author of twelve books, including the novel *Lovingkindness*. She is a contributing editor to the *Jerusalem Report* and a columnist for the *New York Observer*.

**Judy Sirota Rosenthal** is a multimedia artist. Called an "elegant primitive," she focuses her work on Jewish and cross-cultural themes and includes installation, ritual objects, prayers, and blessings in it. Her art has been seen in numerous museums around the country. Judy conducts expressive arts workshops on creativity and spirituality and has a private practice in integrated kabbalistic healing. She lives in Connecticut.

**Gertrude Rubin** is the author of two books of poetry, *The Passover Poems* and *A Beating of Wings*. She went back to school in her mid-fifties, receiving an M.F.A. from the University of Illinois, Circle Campus, in 1978. Her poem "You Never Die at Auschwitz" was published in the *American Yearbook of Poetry* in 1985. At present, Gertrude is a workshop chairman for Poets and Patrons in Chicago.

**Danya Ruttenberg** is the editor of *Yentl's Revenge: The Next Wave of Jewish Feminism*. She also serves as a contributing editor to *Lilith: The Independent Jewish Women's Magazine;* has written for many publications, including *The San Francisco Chronicle, Tikkun, Bitch,* and *Salon;* and lectures nationwide about religion, spirituality, and culture.

**Rabbi Sandy Eisenberg Sasso** has been rabbi of Congregation Beth-El Zedeck in Indianapolis since 1977. She is author of many award-winning children's books, two of which have been selected as Best Books of the Year. Her books include *Cain and Abel: Finding the Fruits of Peace, In God's Name, God's Paintbrush, But God Remembered: Stories of Women from Creation to the Promised Land* (all Jewish Lights Publishing), and *Urban Tapestry: Indianapolis Stories.*

**The Honorable Jan Schakowsky** is United States representative from the state of Illinois. She has been a longtime consumer advocate, grassroots organizer, and activist for social and economic justice.

**Lisa Schlaff** is a graduate student in rabbinic literature at New York University. A noted Jewish educator and lecturer, she is coauthor of *The Orthodox Jewish Woman and Ritual: Options and Opportunities—Birth.*

**Rabbi Susan Schnur's** "paper pulpit" is *Lilith* magazine, where she has committedly worked to boost and enhance women's enfranchisement in Judaism for more than fifteen years. She is also a clinical psychologist and has written a weekly column for the *New York Times.*

**Rebecca Schwartz** is editor of *All the Women Followed Her: A Collection of Writings on Miriam the Prophet and the Women of Exodus* and coauthor of *The Dancing with Miriam Haggadah.* She is currently director of the Peninsula Academy for Jewish Education in the San Francisco Bay Area.

**Jordana Schuster** is a student at the Harvard Divinity School. She grew up in Claremont, California, and studied literature at Williams College. She traveled to Israel via Nesiya and Project Otzma and studied at the Conservative Yeshiva. Jordana served as the program coordinator at Yale Hillel from 2000 to 2002.

**Dr. Susan Sered** is the director of the Religion, Health and Healing Initiative at Harvard University's Center for the Study of World Religions and is associate professor of anthropology at Bar Ilan University in Israel. Dr. Sered's publications include *What Makes Women Sick? Maternity, Modesty and Militarism in Israeli Society* and *Priestess, Mother, Sacred Sister: Religions Dominated by Women.* Currently, she is carrying out a study on the extent and diversity of religious healing in the United States.

**Martha Shelley,** longtime feminist activist, is the author of *Haggadah: A Celebration of Freedom* as well as two books of poetry, *Crossing the DMZ* and *Lovers and Mothers*. Her short stories, essays, and poems have appeared in numerous anthologies. She has just completed the first volume of a forthcoming trilogy, *Jezebel: Queen of Israel*.

**Ellen Siegel** is a longtime Jewish peace activist. Professionally, she is a registered nurse. After working as a nurse in the refugee camps of Sabra and Shatila in Beirut during the massacre in 1982, she testified before the Kahan Commission of Inquiry in Jerusalem. Ellen serves on the Medical Committee of American Near East Refugee Aid.

**Cathy Smith** is a writer living in Scottsdale, Arizona. In 1995, following the death of her twenty-year-old son, she left her practice as a psychotherapist and began to write. Since that time, her articles and poems have appeared in numerous magazines and journals.

**Rabbi Susan Silverman** is the coauthor of *Jewish Family and Life: Traditions, Holidays, and Values for Today's Parents and Children*. She is working on a book on the spiritual journey of international adoption.

**Rabbi Sharon L. Sobel** was appointed executive director of the Canadian Council for Reform Judaism and ARZA Canada in July 2000. Previously, Sharon was the chair of the liturgy committee for Women in Interfaith Dialogue and one of the sponsors of The Legacy of Miriam: A Feminist Seder in Toronto. Selections of her writings for The Legacy of Miriam haggadah are included in *The Women's Seder Sourcebook* (Jewish Lights Publishing). In 1994, Vision TV produced a documentary on Sharon's rabbinate, which has been shown many times on Canadian national television.

**Catherine Spector** attends the University of Chicago Law School. She graduated from Yale University in 2000 with a B.A. in political science. As an undergraduate, she was the coordinator of Jewish Women at Yale and part of the steering committee for Yale's two international conferences on Jewish women. She is coeditor of *The Women's Passover Companion* and *The Women's Seder Sourcebook* (both Jewish Lights Publishing).

**Marcia Cohn Spiegel** holds an M.A. in Jewish communal service from Hebrew Union College–Jewish Institute of Religion and is working to create change in the Jewish community's attitudes toward addiction, violence, and sexual abuse. She founded the Alcoholism/Drug Action Program in Los Angeles and sits on the Jewish Committee of the Center for Prevention of Sexual and Domestic Violence.

**Judith Stein** is a lesbian feminist who views writing as both a politicizing and a community-building activity. She knows there are many ways to work for *tikkun olam,* each path with its own power. Currently working as a human resources consultant and trainer, Judith lives in Cambridge, Massachusetts, with Meridith Lawrence, her partner of twenty years.

**Claire Sufrin,** a graduate student in the Department of Religious Studies at Stanford University, studies modern Jewish thought. She is particularly interested in issues of community, identity, and ways of reading texts. She graduated from Yale University with a B.A. in religious studies in 2000.

**Alana Suskin** will be ordained as a Conservative rabbi in the spring of 2003. She has published her writing, including poetry and essays, in a variety of forums. Her background is in academic philosophy and women's studies, and she has a special interest in Jewish social justice.

**Ela Thier** is a graduate of the Scholars' Circle at the Drisha Institute for Jewish Education, where she studied Talmud and Jewish law and taught Bible and Talmud. Ela is a painter and award-winning screenwriter. She is also a teacher of Re-evaluation Co-Counseling, a grassroots organization that trains people to assist one another in healing from the emotional scars of oppression. She has recently completed her memoir, *Jumping for Joy.*

**Dr. Ellen M. Umansky** is the Carl and Dorothy Bennett Professor of Judaic Studies at Fairfield University in Fairfield, Connecticut. The author of numerous books and articles on modern Jewish history and thought, constructive Jewish theology, and women and Judaism, she has also coedited *Four Centuries of Jewish Women's Spirituality: A Sourcebook.*

**Davi Walders** is a poet, writer, and educator. Her poetry and prose have been published in more than one hundred and fifty anthologies, journals, and magazines. In addition to receiving fellowships from the Maryland State Arts Council, the Alden Dow Creativity Center, CrossCurrents, and the Luce Foundation, she developed and directs the Vital Signs Poetry Project at the National Institutes of Health and its Children's Inn. The project is funded by the Witter Bynner Foundation for Poetry.

**Rabbi Iscah Waldman** is currently director of education and family programming at Ansche Chesed in New York City. Iscah graduated from Columbia University and the Jewish Theological Seminary with bachelor's degrees in Talmud and ancient studies. Ordained from JTS in 1999, she is also pursuing a Ph.D. in midrash there.

**Rabbi Deborah Waxman** is assistant to the president and director of special projects at the Reconstructionist Rabbinical College, where she studied for the rabbinate. She is also enrolled as a doctoral student in American Jewish history at Temple University.

**Rabbi Sheila Peltz Weinberg** was the rabbi of the Jewish Community of Amherst in Massachusetts for thirteen years. She graduated from the Reconstructionist Rabbinical College in 1986. A coteacher of the Mindfulness Leadership Training Program at Elat Chayyim, she is also on the faculty of Metivta Spirituality Institute, a rabbinic training program.

**Dr. Chava Weissler** is professor of religious studies at Lehigh University, where she holds the Philip and Muriel Berman Chair of Jewish Civilization. Among the courses she teaches are Jewish folklore, women and Jewish history, Chasidic tales, and the mystical tradition in Judaism. Her book on the religious lives of Jewish women, *Voices of the Matriarchs,* was a National Jewish Book Award Finalist in Women's Studies in 1999 and won the Koret Foundation Book Award in Jewish History in 2000.

**Cantor Lorel Zar-Kessler** has served as the cantor of Congregation Beth El of the Sudbury River Valley, in Sudbury, Massachusetts, since 1990. She has grown as a Jew, as a teacher, and as a student of Torah by helping her community develop its love of the music of prayer. She lives in Newton, Massachusetts, with her husband, Arnold, and three wonderful daughters: Rachel, Claire, and Shira.

# Permissions

*"Kanfei ha Shekhinah"* and "This Special Occasion" by Stephanie S. Aaron previously appeared in the *Tucson Jewish Feminist Haggadah*. They appear by permission of the author.

"Our Continuing Survival" by Evy Gershon previously appeared in *The Survivors' Haggadah*. © Evy Gershon. It appears by permission of the author. All rights reserved.

"Free to Answer Our Questions" from *Women's Seder* by the Jewish Family Service of Delaware appear by permission of Yvette Rudnitsky, editor of the haggadah.

"Joining Together," "How Far Would We Go?" and "Through Bitter and Sweet" by Sharon Sobel previously appeared in *The Legacy of Miriam* by the Women in Interfaith Dialogue of the League for Human Rights of B'nai Brith Canada. They appear by permission of the author.

"We Will All Remember," "Our Passover Stories," and "Half-Baked Bread" from *Her Seder,* prepared by Commission on Women's Equality of the American Jewish Congress, Pennsylvania Region, 1994, 1998. They appear by permission of Joseph L. Puder, Executive Director. Contact AJC, 2100 Arch Street, Philadelphia, PA 19103 for more information.

"Jocheved Works" by Davi Walders previously appeared in *Midstream*, June/July 1997, and *In Praise of Women Haggadah,* edited by Davi Walders, National Council of Jewish Women, Montgomery County Maryland Branch, 1999. It appears by permission of the author.

"For Equity and Dignity" by Lisa S. Greene previously appeared in *Miriam Sang to Them,* edited by Lisa S. Greene, Project Kesher's Global Women's Pre-Passover Seder. It appears by permission of the author.

*"Maggid"* by Lisa S. Greene appears by permission of the author.

"Opening the Door for Elijah" by Lisa S. Greene previously appeared in *Haggadah* for North Shore Congregation Israel's women's seder. It appears by permission of the author.

"A Passover Prayer to Speak Out For Children" © National Council of Jewish Women appears by permission of Stacy Kass, Acting Executive Director.

"The Telling" by Arielle Derby previously appeared in the *Smith College Haggadah 2001*. It appears by permission of the author.

"Wrought by Humankind" from the Jewish Family Service Women's Seder of the Durham–Chapel Hill Community, 2000, appears by permission of Marjorie Scheer, Director.

"Memory" by Jenny Aisenberg previously appeared in the *Smith College Haggadah 2001*. It appears by permission of the author.

"To Her Grandchild" by Janet Berkenfield previously appeared in *A New Haggadah, A Jewish Lesbian Seder* by Judith Stein. It appears by permission of the author.

"Restoring Wholeness" is reprinted with permission by Gloria Greenfield, chair, *Lichvod Pesach* Committee of the Women's Community Seders, Temple Emunah, Lexington, Massachusetts.

"Those Who Sustain Us" is reprinted with permission by Gloria Greenfield, chair, *Lichvod Pesach* Committee of the Women's Community Seders, Temple Emunah, Lexington, Massachusetts. The ritual was adapted from a reading by Matia Rania Angelou and Janet Berkenfield.

"The Radiance of the Infinite" and "The Fourth Matzah" from the *Williams College Feminist Haggadah* appear by permission of Jordana Schuster, editor of the *1998 Williams College Feminist Haggadah*.

"The Measure of Our Success" previously appeared in "Jewish Feminist Social Responsibility: The Rise of the Global Sweatshop" by Jo-Ann Mort on the web magazine SocialAction.com, published by Jewish Family & Life! (JFL). Reprinted with permission by JFL and the author.

"The Song of Questions" and *"Lo Dayeinu"* from *The Women's Haggadah* by E. M. Broner. © 1993, 1994 by E. M. Broner. Reprinted by permission of HarperCollins Publishers.

"It Would Have Been Enough," "Until All of Us Are Free," and "This is the Way to Experience Bitterness" by Tamara Cohen and "Tremor in the Seed" by Ronnie Horn were previously published in *The Journey Continues: The Ma'yan Passover Haggadah*. © 1999, 2000 by Ma'yan: The Jewish Women's

# Author Index

# Index

Notes

# Notes

Notes

# Notes

Notes

# Notes

# About JEWISH LIGHTS Publishing

People of all faiths and backgrounds yearn for books that attract, engage, educate, and spiritually inspire.

Our principal goal is to stimulate thought and help all people learn about who the Jewish People are, where they come from, and what the future can be made to hold. While people of our diverse Jewish heritage are the primary audience, our books speak to people in the Christian world as well and will broaden their understanding of Judaism and the roots of their own faith.

We bring to you authors who are at the forefront of spiritual thought and experience. While each has something different to say, they all say it in a voice that you can hear.

Our books are designed to welcome you and then to engage, stimulate, and inspire. We judge our success not only by whether or not our books are beautiful and commercially successful, but by whether or not they make a difference in your life.

We at Jewish Lights take great care to produce beautiful books that present meaningful spiritual content in a form that reflects the art of making high quality books. Therefore, we want to acknowledge those who contributed to the production of this book.

*Stuart M. Matlins, Publisher*

PRODUCTION
Sara Dismukes, Tim Holtz,
Martha McKinney & Bridgett Taylor

EDITORIAL
Rebecca Castellano, Amanda Dupuis, Polly Short Mahoney,
Lauren Seidman & Emily Wichland

JACKET DESIGN
Bridgett Taylor

TYPESETTING
Chelsea Cloeter, Tucson, Arizona

JACKET / TEXT PRINTING & BINDING
Lake Book, Melrose Park, Illinois

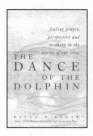 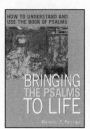   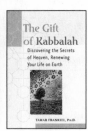

# *Spirituality—The Kushner Series*
## Books by Lawrence Kushner

### The Way Into Jewish Mystical Tradition

Explains the principles of Jewish mystical thinking, their religious and spiritual significance, and how they relate to our lives. A book that allows us to experience and understand the Jewish mystical approach to our place in the world.
6 x 9, 224 pp, HC, ISBN 1-58023-029-6 **$21.95**

### Jewish Spirituality: *A Brief Introduction for Christians*

Addresses Christian's questions, revealing the essence of Judaism in a way that people whose own tradition traces its roots to Judaism can understand and appreciate.
5½ x 8½, 112 pp, Quality PB, ISBN 1-58023-150-0 **$12.95**

### Eyes Remade for Wonder: *The Way of Jewish Mysticism and Sacred Living*
A Lawrence Kushner Reader  Intro. by *Thomas Moore*

Whether you are new to Kushner or a devoted fan, you'll find inspiration here. With samplings from each of Kushner's works, and a generous amount of new material, this book is to be read and reread, each time discovering deeper layers of meaning in our lives.
6 x 9, 240 pp, Quality PB, ISBN 1-58023-042-3 **$18.95**; HC, ISBN 1-58023-014-8 **$23.95**

 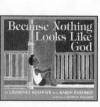  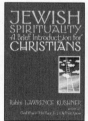 

**Invisible Lines of Connection:** *Sacred Stories of the Ordinary*  AWARD WINNER!
5½ x 8½, 160 pp, Quality PB, ISBN 1-879045-98-2 **$15.95**

**Honey from the Rock:** *An Introduction to Jewish Mysticism*  SPECIAL ANNIVERSARY EDITION
6 x 9, 176 pp, Quality PB, ISBN 1-58023-073-3 **$15.95**

**The Book of Letters:** *A Mystical Hebrew Alphabet*  AWARD WINNER!
*Popular HC Edition,* 6 x 9, 80 pp, 2-color text, ISBN 1-879045-00-1 **$24.95**; *Deluxe Gift Edition,* 9 x 12, 80 pp, HC, 4-color text, ornamentation, slipcase, ISBN 1-879045-01-X **$79.95**; *Collector's Limited Edition,* 9 x 12, 80 pp, HC, gold-embossed pages, hand-assembled slipcase. With silkscreened print. Limited to 500 signed and numbered copies, ISBN 1-879045-04-4 **$349.00**

**The Book of Words:** *Talking Spiritual Life, Living Spiritual Talk*  AWARD WINNER!
6 x 9, 160 pp, Quality PB, 2-color text, ISBN 1-58023-020-2 **$16.95**; HC, ISBN 1-879045-35-4 **$21.95**

**God Was in This Place & I, i Did Not Know:** *Finding Self, Spirituality and Ultimate Meaning*
6 x 9, 192 pp, Quality PB, ISBN 1-879045-33-8 **$16.95**

**The River of Light:** *Jewish Mystical Awareness*  SPECIAL ANNIVERSARY EDITION
6 x 9, 192 pp, Quality PB, ISBN 1-58023-096-2 **$16.95**

**Because Nothing Looks Like God**
by Lawrence and Karen Kushner; Full-color illus. by Dawn W. Majewski
11 x 8½, 32 pp, HC, Full-color illus., ISBN 1-58023-092-X **$16.95**  **For ages 4 & up**

# The Way Into... Series

A major multi-volume series to be completed over the next several years, **The Way Into... provides an accessible and usable "guided tour" of the Jewish faith, its people, its history and beliefs—in total, an introduction to Judaism for adults that will enable them to understand and interact with sacred texts.**

Each volume is written by a major modern scholar and teacher, and is organized around an important concept of Judaism.

*The Way Into...* will enable all readers to achieve a real sense of Jewish cultural literacy through guided study. Available volumes:

### The Way Into Torah
by *Dr. Norman J. Cohen*

What is "Torah"? What are the different approaches to studying Torah? What are the different levels of understanding Torah? For whom is study intended? Explores the origins and development of Torah, why it should be studied and how to do it. An easy-to-use, easy-to-understand introduction to an ancient subject.
6 x 9, 176 pp, HC, ISBN 1-58023-028-8 **$21.95**

### The Way Into Jewish Prayer
by *Dr. Lawrence A. Hoffman*

Explores the reasons for and the ways of Jewish prayer. Opens the door to 3,000 years of the Jewish way to God by making available all you need to feel at home in Jewish worship. Provides basic definitions of the terms you need to know as well as thoughtful analysis of the depth that lies beneath Jewish prayer.
6 x 9, 224 pp, HC, ISBN 1-58023-027-X **$21.95**

### The Way Into Encountering God in Judaism
by *Dr. Neil Gillman*

Explains how Jews have encountered God throughout history—and today—by exploring the many metaphors for God in Jewish tradition. Explores the Jewish tradition's passionate but also conflicting ways of relating to God as Creator, relational partner, and a force in history and nature.
6 x 9, 240 pp, HC, ISBN 1-58023-025-3 **$21.95**

### The Way Into Jewish Mystical Tradition
by *Rabbi Lawrence Kushner*

Explains the principles of Jewish mystical thinking, their religious and spiritual significance, and how they relate to our lives. A book that allows us to experience and understand the Jewish mystical approach to our place in the world.
6 x 9, 224 pp, HC, ISBN 1-58023-029-6 **$21.95**

# Jewish Meditation

## Aleph-Bet Yoga
### Embodying the Hebrew Letters for Physical and Spiritual Well-Being
by *Steven A. Rapp*; Foreword by *Tamar Frankiel & Judy Greenfeld*; Preface by *Hart Lazer*

Blends aspects of hatha yoga and the shapes of the Hebrew letters. Connects yoga practice with Jewish spiritual life. Easy-to-follow instructions, b/w photos.
7 x 10, 128 pp, Quality PB, b/w photos, ISBN 1-58023-162-4 **$16.95**

## The Rituals & Practices of a Jewish Life
### A Handbook for Personal Spiritual Renewal
by *Rabbi Kerry M. Olitzky* and *Rabbi Daniel Judson*; Foreword by *Vanessa L. Ochs*; Illustrated by *Joel Moskowitz*

This easy-to-use handbook explains the why, what, and how of ten specific areas of Jewish ritual and practice: morning and evening blessings, covering the head, blessings throughout the day, daily prayer, tefillin, tallit and *tallit katan*, Torah study, kashrut, *mikvah*, and entering Shabbat. 6 x 9, 272 pp, Quality PB, Illus., ISBN 1-58023-169-1 **$18.95**

Discovering Jewish Meditation: *Instruction & Guidance for Learning an Ancient Spiritual Practice* by Nan Fink Gefen 6 x 9, 208 pp, Quality PB, ISBN 1-58023-067-9 **$16.95**

The Handbook of Jewish Meditation Practices: *A Guide for Enriching the Sabbath and Other Days of Your Life* by Rabbi David A. Cooper
6 x 9, 208 pp, Quality PB, ISBN 1-58023-102-0 **$16.95**

Meditation from the Heart of Judaism: *Today's Teachers Share Their Practices, Techniques, and Faith* Ed. by Avram Davis 6 x 9, 256 pp, Quality PB, ISBN 1-58023-049-0 **$16.95**

The Way of Flame: *A Guide to the Forgotten Mystical Tradition of Jewish Meditation* by Avram Davis 4½ x 8, 176 pp, Quality PB, ISBN 1-58023-060-1 **$15.95**

Minding the Temple of the Soul: *Balancing Body, Mind, and Spirit through Traditional Jewish Prayer, Movement, and Meditation* by Tamar Frankiel and Judy Greenfeld
7 x 10, 184 pp, Quality PB, Illus., ISBN 1-879045-64-8 **$16.95**

Entering the Temple of Dreams: *Jewish Prayers, Movements, and Meditations for the End of the Day* by Tamar Frankiel and Judy Greenfeld
7 x 10, 192 pp, Illus., Quality PB, ISBN 1-58023-079-2 **$16.95**

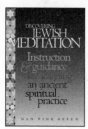   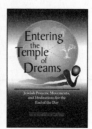 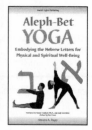

# Ecology

## Torah of the Earth: *Exploring 4,000 Years of Ecology in Jewish Thought*
In 2 Volumes Ed. by *Rabbi Arthur Waskow*

An invaluable key to understanding the intersection of ecology and Judaism. Leading scholars provide a guided tour of Jewish ecological thought.
Vol. 1: *Biblical Israel & Rabbinic Judaism*, 6 x 9, 272 pp, Quality PB, ISBN 1-58023-086-5 **$19.95**
Vol. 2: *Zionism & Eco-Judaism*, 6 x 9, 336 pp, Quality PB, ISBN 1-58023-087-3 **$19.95**

Ecology & the Jewish Spirit: *Where Nature & the Sacred Meet* Ed. and with Intros.
by Ellen Bernstein 6 x 9, 288 pp, Quality PB, ISBN 1-58023-082-2 **$16.95**

# Theology/Philosophy

## Love and Terror in the God Encounter
### The Theological Legacy of Rabbi Joseph B. Soloveitchik
by *Dr. David Hartman*

Renowned scholar David Hartman explores the sometimes surprising intersection of Soloveitchik's rootedness in halakhic tradition with his genuine responsiveness to modern Western theology. An engaging look at one of the most important Jewish thinkers of the twentieth century.
6 x 9, 240 pp, HC, ISBN 1-58023-112-8 **$25.00**

## These Are the Words: *A Vocabulary of Jewish Spiritual Life*
by *Arthur Green*

What are the most essential ideas, concepts and terms that an educated person needs to know about Judaism? From *Adonai* (My Lord) to *zekhut* (merit), this enlightening and entertaining journey through Judaism teaches us the 149 core Hebrew words that constitute the basic vocabulary of Jewish spiritual life. 6 x 9, 304 pp, Quality PB, ISBN 1-58023-107-1 **$18.95**

## Broken Tablets: *Restoring the Ten Commandments and Ourselves*
Ed. by *Rabbi Rachel S. Mikva*; Intro. by *Rabbi Lawrence Kushner*  AWARD WINNER!

Twelve outstanding spiritual leaders each share profound and personal thoughts about these biblical commands and why they have such a special hold on us.
6 x 9, 192 pp, Quality PB, ISBN 1-58023-158-6 **$16.95**; HC, ISBN 1-58023-066-0 **$21.95**

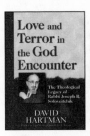 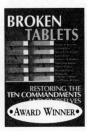 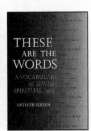 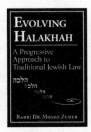 

A Heart of Many Rooms: *Celebrating the Many Voices within Judaism*  AWARD WINNER!
by Dr. David Hartman  6 x 9, 352 pp, Quality PB, ISBN 1-58023-156-X **$19.95**; HC, ISBN 1-58023-048-2 **$24.95**

A Living Covenant: *The Innovative Spirit in Traditional Judaism*  AWARD WINNER!
by Dr. David Hartman  6 x 9, 368 pp, Quality PB, ISBN 1-58023-011-3 **$18.95**

Evolving Halakhah: *A Progressive Approach to Traditional Jewish Law*
by Rabbi Dr. Moshe Zemer  6 x 9, 480 pp, HC, ISBN 1-58023-002-4 **$40.00**

The Death of Death: *Resurrection and Immortality in Jewish Thought*  AWARD WINNER!
by Dr. Neil Gillman  6 x 9, 336 pp, Quality PB, ISBN 1-58023-081-4 **$18.95**

The Last Trial: *On the Legends and Lore of the Command to Abraham to Offer Isaac as a Sacrifice*  by Shalom Spiegel  6 x 9, 208 pp, Quality PB, ISBN 1-879045-29-X **$17.95**

Tormented Master: *The Life and Spiritual Quest of Rabbi Nahman of Bratslav*
by Dr. Arthur Green  6 x 9, 416 pp, Quality PB, ISBN 1-879045-11-7 **$18.95**

The Earth Is the Lord's: *The Inner World of the Jew in Eastern Europe*
by Abraham Joshua Heschel  5½ x 8, 128 pp, Quality PB, ISBN 1-879045-42-7 **$14.95**

A Passion for Truth: *Despair and Hope in Hasidism*  by Abraham Joshua Heschel
5½ x 8, 352 pp, Quality PB, ISBN 1-879045-41-9 **$18.95**

Your Word Is Fire: *The Hasidic Masters on Contemplative Prayer*  Ed. by Dr. Arthur Green and Dr. Barry W. Holtz  6 x 9, 160 pp, Quality PB, ISBN 1-879045-25-7 **$15.95**

# Life Cycle/Grief/Divorce

### Divorce Is a Mitzvah: *A Practical Guide to Finding Wholeness and Holiness When Your Marriage Dies*
by *Rabbi Perry Netter;*
Afterword—"Afterwards: New Jewish Divorce Rituals"—by *Rabbi Laura Geller*
What does Judaism tell you about divorce? This first-of-its-kind handbook provides practical wisdom from biblical and rabbinic teachings and modern psychological research, as well as information and strength from a Jewish perspective for those experiencing the challenging life-transition of divorce.  6 x 9, 224 pp, Quality PB, ISBN 1-58023-172-1 **$16.95**

### Against the Dying of the Light
#### *A Parent's Story of Love, Loss and Hope*
by *Leonard Fein*
The sudden death of a child. A personal tragedy beyond description. Rage and despair deeper than sorrow. What can come from it? Raw wisdom and defiant hope. In this unusual exploration of heartbreak and healing, Fein chronicles the sudden death of his 30-year-old daughter and reveals what the progression of grief can teach each one of us.
5½ x 8½, 176 pp, HC, ISBN 1-58023-110-1 **$19.95**

### Mourning & Mitzvah, 2nd Ed.: *A Guided Journal for Walking the Mourner's Path through Grief to Healing* with *Over 60 Guided Exercises*
by *Anne Brener, L.C.S.W.*
For those who mourn a death, for those who would help them, for those who face a loss of any kind, Brener teaches us the power and strength available to us in the fully experienced mourning process. Revised and expanded.  7½ x 9, 304 pp, Quality PB, ISBN 1-58023-113-6 **$19.95**

### Grief in Our Seasons: *A Mourner's Kaddish Companion*
by *Rabbi Kerry M. Olitzky*
A wise and inspiring selection of sacred Jewish writings and a simple, powerful ancient ritual for mourners to read each day, to help hold the memory of their loved ones in their hearts. Offers a comforting, step-by-step daily link to saying Kaddish.
4½ x 6½, 448 pp, Quality PB, ISBN 1-879045-55-9 **$15.95**

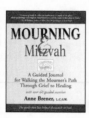

Tears of Sorrow, Seeds of Hope
*A Jewish Spiritual Companion for Infertility and Pregnancy Loss*
by Rabbi Nina Beth Cardin   6 x 9, 192 pp, HC, ISBN 1-58023-017-2 **$19.95**

A Time to Mourn, A Time to Comfort
*A Guide to Jewish Bereavement and Comfort*
by Dr. Ron Wolfson   7 x 9, 336 pp, Quality PB, ISBN 1-879045-96-6 **$18.95**

When a Grandparent Dies
*A Kid's Own Remembering Workbook for Dealing with Shiva and the Year Beyond*
by Nechama Liss-Levinson, Ph.D.
8 x 10, 48 pp, HC, Illus., 2-color text, ISBN 1-879045-44-3 **$15.95**   **For ages 7–13**

# Healing/Wellness/Recovery

## Jewish Paths toward Healing and Wholeness
### A Personal Guide to Dealing with Suffering
by *Rabbi Kerry M. Olitzky*; Foreword by *Debbie Friedman*

Why me? Why do we suffer? How can we heal? Grounded in personal experience with illness and Jewish spiritual traditions, this book provides healing rituals, psalms and prayers that help readers initiate a dialogue with God, to guide them along the complicated path of healing and wholeness.  6 x 9, 192 pp, Quality PB, ISBN 1-58023-068-7 **$15.95**

## Healing of Soul, Healing of Body
### Spiritual Leaders Unfold the Strength & Solace in Psalms
Ed. by *Rabbi Simkha Y. Weintraub, CSW*, for The National Center for Jewish Healing

For those who are facing illness and those who care for them. Inspiring commentaries on ten psalms for healing by eminent spiritual leaders reflecting all Jewish movements make the power of the psalms accessible to all.
6 x 9, 128 pp, Quality PB, Illus., 2-color text, ISBN 1-879045-31-1 **$14.95**

## Jewish Pastoral Care
### A Practical Handbook from Traditional and Contemporary Sources
Ed. by *Rabbi Dayle A. Friedman*

Gives today's Jewish pastoral counselors practical guidelines based in the Jewish tradition.
6 x 9, 464 pp, HC, ISBN 1-58023-078-4 **$35.00**

Twelve Jewish Steps to Recovery: *A Personal Guide to Turning from Alcoholism & Other Addictions—Drugs, Food, Gambling, Sex . . .* by Rabbi Kerry M. Olitzky & Stuart A. Copans, M.D. Preface by Abraham J. Twerski, M.D.; "Getting Help" by JACS Foundation  6 x 9, 144 pp, Quality PB, ISBN 1-879045-09-5 **$14.95**

One Hundred Blessings Every Day: *Daily Twelve Step Recovery Affirmations, Exercises for Personal Growth & Renewal Reflecting Seasons of the Jewish Year* by Rabbi Kerry M. Olitzky  4½ x 6½, 432 pp, Quality PB, ISBN 1-879045-30-3 **$14.95**

Recovery from Codependence: *A Jewish Twelve Steps Guide to Healing Your Soul* by Rabbi Kerry M. Olitzky  6 x 9, 160 pp, Quality PB, ISBN 1-879045-32-X **$13.95**

Renewed Each Day: *Daily Twelve Step Recovery Meditations Based on the Bible* by Rabbi Kerry M. Olitzky & Aaron Z. *Vol. I: Genesis & Exodus; Vol. II: Leviticus, Numbers and Deuteronomy*
*Vol. I:* 6 x 9, 224 pp, Quality PB, ISBN 1-879045-12-5 **$14.95**
*Vol. II:* 6 x 9, 280 pp, Quality PB, ISBN 1-879045-13-3 **$14.95**

# Life Cycle & Holidays

## The Jewish Family Fun Book: *Holiday Projects, Everyday Activities, and Travel Ideas with Jewish Themes*
by *Danielle Dardashti* & *Roni Sarig;* Illustrated by *Avi Katz*

With almost 100 easy-to-do activities to re-invigorate age-old Jewish customs and make them fun for the whole family, this complete sourcebook details activities for fun at home and away from home, including meaningful everyday and holiday crafts, recipes, travel guides, enriching entertainment and much, much more. Illustrated.
6 x 9, 288 pp, Quality PB, Illus., ISBN 1-58023-171-3 **$18.95**

## The Book of Jewish Sacred Practices
### CLAL's Guide to Everyday & Holiday Rituals & Blessings
Ed. by *Rabbi Irwin Kula* & *Vanessa L. Ochs, Ph.D.*

A meditation, blessing, profound Jewish teaching, and ritual for more than one hundred everyday events and holidays. 6 x 9, 368 pp, Quality PB, ISBN 1-58023-152-7 **$18.95**

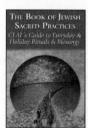    

Celebrating Your New Jewish Daughter: *Creating Jewish Ways to Welcome Baby Girls into the Covenant—New and Traditional Ceremonies*
by Debra Nussbaum Cohen; Foreword by Rabbi Sandy Eisenberg Sasso
6 x 9, 272 pp, Quality PB, ISBN 1-58023-090-3 **$18.95**

The New Jewish Baby Book AWARD WINNER!
*Names, Ceremonies & Customs—A Guide for Today's Families*
by Anita Diamant  6 x 9, 336 pp, Quality PB, ISBN 1-879045-28-1 **$18.95**

Parenting As a Spiritual Journey
*Deepening Ordinary & Extraordinary Events into Sacred Occasions*
by Rabbi Nancy Fuchs-Kreimer  6 x 9, 224 pp, Quality PB, ISBN 1-58023-016-4 **$16.95**

Putting God on the Guest List, 2nd Ed. AWARD WINNER!
*How to Reclaim the Spiritual Meaning of Your Child's Bar or Bat Mitzvah*
by Rabbi Jeffrey K. Salkin  6 x 9, 224 pp, Quality PB, ISBN 1-879045-59-1 **$16.95**

The Bar/Bat Mitzvah Memory Book: *An Album for Treasuring the Spiritual Celebration* by Rabbi Jeffrey K. Salkin and Nina Salkin
8 x 10, 48 pp, Deluxe HC, 2-color text, ribbon marker, ISBN 1-58023-111-X **$19.95**

For Kids—Putting God on Your Guest List
*How to Claim the Spiritual Meaning of Your Bar or Bat Mitzvah*
by Rabbi Jeffrey K. Salkin  6 x 9, 144 pp, Quality PB, ISBN 1-58023-015-6 **$14.95**

Bar/Bat Mitzvah Basics, 2nd Ed.: *A Practical Family Guide to Coming of Age Together*
Ed. by Cantor Helen Leneman  6 x 9, 240 pp, Quality PB, ISBN 1-58023-151-9 **$18.95**

Hanukkah, 2nd Ed.: *The Family Guide to Spiritual Celebration*—The Art of Jewish Living
by Dr. Ron Wolfson  7 x 9, 240 pp, Quality PB, Illus., ISBN 1-58023-122-5 **$18.95**

Shabbat, 2nd Ed.: *Preparing for and Celebrating the Sabbath*—The Art of Jewish Living
by Dr. Ron Wolfson  7 x 9, 320 pp, Quality PB, Illus., ISBN 1-58023-164-0 **$19.95**

Passover, 2nd Ed.: *The Family Guide to Spiritual Celebration*—The Art of Jewish Living
by Dr. Ron Wolfson  7 x 9, 352 pp, Quality PB, ISBN 1-58023-174-8 **$19.95**

# Children's Spirituality

## Cain & Abel  AWARD WINNER!
### *Finding the Fruits of Peace*
by *Sandy Eisenberg Sasso*
Full-color illus. by *Joani Keller Rothenberg*

For ages 5 & up

A sensitive recasting of the ancient tale shows we have the power to deal with anger in positive ways. Provides questions for kids and adults to explore together. "Editor's Choice"—American Library Association's *Booklist*

9 x 12, 32 pp, HC, Full-color illus., ISBN 1-58023-123-3  **$16.95**

## For Heaven's Sake  AWARD WINNER!

For ages 4 & up

by *Sandy Eisenberg Sasso*; Full-color illus. by *Kathryn Kunz Finney*
Everyone talked about heaven, but no one would say what heaven was or how to find it. So Isaiah decides to find out.  9 x 12, 32 pp, HC, Full-color illus., ISBN 1-58023-054-7  **$16.95**

## God Said Amen  AWARD WINNER!

For ages 4 & up

by *Sandy Eisenberg Sasso*; Full-color illus. by *Avi Katz*
Inspiring tale of two kingdoms: one overflowing with water but without oil to light its lamps; the other blessed with oil but no water to grow its gardens. The kingdoms' rulers ask God for help but are too stubborn to ask each other. Shows that we need only reach out to each other to find God's answer to our prayers.  9 x 12, 32 pp, HC, Full-color illus., ISBN 1-58023-080-6  **$16.95**

## God in Between  AWARD WINNER!

For ages 4 & up

by *Sandy Eisenberg Sasso*; Full-color illus. by *Sally Sweetland*
If you wanted to find God, where would you look? This magical, mythical tale teaches that God can be found where we are: within all of us and the relationships between us.
9 x 12, 32 pp, HC, Full-color illus., ISBN 1-879045-86-9  **$16.95**

## Noah's Wife: *The Story of Naamah*

For ages 4 & up

by *Sandy Eisenberg Sasso*; Full-color illus. by *Bethanne Andersen*  AWARD WINNER!
Opens religious imaginations to new ideas about the story of the Flood. When God tells Noah to bring the animals onto the ark, God also calls on Naamah, Noah's wife, to save each plant on Earth.  9 x 12, 32 pp, HC, Full-color illus., ISBN 1-58023-134-9  **$16.95**

## But God Remembered  AWARD WINNER!
### *Stories of Women from Creation to the Promised Land*

For ages 8 & up

by *Sandy Eisenberg Sasso*; Full-color illus. by *Bethanne Andersen*
Vibrantly brings to life four stories of courageous and strong women from ancient tradition; all teach important values through their actions and faith.
9 x 12, 32 pp, HC, Full-color illus., ISBN 1-879045-43-5  **$16.95**

# Children's Spirituality

## In Our Image
### God's First Creatures   AWARD WINNER!

For ages 4 & up

by *Nancy Sohn Swartz*
Full-color illus. by *Melanie Hall*

A playful new twist on the Creation story—from the perspective of the animals. Celebrates the interconnectedness of nature and the harmony of all living things. "The vibrantly colored illustrations nearly leap off the page in this delightful interpretation." —*School Library Journal*
9 x 12, 32 pp, HC, Full-color illus., ISBN 1-879045-99-0 **$16.95**

## God's Paintbrush   AWARD WINNER!

For ages 4 & up

by *Sandy Eisenberg Sasso;* Full-color illus. by *Annette Compton*

Invites children of all faiths and backgrounds to encounter God openly in their own lives. Wonderfully interactive; provides questions adult and child can explore together at the end of each episode.  11 x 8½, 32 pp, HC, Full-color illus., ISBN 1-879045-22-2 **$16.95**

*Also available: A Teacher's Guide:* **A Guide for Jewish & Christian Educators and Parents**
8½ x 11, 32 pp, PB, ISBN 1-879045-57-5 **$8.95**

**God's Paintbrush Celebration Kit**  9½ x 12, HC, Includes 5 sessions/40 full-color Activity Sheets and Teacher Folder with complete instructions, ISBN 1-58023-050-4 **$21.95**

## In God's Name   AWARD WINNER!

For ages 4 & up

by *Sandy Eisenberg Sasso;* Full-color illus. by *Phoebe Stone*

Like an ancient myth in its poetic text and vibrant illustrations, this award-winning modern fable about the search for God's name celebrates the diversity and, at the same time, the unity of all people. 9 x 12, 32 pp, HC, Full-color illus., ISBN 1-879045-26-5 **$16.95**

## What Is God's Name? (A Board Book)

For ages 0–4

An abridged board book version of award-winning *In God's Name.*
5 x 5, 24 pp, Board, Full-color illus., ISBN 1-893361-10-1 **$7.95**  A SKYLIGHT PATHS Book

## The 11th Commandment: *Wisdom from Our Children*

For all ages

by *The Children of America*   AWARD WINNER!

"If there were an Eleventh Commandment, what would it be?" Children of many religious denominations across America answer this question—in their own drawings and words. "A rare book of spiritual celebration for all people, of all ages, for all time."—*Bookviews*
8 x 10, 48 pp, HC, Full-color illus., ISBN 1-879045-46-X **$16.95**

# Children's Spirituality

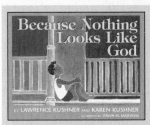

## Because Nothing Looks Like God

by *Lawrence and Karen Kushner*
Full-color illus. by *Dawn W. Majewski*

**For ages 4 & up**

MULTICULTURAL, NONDENOMINATIONAL, NONSECTARIAN

What is God like? The first collaborative work by husband-and-wife team Lawrence and Karen Kushner introduces children to the possibilities of spiritual life. Real-life examples of happiness and sadness—from goodnight stories, to the hope and fear felt the first time at bat, to the closing moments of life—invite us to explore, together with our children, the questions we all have about God, no matter what our age.

11 x 8½, 32 pp, HC, Full-color illus., ISBN 1-58023-092-X **$16.95**

*Also available:* **Teacher's Guide,** 8½ x 11, 22 pp, PB, ISBN 1-58023-140-3 **$6.95** For ages 5–8

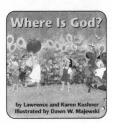

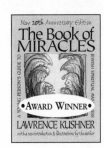

## Where Is God?
## What Does God Look Like?
## How Does God Make Things Happen? (Board Books)

**For ages 0–4**

by *Lawrence and Karen Kushner*; Full-color illus. by *Dawn W. Majewski*

Gently invites children to become aware of God's presence all around them. Three board books abridged from *Because Nothing Looks Like God* by Lawrence and Karen Kushner.
Each 5 x 5, 24 pp, Board, Full-color illus. **$7.95** SKYLIGHT PATHS Books

## Sharing Blessings
### Children's Stories for Exploring the Spirit of the Jewish Holidays

**For ages 6 & up**

by *Rahel Musleah* and *Rabbi Michael Klayman*; Full-color illus.

What is the spiritual message of each of the Jewish holidays? How do we teach it to our children? Through stories about one family's life, *Sharing Blessings* explores ways to get into the *spirit* of thirteen different holidays.
8½ x 11, 64 pp, HC, Full-color illus., ISBN 1-879045-71-0 **$18.95**

## The Book of Miracles  AWARD WINNER!
### A Young Person's Guide to Jewish Spiritual Awareness

**For ages 9 & up**

by *Lawrence Kushner*

Introduces kids to a way of everyday spiritual thinking to last a lifetime. Kushner, whose award-winning books have brought spirituality to life for countless adults, now shows young people how to use Judaism as a foundation on which to build their lives.
6 x 9, 96 pp, HC, 2-color illus., ISBN 1-879045-78-8 **$16.95**

# Spirituality

**My People's Prayer Book:** *Traditional Prayers, Modern Commentaries*
Ed. by *Dr. Lawrence A. Hoffman*

Provides a diverse and exciting commentary to the traditional liturgy, helping modern men and women find new wisdom in Jewish prayer, and bring liturgy into their lives. Each book includes Hebrew text, modern translation, and commentaries *from all perspectives* of the Jewish world.
Vol. 1—*The Sh'ma and Its Blessings*, 7 x 10, 168 pp, HC, ISBN 1-879045-79-6 **$23.95**
Vol. 2—*The Amidah*, 7 x 10, 240 pp, HC, ISBN 1-879045-80-X **$23.95**
Vol. 3—*P'sukei D'zimrah* (Morning Psalms), 7 x 10, 240 pp, HC, ISBN 1-879045-81-8 **$24.95**
Vol. 4—*Seder K'riat Hatorah* (The Torah Service), 7 x 10, 264 pp, HC, ISBN 1-879045-82-6 **$23.95**
Vol. 5—*Birkhot Hashachar* (Morning Blessings), 7 x 10, 240 pp, HC, ISBN 1-879045-83-4 **$24.95**
Vol. 6—*Tachanun and Concluding Prayers*, 7 x 10, 240 pp, HC, ISBN 1-879045-84-2 **$24.95**

**Six Jewish Spiritual Paths:** *A Rationalist Looks at Spirituality*
by Rabbi Rifat Sonsino
6 x 9, 208 pp, Quality PB, ISBN 1-58023-167-5 **$16.95**; HC, ISBN 1-58023-095-4 **$21.95**

**Becoming a Congregation of Learners**
*Learning as a Key to Revitalizing Congregational Life* by Isa Aron, Ph.D.;
Foreword by Rabbi Lawrence A. Hoffman, Co-Developer, Synagogue 2000
6 x 9, 304 pp, Quality PB, ISBN 1-58023-089-X **$19.95**

**Self, Struggle & Change**
*Family Conflict Stories in Genesis and Their Healing Insights for Our Lives*
by Dr. Norman J. Cohen  6 x 9, 224 pp, Quality PB, ISBN 1-879045-66-4 **$16.95**

**Voices from Genesis:** *Guiding Us through the Stages of Life*
by Dr. Norman J. Cohen  6 x 9, 192 pp, Quality PB, ISBN 1-58023-118-7 **$16.95**

**Ancient Secrets:** *Using the Stories of the Bible to Improve Our Everyday Lives*
by Rabbi Levi Meier, Ph.D.  5½ x 8½, 288 pp, Quality PB, ISBN 1-58023-064-4 **$16.95**

**The Business Bible:** *10 New Commandments for Bringing Spirituality &
Ethical Values into the Workplace*
by Rabbi Wayne Dosick  5½ x 8½, 208 pp, Quality PB, ISBN 1-58023-101-2 **$14.95**

**Being God's Partner:** *How to Find the Hidden Link Between Spirituality and Your Work*
by Rabbi Jeffrey K. Salkin; Intro. by Norman Lear  **AWARD WINNER!**
6 x 9, 192 pp, Quality PB, ISBN 1-879045-65-6 **$16.95**; HC, ISBN 1-879045-37-0 **$19.95**

**God & the Big Bang**
*Discovering Harmony Between Science & Spirituality* **AWARD WINNER!**
by Daniel C. Matt  6 x 9, 224 pp, Quality PB, ISBN 1-879045-89-3 **$16.95**

**Soul Judaism:** *Dancing with God into a New Era*
by Rabbi Wayne Dosick  5½ x 8½, 304 pp, Quality PB, ISBN 1-58023-053-9 **$16.95**

**Finding Joy:** *A Practical Spiritual Guide to Happiness* **AWARD WINNER!**
by Rabbi Dannel I. Schwartz with Mark Hass
6 x 9, 192 pp, Quality PB, ISBN 1-58023-009-1 **$14.95**; HC, ISBN 1-879045-53-2 **$19.95**

# Spirituality & More

## The Jewish Lights Spirituality Handbook
### A Guide to Understanding, Exploring & Living a Spiritual Life
Ed. by *Stuart M. Matlins, Editor in Chief, Jewish Lights Publishing*

Rich, creative material from over fifty spiritual leaders on every aspect of Jewish spirituality today: prayer, meditation, mysticism, study, rituals, special days, the everyday, and more.
6 x 9, 456 pp, Quality PB, ISBN 1-58023-093-8 **$18.95**; HC, ISBN 1-58023-100-4 **$24.95**

## The Story of the Jews: *A 4,000-Year Adventure—A Graphic History Book*
Written and illustrated by *Stan Mack*

Through witty cartoons and accurate narrative, illustrates the major characters and events that have shaped the Jewish people and culture. For all ages.
6 x 9, 304 pp, Quality PB, Illus., ISBN 1-58023-155-1 **$16.95**

## The Jewish Prophet: *Visionary Words from Moses and Miriam to Henrietta Szold and A. J. Heschel*
by *Rabbi Dr. Michael J. Shire*

This beautifully illustrated collection of Jewish prophecy features the lives and teachings of thirty men and women, from biblical times to modern day. Provides an inspiring and informative description of the role each played in their own time, and an explanation of why we should know about them in our time. Illustrated with illuminations from medieval Hebrew manuscripts.
6½ x 8½, 128 pp, HC, 123 full-color illus., ISBN 1-58023-168-3 **$25.00**

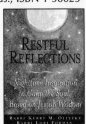

**The Enneagram and Kabbalah:** *Reading Your Soul*
by Rabbi Howard A. Addison  6 x 9, 176 pp, Quality PB, ISBN 1-58023-001-6 **$15.95**

**Cast in God's Image:** *Discover Your Personality Type Using the Enneagram and Kabbalah*
by Rabbi Howard A. Addison  7 x 9, 176 pp, Quality PB, ISBN 1-58023-124-1 **$16.95**

**Mystery Midrash:** *An Anthology of Jewish Mystery & Detective Fiction*  AWARD WINNER!
Ed. by Lawrence W. Raphael  6 x 9, 304 pp, Quality PB, ISBN 1-58023-055-5 **$16.95**

**Criminal Kabbalah:** *An Intriguing Anthology of Jewish Mystery & Detective Fiction*
Ed. by Lawrence W. Raphael; Foreword by Laurie R. King
6 x 9, 256 pp, Quality PB, ISBN 1-58023-109-8 **$16.95**

**Sacred Intentions:** *Daily Inspiration to Strengthen the Spirit, Based on Jewish Wisdom*
by Rabbi Kerry M. Olitzky & Rabbi Lori Forman
4½ x 6½, 448 pp, Quality PB, ISBN 1-58023-061-X **$15.95**

**Restful Reflections:** *Nighttime Inspiration to Calm the Soul, Based on Jewish Wisdom*
by Rabbi Kerry M. Olitzky & Rabbi Lori Forman
4½ x 6½, 448 pp, Quality PB, ISBN 1-58023-091-1 **$15.95**

**Embracing the Covenant:** *Converts to Judaism Talk About Why & How*  Ed. by Rabbi Allan Berkowitz & Patti Moskovitz  6 x 9, 192 pp, Quality PB, ISBN 1-879045-50-8 **$16.95**

**Wandering Stars:** *An Anthology of Jewish Fantasy & Science Fiction*  Ed. by Jack Dann; Intro. by Isaac Asimov  6 x 9, 272 pp, Quality PB, ISBN 1-58023-005-9 **$16.95**

**Israel—A Spiritual Travel Guide:** *A Companion for the Modern Jewish Pilgrim*  AWARD WINNER!
by Rabbi Lawrence A. Hoffman  4¾ x 10, 256 pp, Quality PB, ISBN 1-879045-56-7 **$18.95**

# *Women's Spirituality*

## The Women's Passover Companion
### *Women's Reflections on the Festival of Freedom*
Ed. by *Rabbi Sharon Cohen Anisfeld, Tara Mohr, & Catherine Spector*

The companion volume to *The Women's Seder Sourcebook*. Offers an in-depth examination of the roots and meanings of women's seders, including how the themes of Exodus and exile relate to women's lives today. 6 x 9, 352 pp, HC, ISBN 1-58023-128-4 **$24.95**

## The Women's Torah Commentary: *New Insights from Women Rabbis on the 54 Weekly Torah Portions* Ed. by *Rabbi Elyse Goldstein*

For the first time, women rabbis provide a commentary on the entire Five Books of Moses. These inspiring teachers bring their rich perspectives to bear on the biblical text, in a week-by-week format; a perfect gift for others, or for yourself. 6 x 9, 496 pp, HC, ISBN 1-58023-076-8 **$34.95**

## Women of the Wall: *Claiming Sacred Ground at Judaism's Holy Site*
Ed. by *Phyllis Chesler & Rivka Haut*

Documents the legendary grassroots and legal struggle of Jewish women to win the right to pray out loud together as a group, according to Jewish law; wear ritual objects; and read from the Torah scrolls at the Western Wall. 6 x 9, 496 pp, b/w photos, HC, ISBN 1-58023-161-6 **$34.95**

  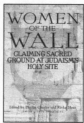  

Pray Tell: *A Hadassah Guide to Jewish Prayer* by Rabbi Jules Harlow, with contributions from many others 8½ x 11, 400 pp, Quality PB, ISBN 1-58023-163-2 **$29.95**

Moonbeams: *A Hadassah Rosh Hodesh Guide* Ed. by Carol Diament, Ph.D.
8½ x 11, 240 pp, Quality PB, ISBN 1-58023-099-7 **$20.00**

Lifecycles In Two Volumes **AWARD WINNERS!**
V. 1: *Jewish Women on Life Passages & Personal Milestones*
Ed. and with Intros. by Rabbi Debra Orenstein
V. 2: *Jewish Women on Biblical Themes in Contemporary Life*
Ed. and with Intros. by Rabbi Debra Orenstein and Rabbi Jane Rachel Litman
V. 1: 6 x 9, 480 pp, Quality PB, ISBN 1-58023-018-0 **$19.95**
V. 2: 6 x 9, 464 pp, Quality PB, ISBN 1-58023-019-9 **$19.95**

ReVisions: *Seeing Torah through a Feminist Lens* **AWARD WINNER!**
by Rabbi Elyse Goldstein 5½ x 8½, 224 pp, Quality PB, ISBN 1-58023-117-9 **$16.95**;
208 pp, HC, ISBN 1-58023-047-4 **$19.95**

The Year Mom Got Religion: *One Woman's Midlife Journey into Judaism*
by Lee Meyerhoff Hendler 6 x 9, 208 pp, Quality PB, ISBN 1-58023-070-9 **$15.95**

*Or phone, fax, mail or e-mail to:* **JEWISH LIGHTS Publishing**
Sunset Farm Offices, Route 4 • P.O. Box 237 • Woodstock, Vermont 05091
Tel: (802) 457-4000 • Fax: (802) 457-4004 • www.jewishlights.com
*Credit card orders:* (800) 962-4544 (8:30AM–5:30PM ET Monday–Friday)
Generous discounts on quantity orders. SATISFACTION GUARANTEED. Prices subject to change.